MPs for Hire

MPs For Hire

The Secret World of Political Lobbying

Mark Hollingsworth

BLOOMSBURY

First published 1991
Copyright © 1991 by Mark Hollingsworth

The moral right of the author has been asserted.

Bloomsbury Publishing Ltd, 2 Soho Square, London W1V 5DE

A CIP catalogue record for this book is available from the British Library

ISBN 0 7475 1055 5

Photoset by Rowland Phototypesetting Ltd,
Bury St Edmunds, Suffolk
Printed in Great Britain by
Clays Ltd, St Ives plc

Contents

So they came to Jerusalem, and Jesus went into the temple and began driving out those who bought and sold in the temple. He upset the tables of the money-changers and the seats of the dealers in pigeons, and he would not allow anyone to use the temple court as the thoroughfare for carrying goods. Then he began to teach them and said: 'Does not Scripture say my house shall be called a house of prayer for all the nations? But you have made it a robbers' cave.'

Mark, 11:15–18

Acknowledgements

This book really belongs to Elizabeth Jowett, the former wife of John Browne, the Conservative MP for Winchester. When I first met her in December 1986, I had intended only to discuss her controversial divorce case, which had just ended in the High Court, but as I covered the story over the next three years for TVS, the *Observer* and Granada Television, it was apparent that she was also deeply concerned about the role of MPs in the business world.

Over the years she has put up with my endless questions and requests for information with great courtesy and patience during our countless meetings. It is no exaggeration to say that without her this book would never have been published.

There are a number of other people I would like to thank, in particular my outstanding researcher, Jon Lewis, who once again did excellent work in tracking down the minutiae and historical aspects of the story. I am grateful to my brother, Daniel Hollingsworth, for his expert advice and research on the chapter dealing with City affairs. I should also like to thank my father, Roy Hollingsworth, for his constructive suggestions for the same chapter. I hope he forgives me for not including all his amendments.

For much of the historical material I am indebted to Alan Doig and his superb book *Corruption and Misconduct in Contemporary British Politics* (Penguin Books, 1984). The other major work on this subject is *Corruption in British Politics, 1895-1930* by G. R. Searle (Clarendon Press, 1987).

I should also like to acknowledge Andrew Roth, whose detailed knowledge of the parliamentary and political world is unsurpassed. His *Parliamentary Profiles* are indispensable to any serious political journalist and researcher.

For their unstinting support and commitment, I should like to thank my editors and colleagues at Granada TV's *World In Action* – one of the last bastions of independent investigative journalism.

I interviewed dozens of people for this book, and I am particularly grateful to Ruth Rees, Rob Edwards, Nigel Griffiths and Christopher Hird. Labour MPs Bob Cryer and Dale Campbell-Savours also deserve credit for their relentless campaigning on this issue.

Finally, I should like to thank Anne McDermid, my agent, Alison Mansbridge, my copy-editor, and in particular Liz Calder, my commissioning editor.

Mark Hollingsworth, London 1991

CHAPTER 1

If the Price is Right

'A little hush money can do a lot of talking.'
– Tory MP

When Dudley Fishburn arrived at the House of Commons in the summer of 1988 after winning the Kensington by-election, he received some curious advice. The newly elected Conservative MP was told by his fellow back-benchers to 'get a job'. His colleagues suggested it 'would help with the bank account' as well as 'raise his intellectual sights'.[1]

Fishburn was already a director of the market-research firm MIL Group PLC but decided to follow this helpful guidance and soon got to work. He became consultant to the international law firm Pepper, Hamilton and Sheetz and a director of the American bank J. P. Morgan, as well as joining the board of the ambitious UK bank HFC PLC.

Most voters, and no doubt many of Fishburn's west London constituents, will be bemused to learn that being a Member of Parliament is not a full-time job. But, according to Fishburn, MPs are 'permitted, even encouraged to take on outside employment'.[2]

It is these paid business interests which are threatening to strike at the heart of British democracy. The House of Commons is fast becoming a market-place with the politician as the commodity. Instead of representing the public and their constituents, MPs are increasingly hiring themselves out to the business world by acquiring consultancies, directorships and shareholdings. In January 1991 there were 384 MPs with commercial interests, holding 522 directorships and 452 consultancies.[3] Not only are they paid substantial fees, they also lobby Parliament and Whitehall and provide information for their clients.

This book is about that commercial relationship. It will reveal how MPs are hired, who is paying them, what MPs do for the money and how their links with companies are sometimes kept secret from the public. It also examines their dealings with the lobbying firms which act as brokers between the twilight worlds of business and politics.

Judges in their own cause

It was during the reign of Charles II (1660–85) that the Palace of Westminster was first infected by the stench of corruption. Influence-peddlers were seen on the stairs of the House of Commons and inducements were far from subtle. A favourite ploy was discreetly to slip parcels of guineas under the dinner-plates of MPs during banquets.[4]

William III's rule was little better. In 1694 the Treasury Secretary, Henry Guy, was committed to the Tower of London for taking a 200-guinea bribe from a middleman contracted to provide troops with money and supplies.[5] The following year the Speaker of the House, Sir John Trevor, was expelled for accepting a £1,100 bribe from the City of London to pass a bill. The chairman of the committee examining that bill was also thrown out for corruption.[6] Scandalised, the Commons passed perhaps the most decisive ruling yet on MPs' financial interests by declaring that 'the offer of any money, or other advantage, to a Member of Parliament for the promoting of any matter whatsoever depending or to be transacted in Parliament, is a high crime and misdemeanour and tends to the subversion of the English Constitution'.[7] For the past 300 years that resolution has never been taken seriously by Parliament. The central privilege granted to MPs exists to this day – namely, that MPs can vote and lobby for legislation in which they have a financial interest.

It was not until the early 19th century that the Commons was roused from its complacent slumber. In 1811, the votes of four MPs were disallowed because they had a direct commercial stake in a bill which helped companies manufacturing flour, wheat and bread.[8] Mr Speaker Abbot ruled that 'no MP who has a direct pecuniary interest in a question shall be allowed to vote upon it'. But that applied only to private bills (proposed laws sponsored by companies). The vast bulk of legislation is in the form of public bills, and so MPs continued to be allowed to vote for laws that benefited their commercial clients.

As parliamentary authorisation for commercial activity became increasingly important in the 19th century, so did lobbying and the hiring of MPs. In the 1840s over 150 MPs became shareholders in the new booming railway companies. Their chief promoter was George Hudson. His 'job' as an MP was 'to pilot through both Houses the innumerable railways bills in which he was interested and to watch over railway interests as a whole in Parliament. To this was attached a considerable amount of committee work, much wire-pulling behind the scenes and a necessary routine of social duties and entertainment.'[9]

The ancient principle of justice, that 'no man shall be a judge in his own cause', continued to be ignored. In 1852 Lord Chancellor Cottenham decreed during a court case in favour of the Grand Junction Canal company in which he was a shareholder.[10] Once again fine-sounding motions were passed in Parliament. After allegations that MPs were being bought by the Indian Raj to promote their land claims, it was resolved that no MP should 'promote or advocate in this House any proceeding or measure in which he may have acted or been concerned for or in consideration of any pecuniary fee or reward'.[11]

It is true, of course, that until 1911 MPs were unpaid and so relied on outside business fees if they had no private income. But by the turn of the 20th century the conflict between their political duties and private interests had become starkly apparent. In 1900, 30 per cent of MPs were directors of public companies. They were to be found mainly in the Liberal Unionist Party (4.75 companies per MP), followed by the Conservatives (2.5) and Liberals (1.75).[12]

Senior politicians like Herbert Asquith, from 1908 the Liberal Prime Minister, identified the inevitable problems, but many MPs carried on regardless. In 1896, Sir William Houldsworth, a Conservative MP, voted for the London and North-Western Railway Bill. This was while he was a director of the London and North-Western Railway Company – the very firm sponsoring the bill. Despite long and loud protests, no action was taken against Sir William.[13]

Some MPs were simply corrupt. In the late 1890s Henri Labouchère was one of London's most colourful characters as a celebrated theatre critic, society wit and Liberal MP. He also ran his own newspaper, with the extravagantly ironic title of *Truth*. This was far from a journal of record. Instead, it was used mainly to promote and praise shares held by Labouchère himself. 'What greater proof can I give of my belief in the shares that I write up than buying them,' he replied to a critic. Eventually, in 1905, his share-dealing racket was exposed and Labouchère never stood for Parliament again.[14]

Others circumvented their own legislation in order to pursue their business activities. Under the 1782 Contractors Act an MP was required to resign his seat if he was a partner of a company with government contracts. The Liberal MP Weetman Pearson neatly side-stepped this by converting his family firm, S. Pearson and Co., into a limited liability company. He was then able to continue tendering for government business.[15]

In the years before the outbreak of the First World War, armaments firms deliberately stirred up international tension. As Lord Welby, a former Treasury permanent secretary, said: 'We are in the hands of an organisation of crooks. They are politicians, generals, manufacturers of armaments and journalists. All of them are anxious for unlimited expenditure and go on inventing scares to terrify the public and Ministers.'[16]

MPs were particularly useful to munitions contractors. They could press for an increase in the Arms Estimates, lobby to prevent regulatory control of munitions manufacturers and try to influence the government's foreign policy. In 1914 Philip (later Lord) Snowden declared in the Commons: 'Now, who are the shareholders [of the arms firms]? . . . I find that honourable Members in this House are largely concerned. Indeed, it would be impossible to throw a stone on the benches opposite without hitting a Member who is a shareholder in one or other of these firms.'[17]

Snowden disclosed that one MP, a director of Cammell Laird and a shareholder in two arms firms, had spoken in every debate on munitions spending, while another, a shareholder in Vickers and Cammell Laird, lobbied the Admiralty to give armour-plate contracts to British firms.

After the Great War MPs paid homage to what the Tory MP Lord Bentinck called 'The Golden Calf' – the post-war contracts. 'Those who worship,' he wrote, 'will be rewarded with the crumbs that fall from the rich man's table, while those who refuse will be denounced as Pacifists and Bolsheviks.'[18]

MPs continued to do much as they pleased. The rules on their financial interests were governed more by custom and the assumption that all MPs are 'honourable members'. Hence criminals like Horatio Bottomley could remain in the Commons while spending much of his time in the courts defending his crooked lotteries and sweepstakes. Even after being successfully sued for swindling £50,000 from an elderly man, he remained an MP. It was his use of his own magazine, *John Bull*, to lure readers into investing in government bonds during the First World War that brought about his downfall. This was shown to be a racket, designed to divert much of the money for his own use, and in 1922 he received a seven-year jail sentence after being found guilty on twenty-three counts of fraud. Only then was he expelled from the Commons in disgrace.

Other MPs spent their time rather differently. Colonel Sir Walter De Frece, Conservative MP from 1920 to 1931, first for Ashton-under-Lyne and then Blackpool, actually lived permanently, in some luxury, at the Park Palace in Monte Carlo. Apart from election campaigns, he visited Britain only twice a year – for the Budget debate in March and for Ascot in July. In his later years De Frece, married to the wealthy music-hall male-impersonator Vesta Tilley, managed to represent his Lancashire constituents from Monaco by employing a young lobbyist, Commander Christopher Powell, later to become the doyen of parliamentary lobbyists (see chapter 6), to act as his surrogate MP.

All of De Frece's constituency mail was answered by Powell on sheets of signed Commons note-paper thoughtfully provided for him by the MP. The lobbyist even submitted written parliamentary questions on subjects of interest to his unsuspecting Lancashire constituents, and the replies were often reported in the local press. Consequently, recalls Powell, De Frece 'was considered quite a good constituency MP'.[19] His only political activity appeared to be as chairman of the Parliamentary Entertainment Commission.

However, for most MPs in the 1930s lobbying Parliament was a serious business. Maurice Hely-Hutchinson, Tory MP for Hastings, wrote in 1933: 'It is not the fault of politicians that their trade is what it is. Let us consider the nature of that trade. The politician comes to the market representing an *interest*, a group of people who have an end to serve and consider him to be the man to appear as their broker-advocate, to negotiate with other groups on their behalf.'[20]

One group who felt they needed an MP as their power-broker was made up of a number of Czechs living in Britain. In the spring of 1939 their assets held in London were frozen by the Bank of England in retaliation for the German invasion of their homeland. To qualify for compensation the Czechs needed to prove they had business interests in Britain, and so a group of claimants was set up to lobby the Treasury. Their chairman and most enthusiastic supporter was the Conservative MP Robert Boothby.

What the members of that group did not realise was that Boothby himself had a financial interest in their success. Earlier that year his merchant bank ran into financial problems and Boothby had to borrow heavily to keep afloat. To pay off his debts, he called in a promised £20,000 commission payment from a Czech businessman, Richard Weininger, earned for transferring Weininger's family assets from Prague to London. Now, his assets frozen by the British government, Weininger, who had bought an off-the-shelf company as 'proof' of his UK business status, promised to pay the MP the £20,000 plus interest. In return, Boothby agreed to make speeches and lobby Treasury ministers and officials on behalf of Weininger and the Czech claimants. This he duly did – but without declaring his interest.[21]

Boothby's activities were revealed in 1940, when Weininger was arrested under the Aliens Act and his papers were discovered. Although a select committee inquiry did find that Boothby had financial expectations and the House accepted their report, the MP received no punishment.

In the 1940s, when MPs continued to be badly paid, a different kind of lobbying pressure was applied. Like many Labour MPs, much of Alderman Robinson's salary was paid by a trade union. In 1944 Robinson's benefactor, the National Union of Distributive and Allied Workers, wrote to him saying they were dissatisfied with his performance as their MP. They demanded his resignation and threatened to withdraw funding. Robinson refused, and so the union stopped the payment.[22] A similar case involved the Civil Service Clerical Association, which tried to influence the MP whose salary they paid, William Brown. They terminated his salary, car and expense-allowance because he was loudly critical of Labour and TUC policies. Again the MP refused to back down.[23]

A subsequent inquiry identified the essence of the problem. It concluded:

> It is inconsistent with the dignity of the House, with the duty of a Member to his constituents, for any Member of this House to enter into any

contractual agreement with an outside body, controlling or limiting the Member's complete independence and freedom of action . . . The duty of a Member is to his constituents and to the country as a whole, rather than to any particular section.

Again, this was largely ignored. MPs continued to take money covertly in return for favours. This was the case with Labour MP Gerry Allighan, who in 1947 claimed that newspapers like the *Evening Standard* obtained inside information about private political meetings by bribing MPs with retainers, cash payments for stories and promises of personal publicity. For good measure he added that it was not unknown for honourable members to be absorbing large quantities of alcohol in the presence of journalists – 'lubricated into loquacity' he called it.[24]

Allighan's allegations were investigated by the Privileges Committee. Most editors and journalists denied bribing MPs for stories. However, the editor of the *Evening Standard*, Herbert Gunn, admitted paying Transatlantic Press Agency £120 a month for regular political reports supplied by 'an MP'. Who was the culprit? Gunn was pressed further, and the MP in question turned out to be none other than Allighan himself, who also held a 65 per cent shareholding in the news-agency.[25]

Allighan admitted the offence and pleaded in mitigation 'mental strain'; he even claimed that he was performing a public duty by revealing the practice! The Commons, for once, were not impressed by this defence and Allighan was expelled, ending his days as principal of the Premier School of Journalism in Johannesburg, South Africa.

As the role of government in business affairs expanded in the 1950s and 1960s, so did the role of MPs as hired guns, acting as intermediaries between companies and government. One of them, Anthony Courtney, recalled what he was able to do for his clients: 'Election to the House of Commons not only consolidated, but also improved my business affairs. I had acquired for the benefit of the firms with which I was connected improved personal contact with the Board of Trade and other ministers.' He said that he created for his clients' overseas activities 'an aura of official government blessing through the fact I was now a Member of Parliament'.[26]

It was a scandal born out of this type of business relationship that sparked off, in 1969, the first parliamentary inquiry into lobbying. The scandal involved the Labour MP Gordon Bagier and his consultancy with a PR agency working for the controversial Greek junta (see chapter 6 for details), but the inquiry did little to confront the fundamental problem – that MPs were receiving secret payments to represent outside commercial bodies. Specific cases were excluded from investigation, as ministers believed this could damage the then Labour government. The report did oppose MPs acting as paid advocates and established a Select Committee on Members' Interests. But its recommended 'code of conduct' only reinforced the notion that the obligation to declare financial interests should be a custom rather than a strict rule.[27]

'We are not crooks'

It took the corruption scandals of the 1970s for Parliament finally to be galvanised into action. This was a time of intrigue and controversy. In 1972 the MP Geoffrey Rhodes claimed he was offered a £12,000 'business proposition' to persuade British airlines to transfer their major Italian landing from Rome to Brindisi in the south.[28]

One of the most vigorous lobbying campaigns was by the National Association of Bookmakers. In November 1971 the government introduced a bill which would enable the Tote (the regulatory body which ensures fair odds for punters) to set up betting shops on high streets. The bookmakers reacted angrily because it meant a loss of millions of pounds in their profits. Discreet lunches and drinks receptions were held for MPs. Soon the bill was obstructed by filibustering and flooded by thousands of amendments. One of the MPs who backed the bookmakers' case was Labour's Brian Walden. In February 1972 he said: 'I have no financial interest, direct or indirect, in the bookmaking industry or in any allied industry. I am neither for nor against bookmaking in any financial sense, but I care about justice for individuals. I suspect that certain private bookmakers will be unjustly treated as a result of this legislation.'[29]

Walden became a member of the Commons Committee examining the bill and so was in an influential position. The National Association of Bookmakers were impressed by his advocacy of their case and immediately offered him a deal – a £25,000 contract as their parliamentary consultant over five years. This was negotiated while the bill was passing through Parliament.

Walden immediately announced the job, stressing that his role was to provide political advice, not to lobby MPs. But he continued to oppose the bill, which staggered along to its third reading. Then the central clause – concerning the setting up of betting shops in high streets – was suddenly curtailed by the Home Office after talks with the National Association of Bookmakers. This removed the whole purpose of the bill, and it collapsed.[30]

One MP who was infuriated by the bookies' lobbying tactics and his fellow back-bencher's role in the proceedings was Labour's Joe Ashton. He had long felt there needed to be tougher regulation against what he claimed amounted to political corruption. His own first experience of it was in 1969, a year after he won the Bassetlaw by-election, when he was walking down a Commons corridor. A hand dropped on his shoulder and he turned to see a fellow Labour MP.

'Joe, you've got a lot of slag heaps in Nottinghamshire haven't you?' asked his colleague.

'I have that,' replied Ashton.

'Well, there's this friend of mine who shifts slag heaps and he wants somebody to mount a campaign. What it is, you see, the Durham County Council have started to levy rates on his activities by calling it quarrying. That means there is a lot less profit in it. He wants somebody to kick up a fuss and get the rating stopped.' The MP paused and added: 'What's more, he's willing to pay.' Ashton was not so hesitant. He used the most economic device available in the English language to reject the offer – a four-letter word, followed by a sharp three-letter word. But then, a few days later, he was shocked to notice another back-bencher who had no slag heaps within miles of his constituency eagerly imploring the minister that this particular rate should be abolished.[31]

Ashton began to campaign for MPs to be more open about their business interests. On 26 April 1974 he wrote an article stating: 'The number of Labour MPs who can be hired can be counted on the fingers of one hand. And the rest of us know who they are. But often their constituents and constituency parties don't. Despite the fact that MPs are supposed to declare their interests if they have a financial involvement, a few of them rarely do.'[32]

Ashton's misfortune was that his article was published on the same day that T. Dan Smith, the PR sidekick of the architect John Poulson, was sentenced to six years in jail on four counts of corruption. Ashton's remarks caused an outcry. He was besieged by the media,

who called on him to 'Name the Guilty Five'. Ashton was unrepentant and explained later that day that his remarks were intended to
speed up reform of disclosure, not accuse MPs of being crooks.
But his colleagues were unconcerned about his motives and he was
reported to the Commons Privileges Committee for 'contempt of the
House'.

Usually when MPs are summoned before the Committee they are
quick to apologise. But Ashton soon made the members of this august
body very nervous by declaring that he would prove MPs were being
hired. He also began to gather evidence about lobbying companies
paying MPs £350 a time to book banqueting rooms at the Commons. But when he asked for the records of which firms were sponsoring MPs in this way, he was refused the information and was
even barred from the Commons Services Committee office. To this
day, that information remains unavailable to the public.

Ashton was determined to defend himself. But as the crucial general election drew near in October 1974, he came under heavy
pressure from his Labour colleagues to back down. The election was
going to be closely fought and his fellow back-benchers were worried
that if he identified the culprits the scandal would damage their
chances. Eventually Ashton agreed to succumb. He apologised and
was censured by the House. 'The affair was very embarrassing to my
constituency party,' recalled Ashton. 'It left a stain on my character for
ever and I believe it finished my chances of a ministerial career.'

Ashton was later proved right, as several MPs were shown to have
been hired in dubious circumstances.[33] But in the spring of 1974 his
main concern was for a Register of Members' Interests to be set up.
He had an ally in Eddie Milne, a fellow MP, and although this was
not a popular cause at Westminster, eventually a packed meeting of
the Parliamentary Labour Party voted for a register. Only one MP
spoke out against the idea. He made an impassioned speech, bitterly
objecting to this 'unwarranted intrusion' into the privacy of MPs,
and stormed out of the meeting. His colleagues were not to know
that the speaker's own companies were at the time being investigated
by Department of Trade and Industry (DTI) Inspectors. Two years
later the MP was jailed for seven years for forgery, theft and fraud
offences. His name was John Stonehouse.

In May 1974 the Commons finally agreed to a Register of
Members' Interests and to new requirements on declaring financial
interests. The debate was notable for a peculiar mixture of genuine

concern and complacency. Many senior M Ps clearly saw the Register as an intrusion into the affairs of what was in effect one of their private clubs. One Labour M P remarked to his colleague Bob Cryer: 'Don't worry, old boy, we know the wrong 'uns in here. We can pick them out. We do not need a register.'[34] James (now Lord) Prior, Leader of the Commons until the Conservatives' general election defeat three months earlier, said:

> Should the public know of our outside interests? My answer, strictly speaking, is 'No'. Why should they? There is no opportunity for corruption and precious little opportunity for influence . . . We are not crooks and we want it to be seen that we are not crooks. We are in the public eye and we hold jobs which in the eyes of the public are very important.[35]

Despite such reservations, a Register was set up a year later. Its function was: 'To provide information of any pecuniary interest or other material benefit which a Member may receive which might be thought to affect his conduct as a Member or influence his actions, speeches or vote in Parliament.' The House also resolved that in Commons debates, committee proceedings or letters with ministers or fellow back-benchers, M Ps should 'disclose any relevant pecuniary interest or benefit of whatever nature, whether direct or indirect, that he may have had, may have or may be expecting to have'.[36]

Like most self-regulating systems, it was wide open to abuse. Many M Ps were at first dismissive. One Labour M P from a mining constituency remarked that when it was his turn to fill in the Register, he would write 'Whippets and Women' and leave it at that.[37] Other objections were more serious. Enoch Powell refused, much to the fury of fellow M Ps, to declare his interests. When the structure of the Register was debated in June 1975 he described the proposal as 'ineffective, degrading and unconstitutional'. Powell's view was that declaring interests was 'a requirement of honour not registration', adding: 'It is an assumption which is accompanied by a safeguard. We do not live or debate as strangers to one another. A sufficient number of honourable members know very well quite enough about the background of their colleagues in this House to judge what motives and credibility may attach to the contributions which we make to debate.'[38] He declined to assess how the *public* were able to know about the background of their elected representatives without a Register. Instead, he remained defiant: 'I shall not consider it right to comply with this order of the House if such an order is made.'[39]

Demands for the government to take action against Powell were stonewalled by Michael Foot, then Leader of the Commons. For four years the Labour government failed to implement its own law and publish the updated Register. They were aided by MPs like Anthony Grant, who asked Foot: 'In view of all the other pressing commitments which the government and House have before them, will the right honourable gentleman undertake to waste not one second more time on such an utterly trivial matter?'[40]

Inside Poulson's pocket but outside the law

The major catalyst for the setting up of a Register of Members' Interests had been the petition for bankruptcy filed at Wakefield Crown Court by the architect John Poulson. The 27,000 documents presented at the hearing revealed a swamp of corruption that sucked in senior civil servants, local government officials, councillors and, most notably, MPs. To win contracts, Poulson paid them cash retainers and provided overseas holidays, gifts and free accommodation. The MPs concerned were Albert Roberts, Reginald Maudling and John Cordle.

The Labour MP for Normanton, Albert Roberts, came to the attention of Poulson at a time when the architect needed well-placed contacts for securing business with foreign governments. Roberts had useful overseas connections, particularly in Spain, and so Poulson paid him £2,500 a year as a consultant.

Roberts provided two services. The first was inside political information. Roberts was once asked by his colleague Austin Mitchell what he provided in return for being on the Poulson payroll. 'My intelligence,' he replied, and he wasn't referring to his IQ level.[41] The second was 'liaison work'. This meant acting as a political middleman on behalf of Poulson. Roberts telephoned the Crown Agents, one of whose functions was to advise Commonwealth governments on the selection of consultants, to question why Poulson was not on an approved list of architects. He also signed a letter (dictated by Poulson and typed by one of his employees on Commons notepaper) urging the Maltese Minister of Works to appoint Poulson as architect consultant for a major hospital contract.[42] Over a four-year period Roberts received £11,508 as a consultant to Poulson's company, Construction Promotions Ltd. In 1966 Roberts introduced a new client to Poulson – Reginald Maudling.

By the time Maudling met Poulson he had already been a Cabinet minister for nine years. He was Chancellor of the Exchequer when the Conservatives lost the 1964 election and the following year unsuccessfully stood against Edward Heath for the leadership of the Party. Maudling believed this period in opposition entitled him, as he later recalled, 'to build up a little pot of money for my old age'.[43] But the Shadow Foreign Secretary went much further than securing for himself a handsome financial legacy. He acquired so many business interests that when he met Poulson he was already earning four times as much as his ministerial salary.

But Maudling wanted more. He became 'a hungry crocodile', as Poulson later remarked.[44] And the ambitious Yorkshire architect was more than happy to feed the insatiable politician. In return, the MP agreed to promote and nurture Poulson's enterprises.

Maudling became a director of three Poulson companies. But his key role was as chairman of International Technical and Construction Services, a Poulson front company that sought hospital contracts in the Mediterranean and Middle East. The Shadow Foreign and Commonwealth Secretary set out to earn his promised £9,500 a year by visiting and lobbying foreign governments. His most notable effort was to win for Poulson a contract to build a new hospital on the island of Gozo in Malta.

He made speeches in the Commons – without declaring his financial interest – calling for greater British expenditure in Malta. Then, as the *World In Action* programme 'Business In Gozo' revealed, Maudling wrote a series of letters to Maltese government and civic figures, including the Prime Minister, promoting the Poulson case. This was also done without declaring his full commercial relationship with Poulson. According to John Abela, a local construction supplies merchant, the MP's intervention was crucial. He told Poulson: 'What has caused an immediate reaction are the letters which Sir R. Maudling has signed. I can assure you that the impression of his signature has greatly influenced one and all.'[45]

As well as securing the Gozo contract, Maudling was instrumental in clearing British government grants. Poulson was suitably grateful. 'I came to the conclusion,' he wrote to the MP, 'that if I didn't bring somebody like you into it, I was going to be played around for the next month or two.'[46]

In 1972 Maudling resigned as Home Secretary. He was directly responsible for the Metropolitan Police, and their Fraud Squad had just begun a corruption inquiry into Poulson companies. In effect, the police were investigating the Home Secretary's own business activities. But in his resignation letter Maudling claimed: 'Before I accepted his invitation to become chairman of an export company, for which post I took no remuneration, he [Poulson] had made a convenant in favour of a charitable appeal which had my support. I do not regard this as a matter either for criticism or investigation.'[47] This statement was economical with the truth, as a Select Committee report later showed. Not only had Maudling received directors' fees from three other Poulson companies, he was promised £9,500 a year from the 'export company'. The architect also built, free of charge, a swimming pool and an extension on the MP's house.[48] Despite severe criticism from the Select Committee, Maudling escaped punishment.

Throughout that period Maudling had been under investigation by the authorities for possible illegality. A senior inspector in the Department of Trade, A. S. Ford, made a preliminary examination of Poulson's companies. His report cited five possible criminal offences committed by Maudling, including conspiracy, two counts of perjury and fraud.[49] Within a few days of his assessment's delivery to the Director of Public Prosecutions (DPP), Ford was taken off the police inquiry and dispatched to a new job in the provinces.

This was not the only report into the Maudling case received by the DPP. According to Ray Fitzwalter and David Taylor, two eminent QCs, John Cobb and Peter Taylor, also examined Maudling's business activities. The two lawyers suggested that if he had been a civil servant there would have been a prima-facie case of corruption: 'There is abundant evidence that Mr Maudling was doing his utmost to advance the interests of Poulson, to recommend him to Maltese ministers, to use his name to add weight to the recommendations and to secure the payment to Poulson of fees.'[50]

The inclusion of John Cordle in the Poulson payroll was, on the face of it, more surprising. An active churchman and evangelical Christian, Cordle had spent much of his parliamentary career loudly lamenting the decline in the moral standards of people in public life. His set speech was that Britain's problems were due to Christian values not being maintained: 'Economically we are nearly bankrupt, but we are certainly morally, if not spiritually, bankrupt. Since the war there has been a collapse of the moral Christian principles which this country has enjoyed over the centuries.'[51]

Cordle's concern for the moral probity of public figures did not, however, extend to his own affairs. When the first of his three wives attempted to send him to prison for contempt of court, he claimed that 'parliamentary privilege' placed him outside the court's jurisdiction. During his second marriage, Cordle hired security guards to prevent his mother-in-law from entering his house.[52] However, it was his business activities that made the MP's public pronouncements sound hollow.

As well as being a broker in Lloyd's, a director of three companies and chairman of another five, Cordle also ran a textile firm. He specialised in the export trade, particularly to West Africa, where he had built up extensive business contacts, aided by his chairmanship of several key parliamentary committees. In the mid-1960s, keen to secure contracts in that region, Poulson hired Cordle to promote and represent his firm Construction Promotions Ltd in West Africa for £500 a year plus expenses. In return the MP set up business lunches for Construction Promotions in the Commons, lobbied ministers and Crown Agents and used his position on West African parliamentary committees 'to give me a further entrée in that region'.[53] He also made speeches in the Commons on Poulson's behalf without declaring his commercial interest. In 1964 he urged the government to finance a development scheme in Gambia, where Poulson was a potential contractor: 'I believe that it would please the British taxpayer if they knew that such money, as was being provided by HMG, was finding its way into the pockets of British contractors, who could undertake many of the civil engineering developments, rather than into the pockets of local governments.'[54]

The evidence that this speech was motivated by his commercial gain was a letter written by Cordle to his paymaster and later published by the *Observer*. The MP wrote to Poulson stating that:

> It was largely for the benefit of Construction Promotions that I took part in a debate in the House of Commons on The Gambia and pressed for HMG to award construction contracts to British firms . . . I have advocated that you should be consulted on all construction planning and be appointed consultant architect to the Gambian government.[55]

Cordle concluded by complaining: 'I feel that the expenses cheque so far paid of £150 is somewhat uncomplimentary to myself.'

A month later the MP again wrote to Poulson, but this time his tone was more sanguine.

> I want to thank you again and express my sincere wish to be of continued and positive assistance to you and Construction Promotions Ltd. I was particularly grateful to you for confirmation of our original discussion at the Dorchester Hotel which dealt with the main points for the service agreement.
>
> It was agreed that a retaining fee of £1,000 per annum should be paid to me for five years from 1 January 1965, and that a 1 per cent commission will be paid on all projects which I am able to introduce and facilitate to your companies . . . Over the past fifteen months I have done what was asked of me and to the best of my ability. I shall continue with renewed vigour knowing that I am in your hands and under your watchful eye. My endeavours for you and Construction Promotions will be maintained throughout.[56]

Cordle continued his endeavours for the corrupt architect for five more years, collecting £5,628.

When the Royal Commission on Standards of Conduct in Public Life examined the Poulson payments to the three MPs in 1976, they were shocked, particularly by Cordle's activities.[57] The legal opinion was equally damning. The QCs, Peter Taylor (now Lord Justice Taylor) and John Cobb, who had also examined the Maudling case, said that there were five possible criminal charges. However, they considered that Cordle could not be prosecuted because the 1889 and 1906 corruption acts gave MPs a legal immunity: 'What then is the position if an MP receives a sum of money knowing its purpose to be to secure for reward his influence, his vote or, as the case may be, in relation to some proceedings in Parliament in connection with his "status" as a Member of Parliament? As the law now stands, he commits no crime.'[58]

The Royal Commission was dismayed by the immunity from prosecution enjoyed by MPs. Its report, published in 1976, advocated: 'Parliament should consider bringing corruption, bribery and attempted bribery of a Member of Parliament, acting in his parliamentary capacity, within the ambit of the criminal law.'[59] But the Labour government refused to implement this proposal. The Prime Minister himself, James (now Lord) Callaghan, led the retreat. He said these were 'very difficult issues' and that 'it may be as well to focus on the practice for the future rather than to re-run the past'.

He dismissed the Royal Commission's proposal as a 'rather obscure recommendation'.[60]

This response caused an immediate outcry. The next day the Prime Minister reluctantly agreed to a select committee inquiry into Roberts, Cordle and Maudling's conduct. Their remit was based on two Commons resolutions which could have been copied from the rule-book of any gentleman's club: firstly, whether the MPs' activities 'amounted to a contempt of the House'; and secondly, whether their conduct 'was inconsistent with the standards which the House is entitled to expect from its members'.[61]

Eight months later the select committee reported and found that all three MPs had failed to declare their interests. Cordle was also found guilty of 'contempt of the House' for 'raising a matter in Parliament for reward'. The committee managed to conclude that this did not 'amount to corruption or corrupt conduct'. Maudling was rebuked for 'lacking in frankness' in his resignation letter as Home Secretary.[62] The committee also noted that there had been 'a close interlocking of actions' between his lobbying and Poulson's payments.

Cordle resigned before the report was debated in the Commons. He claimed, bizarrely, 'a vindication after trial by media'.[63] Maudling was unrepentant, saying the criticism of him was 'outrageous'. He remained in the Commons and the libel writs he issued prevented further disclosure of his business affairs. Only Albert Roberts was magnanimous enough to tell the select committee that he 'may have been a little bit unethical at times'.[64] He later apologised for having 'transgressed in shallow waters'.[65]

However, MPs voted to merely 'take note' rather than 'endorse' the committee's conclusions about their colleagues' conduct. No action was taken. The tone of the debate was that the MPs' offences were not that serious and that, as in all clubs, any punishment should be minimal and privately administered. As Michael Foot, then Leader of the Commons, told the House: 'I believe that the right honourable gentleman and my honourable friend have suffered sufficiently. I do not believe that in addition they should have a penalty imposed by the House of Commons ... We can act wisely and intelligently without any sort of vindictiveness.'[66]

This was contrary to the judgement of those outside who examined the evidence independently. They included eminent QCs, police officers, civil servants and members of the Royal Commission on

Standards of Conduct in Public Life. It was their view that criminal charges should have been brought against Cordle and Maudling and that the real problem was the legal immunity enjoyed by MPs.

That legal loophole was the main recommendation of the Royal Commission's report, published on 15 July 1976, before the select committee inquiry. It took nearly three years before either Labour or Conservative administrations made a statement about the Royal Commission report, claiming 'consultations' were taking place. Eventually, on 11 June 1979, the Home Secretary William (now Lord) Whitelaw said: 'The main recommendations not yet implemented [amending the corruption law to include MPs] would require legislation and I cannot at present see any prospect of this during the current session.'

Four days later, Whitelaw was asked what policies he had in mind to improve the standards of conduct in public life. He replied: 'To set a good example to others.'[67] Eleven years later that remains the position.

The money-changers enter the Temple

The decade since the publication of the Register of Members' Interests has seen a considerable increase both in lobbying and in consultancies and directorships taken on by MPs. In 1980 the total was 541. By 1990 this had risen to 974. Consultancies alone have more than doubled.

A major reason for this phenomenon is the government's divestment of state monopolies, which has created vast opportunities for the commercial sector, involving not only private firms but also stockbrokers, merchant banks and investment companies. With government decisions increasingly affecting the private sector, companies saw MPs as useful assets.

This was illustrated by an account of a lunch meeting involving the MP Anthony Steen, barrister, Lloyd's underwriter and chairman of the Conservative back-bench Committee on Urban Affairs. In the spring of 1980 he spent two hours with three members of the Association of Consultant Architects. Under the heading 'MPs' Time', the report of their discussion recorded Steen's comments:

It is apparently a fact of life that MPs have little opportunity on their own to concentrate on any one group's interests or problems unless they have a special reason for doing so. They are bombarded with material every day in large quantities. If, however, a special-interest group is prepared to sponsor MPs, to pay them fees for their care and attention, this has proved to be an effective method. The sort of fee that an MP would expect from a special-interest group for special care and attention to their problems would be between £5,000 and £10,000.

The benefits which could flow from such an arrangement are that the MPs could, at the ear of government, explain problems with particular care to ministers, take the extra trouble required to put down questions, to prepare speeches on special interests which would otherwise go by default.[68]

Steen accepts this account of the meeting as 'broadly accurate'. But he said he had been invited to the lunch for his knowledge and expertise in inner-city planning. 'They asked me for advice,' he recalled. 'In no way did I say to them that I was out for tender.' This was later confirmed by one of those present.

Steen debarred himself on this occasion, but there is no doubt that many MPs will often lobby for companies only if they are paid. This is confirmed by the experienced political lobbyist John Russell from his own dealings with MPs: 'I know of two cases where MPs have said: "I will help you, but I would not do it normally and it is going to cost you money."'[69] According to Russell, many MPs use stock phrases to indicate their desire for cash – 'There is pressure on my time', 'My time is valuable', 'I can only afford to take an interest in a limited number of subjects'.[70]

Russell also has knowledge of MPs 'canvassing for jobs'. He puts the number at 300 and says MPs often act after receiving letters from companies. They will either write back offering their services or mention their interest in consultancy work in casual conversation. 'Let me know if I can be of any assistance' is the much-loaded parting comment from MPs, according to Russell.

One such MP was Sir Alex Fletcher, a junior minister at the DTI from June 1983 until September 1985. Part of his responsibility was City and Corporate Affairs, particularly take-over bids. His ministerial tenure was not a notable success, although he did receive a knighthood on leaving office.

Five months later his former ministry was under fire for negotiating the sale of British Leyland's truck and Land-Rover divisions to General Motors of Detroit. News of the bid was greeted with patriotic outrage in the Commons. But some British companies reacted rather differently. The Dutton-Forshaw Motor Group, a subsidiary of Lonrho, saw the deal as an opportunity to collaborate with the American car giant and buy up one of British Leyland's subsidiaries. Dutton-Forshaw also believed that a knowledgeable MP could help them negotiate favourable terms with the government, and so a group of their executives met Sir Alex Fletcher to discuss a consultancy deal. Sir Alex was interested and wrote a letter to the company outlining his terms. He offered to help with their 'negotiations with the government, BL and other parties regarding the proposed acquisition . . . of the Land-Rover subsidiary of British Leyland'. The MP then came to the subject of his fees:

> Obviously I must learn something about the business and its markets before I begin. I would therefore suggest a briefing fee of £5,000 and a monthly retainer of £5,000 plus expenses. I would suggest also a minimum guaranteed fee of £15,000 if no deal is concluded. In the event of a transaction taking place, I would suggest a bonus of £25,000 in addition to the briefing fee and monthly retainers.[71]

Sir Alex did not get his £25,000 bonus or consultancy, as the government decided not to sell off BL. But it was a classic contemporary case of an MP offering himself as a lobbyist – at a price.

A more transparent method was used by the Conservative MP and solicitor Richard Alexander. In July 1989, just before the Commons summer recess, he placed an advertisement in the 'Situations Wanted' column of the parliamentary *House Magazine*. It stated: 'Hardworking back-bench Tory MP of 10 years standing seeks consultancy in order to widen his range of activities. Please contact Richard Alexander at the House of Commons on 01 219 4207.'[72]

Alexander, already a consultant to the import-export firm Rindalbourne Ltd since 1985, explained why he inserted the advertisement:

> I had not at that time many outside interests and I thought advertising was one way of making it clear to others that I was available to be their spokesman if they wished . . . It was one way of drawing the nation's attention to the fact that I only had one consultancy and could take on more if they wished.[73]

The MP received three offers. He rejected two, considered one, but did not take it up.

As well as canvassing for jobs, MPs also receive direct propositions. When Robin Maxwell-Hyslop was first elected the Conservative MP for the Devon seat of Tiverton, he was offered two contracts that he regarded as 'manifestly corrupt'. One was a £1,200 a year consultancy from a firm of stockbrokers who wanted him to write reports on Tory Party Finance Committee meetings, particularly just before the budget. The other was a directorship with a private company which was just about to go public with a share issue and wanted an MP to decorate its board.[74] Maxwell-Hyslop rejected both of them and has since consistently refused to have any outside business interests.

For the MPs who do accept outside paid jobs, the time devoted to these other employers varies. But Sir Marcus Fox, the Tory MP for Shipley and vice-chairman of the back-bench 1922 Committee, is typical of the new breed of business-friendly MPs. He has six consultancies and three directorships. This is how he divides up part of his time:

> I have board meetings perhaps two and a half days a month in London and go down to Bournemouth for the odd half day. But as I live in the constituency, I'm back there at weekends and hold two or three surgeries a month. What I don't have are arrangements which mean I have to be in the City for a set number of hours a day.[75]

As regards payment, the going rate for a top-rate non-executive directorship is between £12,000 and £15,000 a year, and between £6,000 and £12,000 for a consultancy. One MP disclosed how his two outside jobs generated £22,000 a year for less than a day's work a week.[76] By the end of his parliamentary career in 1987, Geoffrey (now Lord) Rippon, QC, had collected forty-eight directorships, notably the chairmanship of the financial services group Britannia Arrow, for which he was paid £60,000 a year. Most MPs with business interests have at least three paid positions and so easily double their parliamentary salary of £28,970 a year.[77]

However, it is what MPs actually do for their paymasters that is of greatest concern. The fear, shared by many MPs as well as outside critics, is that an MP's independence is compromised and allegiance placed in doubt once they receive payment. 'It's difficult to imagine,' said former right-wing Tory MP Piers Merchant, 'how an MP who is involved with a company, an interest group or a trade union can be utterly impartial when it comes to making decisions.'[78]

This view is shared by another Conservative MP, James Cran, a former CBI director and a member of the Commons Trade and Industry Select Committee. Since his election in 1987 he has refused to acquire any business interests, explaining that: 'My constituents back in Beverley send me to the House of Commons to use my judgement and I do not see how I could be expected to use my judgement if I am prepared to accept money from this or that outfit ... As soon as one accepts money for something, one ceases to use one's own independent mind.'[79]

When Cran sits in the Commons chamber and an MP begins making a speech on an issue after declaring a commercial interest, this is his reaction:

> I cease to listen to it and I think that's the case for many of my colleagues on the back-benches. If it's known that an MP is merely standing up, if you like, to earn his corn and to be seen by whoever is paying him to raise this issue in the Commons, then frankly it's rarely worth listening to. I think that those members who accept money for this sort of thing should consider the reaction they're getting because, I assure you, it tends to make colleagues look down on those MPs.[80]

MPs can do much more than make speeches on behalf of their commercial clients. They can sponsor bills, put down motions, make interventions, ask questions and then vote for acts of Parliament (the last four of these actions without having to declare an interest). There is also the more subtle, secret lobbying of civil servants and ministers either by correspondence or by discreet conversations.

This book is an investigation into such activity and asks the question: should elected public servants also be the paid advocates of outside organisations?

Some MPs believe their business activities should be kept private from the electorate. Sir Patrick McNair-Wilson, Conservative MP for the New Forest and a public-relations consultant whose clients include Union Carbide and Re-Chem International, said in July 1989: 'The public does not have an automatic right to know what Members of Parliament get up to.'[81] I hope this book will serve as a democratic riposte to that contention.

CHAPTER 2

Abroad on Business

'The directors consider any disclosure of the geographical breakdown of turnover prejudicial to the interests of the company.'
Annual accounts of Falcon Finance Management Ltd (1983,
1984, 1985), consultancy company of John Browne, MP for
Winchester.

I n May 1985, eleven members of the Commons Trade and Industry
Select Committee embarked on an official 'fact-finding' trip to
China. The two-week visit was designed to improve trade relations
and help British industry take advantage of China's new 'open-door
policy'. But for some of the MPs rather more private commercial
interests were being pursued – their own.

There were numerous receptions and seminars with Chinese
government officials, ministers and businessmen. The British MPs
'were treated like royalty', according to one of the guests. But they
introduced themselves not by asking questions about their host
country's economy. Instead some of the MPs presented details of
their own financial portfolios.

Interpreters were used, much to the embarrassment of those
present, to explain the range of consultancies and services those
MPs could provide. Some back-benchers sidled up to guests, seeking
information for their own commercial interests. One MP even
handed round his business card, which had been specially printed in
Chinese for the occasion. Another went off to Shanghai to check on
investments in telecommunications. By the end of the trip only five
had completed the itinerary, as one by one the remaining MPs had
taken off for Hong Kong.

Those present were appalled at such canvassing for private profit
during an official, all-expenses trip paid for from the public purse.
But MPs have always looked to foreign governments and companies
for lucrative consultancies, one-off payments and free holidays. In

the past it was countries like East Germany, Nigeria and Israel that handed out such inducements.[1] In more recent years MPs have turned their attention to the oil-rich countries of the Middle East.

Middle Eastern promise

One MP who cashed in on his Middle East contacts was an ambitious former Guardsman called John Browne. Before entering the Commons, Browne had spent four and a half years with a merchant bank, the European Banking Company, as director of their Middle East operations. He travelled extensively, building up contacts with eighty-two banks in eleven Arab countries. It was during this time that, on 21 June 1977, Browne was selected as the parliamentary candidate for the safe Conservative seat of Winchester.

His plan was to set up his own company as a vehicle for his business interests by the time of the election. As this was expected in the autumn of 1978, Browne resigned from the European Banking Company on 19 June. The bank offered 'generous terms' to retain him while he was in Parliament. But he refused, explaining that he preferred to set up 'a private firm of my own'. Three weeks later Falcon Rose Ltd was formed.

This company was to be the conduit for Browne's consultancy work while he remained in the Commons. Based at his house at 12 Eaton Mews South, in the heart of Belgravia, the office consisted of three rooms. One was a converted garage which served as a general office. Another was the first-floor drawing room where Browne held regular business meetings starting at 10.30 a.m. And behind the garage was a converted bedroom which the MP used as his private office. There was also an elaborate intercom system which Browne used to summon his secretary to dictate letters in the mornings – often from his second-floor bedroom.

The house, owned by his wife Elizabeth, was effectively a company head office. Much of the company expenditure – office equipment, research assistance, travel and entertainment – was met by his wife. However, although she was also a director and owned 25 per cent of the shares, Falcon Rose was very much John Browne's company. He held a 50 per cent stake (later increased to 75 per cent) and was managing director. 'It is very much a one-man company,' his lawyers later stated.[2]

From its inception Falcon Rose made substantial amounts of money. Yet Browne failed to declare his controlling shareholding to Parliament for eight years. He later claimed: 'I understood you did not declare shares which were valueless.'[3] But, as a select committee report later found, this failure to disclose his shareholding prevented the public from knowing about the MP's direct personal control over Falcon.[4]

Browne's first major client was Barclays Bank International, who paid him £20,000 a year. This was reduced to £9,000 when he was elected in May 1979. A year later he renegotiated his contract. He wrote a memorandum suggesting 'what services I could provide' and listed 'the skills and contacts I have to offer so you can evaluate where and how BBI may wish to use and pay for them'.[5] This consisted mainly of his business background and contacts in the Middle East. He went on to become an adviser to the Barclays Group itself and in 1981 made a number of speeches defending the clearing banks against criticism.[6] For example, in the Budget debate he attacked the tax on windfall profits made by banks. Two months later he moved an amendment on the Finance Bill, arguing that the banks' profits were 'not excessive' but 'cyclical'.[7] During his speech he declared a general interest 'as a consultant and director in the banking industry'.

Browne's other clients included oil companies, foreign banks and the private security firm Control Risks (£200 a day plus VAT). From 1985 to 1989 he was also a consultant to the American International Group, the giant insurance corporation. He was paid £10,000 a year by their subsidiary company based in Pembroke, Bermuda. In return the MP supplied briefings on the British economy and in 1987 lobbied ministers on health insurance and British involvement in US defence programmes.[8]

Falcon Rose was also the front company for Browne's work as an investment adviser in gold, gemstones, currency, Eurobonds, UK government gilt-edged stock and UK and US real estate.[9] He even opened a Falcon 'representative office' in Denver, Colorado, 'to cater for investments into the United States, particularly in the oil, gas, high technology and real estate fields'.[10]

By 1981 Browne had acquired an impressive range of contacts and contracts in the Arab banking community and was on friendly terms with the Saudi royal family. He had also joined the board of the Churchill Private Clinic, an Arab-owned hospital based in London, at £2,000 a year. An indication of the nature of his clientele was that the company name was changed to Falcon Finance Management Ltd (Falcon Rose having Jewish connotations).

One of Browne's most revealing associations was with the Lebanese businessman Charles C. El Chidiac. Chidiac was the classic example of a 'middleman' – an agent who lobbies for large corporations in their pursuit of contracts and then receives a commission if the bid is successful. A Maronite Christian, he had set up his own company, Selco East Consultants, in Beirut in 1966. Within ten years offices had been established in eleven countries, including the Gulf states, Hong Kong and the United States. His many clients were oil and construction corporations, notably Trafalgar House, and he specialised in doing business in Saudi Arabia. He was also active in the political arena. His uncle, Camille Chamoun, was President of Lebanon in the 1950s. Chidiac himself later tried to run for President and set up his own party, the Lebanese Arab Progressives. But his forte was commercial lobbying of foreign governments, sometimes working on fifty contracts at the same time.[11]

In 1976 Chidiac's attention turned to the United Kingdom. He moved to London and hired a public-relations consultant, Lady Edith Foxwell, to introduce him to the British business and political community. She organised grand dinner parties for him at his house at 21 Kensington Park Gardens, off Ladbroke Square. Guests included Cecil Parkinson, then an Opposition Trade spokesperson, Tory MPs Nicholas Ridley, Anthony Kershaw and Julian Amery, American businessmen, Saudi princes and intelligence officers.

It was during one of these formal parties, in 1978, that Chidiac was introduced to John Browne. The two immediately hit it off. They had a mutual interest in politics and business, especially the Middle East, and Chidiac would often ask the MP for advice. For the next two years they regularly met for dinner, either at their homes or at Cecconi's restaurant in Burlington Gardens, off Bond Street. Browne was also a guest at Chidiac's house in Honolulu, Hawaii. It was not until February 1981, however, that a business relationship was cemented. A year earlier Chidiac had set up a London office for his company in a converted flat at 33 Barrie House, Lancaster Gate. He hired his brother Philip, a banker, and brought him over from Montreal, Canada, to be one of the directors. His other brother, Caesar, a doctor, was also a director but remained in Beirut. For tax reasons, Charles Chidiac was only a consultant.

Browne was hired by Chidiac's London company, Selco East, for his 'exclusive services' as an adviser and paid a retainer of £200 a month plus VAT. His job involved attending business meetings, providing briefings on banking and currency issues, and securing introductions for Selco East executives. He also signed a secrecy clause pledging 'not to disclose to any person whatsoever during or after the termination of this Agreement any information relating to the Company, its business or trade secrets'.[12]

From now on the two met more frequently. Chidiac visited Browne in the mornings for coffee at his Belgravia home and they would talk once a week on the telephone. On at least one occasion, on 2 July 1981, they had dinner at the House of Commons with an American client.

It was during this period that Browne's lobbying activities came to fruition. In February 1981, he wrote to Mrs Thatcher offering advice for her forthcoming Middle East tour. She agreed to see him and they met six weeks later, on the evening of 30 March. Part of the meeting was spent discussing whether the Prime Minister could make a good impression in Saudi Arabia by talking about falconry. The next day Browne wrote gratefully: 'I only hope that I did not stay too long.' Enclosed was a confidential paper in which he outlined who should be given presents and how to handle industrial contracts.

At the time Chidiac was a consultant for the engineering company Davy McKee, who were bidding for a $350 million contract to build a petro-chemical plant in Bahrain. Chidiac mentioned the project to Browne. After a meeting with Davy McKee, the MP dispatched an ugent letter to Mrs Thatcher while she was in the Middle East: 'I have located a project in which I believe you could play a critical role in winning for Great Britain . . . It is an important project and I believe that you would be very well advised to make a stop-over in Bahrain, if only for a few hours, to see Sheikh Issa.'[13] He enclosed a two-page memorandum extolling the virtues of Davy McKee, and concluded in capital letters: 'It is my belief that a key role can be played by the Prime Minister in getting this contract awarded to a British contractor by exerting influence on HH Sheikh Issa.'

The next day Browne wrote a similar letter to Cecil Parkinson, then a minister at the Department of Trade and a friend since the mid-1970s, when they took Swiss skiing holidays together. Douglas Hurd, then a Foreign minister, and Lord Selsdon, chairman of the Committee for Middle East Trade, also received letters from Browne informing them that 'political influence may well prove decisive'.

Davy McKee clearly saw Browne's support as crucial. The company's associate director, Peter Dance, sent the MP a formal letter that afternoon which concluded: 'Whilst we will do everything in our power to secure this contract, it would certainly be beneficial if the maximum political assistance could be made, not only at the highest but at all levels of Government influence.'[14]

Unfortunately for Davy McKee, Mrs Thatcher did not visit Bahrain. Six days later, on 23 April, Browne and Chidiac dined together at the House of Commons. The two must have been concerned, as the next morning Browne wrote to Mrs Thatcher's parliamentary aide, Ian Gow: 'I feel that the Prime Minister could exercise decisive influence . . . She may be able to telephone Sheikh Issa direct.' Two weeks later Parkinson responded. He explained that two other companies were bidding for the contract but agreed that his officials should meet Davy McKee to discuss the project. This meeting took place the following week and John Biffen, the Trade Secretary, wrote to Browne with a detailed account of the negotiations. But that proved to be the last chance for Davy McKee, as they failed to win the contract.

Mrs Thatcher did visit Bahrain, but not until September, five months later. She had been, according to Biffen, 'interested to know about this project, but in the circumstances no action on her part seemed necessary' to secure the contract.[15]

Browne did not disclose in this correspondence that he was paid a retainer by Chidiac's company, Selco East. Nor did he declare his consultancy in the Register of Members' Interests.

Browne engaged in a different kind of lobbying when a contract to build nuclear aircraft shelters for the Iraqi airforce became available. Tarmac International were interested in bidding and so Browne introduced two of their executives, Jack Codd and Bernard Woodman (an old contact), to Chidiac. On 23 March 1981, the four met at Tarmac's new offices on Great Western Road, near Heathrow airport. Codd 'explained that whilst he and many of his colleagues in Tarmac International were very keen to start operations in Iraq, they still had to persuade their main Board'.[16]

The negotiations became protracted, and for the next two months Browne, Chidiac and Codd met only informally, usually for drinks at the Churchill Hotel in Portman Square. Then, in the first ten days of June, two Tarmac executives embarked on a Middle East tour which included Baghdad, Iraq's capital. On 5 June 1981, an agreement between Chidiac's Beirut company, Selco Construction, and Tarmac was finalised. Chidiac was hired to represent Tarmac if they tendered for the Iraqi aircraft shelters contract. That same day Browne wrote to Stephen Egerton, the British ambassador in Iraq, requesting a meeting between him and the two visiting Tarmac directors. He concluded: 'The purpose of their visit is to look for opportunities in the construction field. As you will know, we are very anxious to help Iraq. I would be very grateful for any help and assistance you can give Tarmac.'[17]

Again the MP's commerical interest was not declared. As it turned out, Tarmac did not tender for the contract and Chidiac received no fees.

Browne's consultancy with Chidiac's company was terminated when another of the MP's clients, Barclays Bank International, objected. In November 1981, Chidiac asked Browne to open a Barclays bank account for him in Atlanta, Georgia. Browne telexed with instructions. But it was not a smooth transaction. Barclays were reluctant to open the account and Chidiac exchanged harsh words with their Atlanta branch manager. Then, when Selco East established 'a business relationship' with Barclays in February 1982, the bank took exception to the MP's consultancy with the Chidiac firm. There was, said Barclays, 'an unacceptable conflict of interest'.[18] Browne promptly resigned from Selco East.

Browne has always maintained that his lobbying for Chidiac involved no financial gain for himself – either actual or potential. 'There was no benefit to me. At the most, a drink,' he remarked.[19] But Chidiac has admitted that if he had secured the Davy McKee contract, he would have offered to give the MP a gift: 'The deal would have been worth $114 million. My commission on that would have been 2 per cent and I would have offered Mr Browne a cheque for perhaps $250,000 as a present.'[20] He added that the MP 'did not know of this and I had no idea whether he would have accepted it or not'.[21]

Browne also argued that his lobbying for Chidiac was motivated purely by patriotism and that it was completely separate from his consultancy with Selco East:

Selco East was a normal commercial client of Falcon Finance Management [Browne's firm] and, as the work did not relate to Parliament, I believed that the interest need not be declared . . . Charles Chidiac had a consultancy relationship with Selco East in London . . . He himself also traded using a corporate vehicle, again known as Selco East. However, I believe that this company was registered in Lebanon.[22]

Essentially, Browne's case was that the London company, Selco East Consultants Ltd, was a separate entity and not controlled or owned by Charles Chidiac. However, this is contradicted by the company's own documents. The most damning evidence was a letter from Charles Chidiac to Browne: 'This letter is to confirm that *our company*, Selco East Consultants Ltd, employed your services as a consultant' (my emphasis). It was signed by Charles Chidiac 'For Selco East Consultants Ltd'.[23] What is more, Selco's note-paper contained the epithet 'From the desk of Charles Chidiac'. Not only did Charles operate from Selco's office in London, but when Browne resigned his consultancy he began his letter: 'In Charles's absence abroad . . .'[24] Finally, Browne himself stated that he had 'business meetings' with Charles Chidiac.[25]

All this evidence indicates that Selco East in London was a mere branch of Chidiac's holding company, registered in the Lebanon. Indeed, the note-paper states that Selco's head office was in Beirut. As a source close to the Chidiac family told me: 'Charles was the company.'

A more lucrative Middle East client for Browne was the Saudi Arabian Monetary Agency, the Saudi central bank. Browne had worked with them in the mid-1970s while at the European Banking Company and he then retained them for his own firm, Falcon Finance Management.

In the spring of 1982 a Saudi banker representing the Saudi Arabian Monetary Agency flew in from Riyadh to visit the MP in London. Browne was commissioned to produce a special report on the consequences for Saudi Arabia if foreign banks froze financial assets held in their UK branches. The Agency was concerned this would happen in the event of a Middle East upheaval, as it did when the Americans froze Iranian assets in London during the 1979 hostages crisis. The project was code-named 'Deep Freeze' and Browne was to be paid £57,188 for his part in it.

The Saudi banking authorities have a passion for secrecy rivalled only by the Swiss. When Browne visited Saudi Arabia for a briefing on his report, he was told the meeting was too sensitive to be held at the Saudi Arabian Monetary Agency's head office in Airport Road, Riyadh. Instead, he met the governor and vice-governor of the agency at the Finance Minister's private residence. Browne himself regarded the commission as 'top secret', and during a later legal action he requested that SAMA should not be uttered in open court.[26]

Browne's concern for secrecy was almost certainly the reason for not declaring the agency as a client in the Register of Members' Interests. He also twice raised the issues behind 'Deep Freeze' in the House of Commons without disclosing his commercial involvement. On 30 July 1982, Browne was granted his own adjournment debate. During a forty-minute speech he asked ten questions of the Treasury Minister, the late Jock Bruce-Gardyne, who attended the debate. One of them was:

Will the Government support the establishment of a code of conduct to be observed by all IMF-member banks in the event of their freezing the financial assets of another government? Could such a code of conduct be designed to prevent extra-territorial claims, the right of set-off and the waiving of sovereign immunity as was exercised by the US government in the freezing of Iranian assets?[27]

Browne declared only a general interest, as 'a director and adviser to companies within the UK's financial and banking industries'.[28] There was no mention of his client, the Saudi Arabian Central Bank. Nor was there any declaration four months later, when he asked the Prime Minister:

Despite the problems that are facing various international financial centres, will my right hon. friend please assure the House that under no circumstances whatever will Her Majesty's Government tolerate an extra-territorial freeze on financial assets in the British branches of foreign banks, as took place in the Iranian asset freeze?

Mrs Thatcher assured him: 'We shall continue to resist attempts by overseas governments to apply their jurisdiction to the United Kingdom.'[29]

Given the importance of London as a financial market, and the strong presence of US banking interests and Saudi investments, this confirmation of government policy would have been of great interest to the Saudi Arabian Monetary Agency.[30] Technically, Browne was not obliged to declare an interest as in both cases he was asking a question. But it does show how the project involved parliamentary lobbying.

Browne denied this: 'There were many different investors round the world who were deeply concerned by the American—US—Iranian asset freeze. I saw an opportunity to boost Britain as a financial centre . . . My motivation for asking that question was not to do with anything for Saudi Arabia but to do good for Britain.'[31] However, he acknowledged that: 'I knew the Saudis were very worried about the American freeze on assets.'[32] This was, of course, why the agency commissioned the study.

Three months after asking his question, Browne submitted the 'Deep Freeze' report. The invoice requested that the fee be paid to Falcon Finance Management. This was because his then wife Elizabeth, a director and shareholder of his company, had lent him £20,000 as an advance on expenses. Browne had agreed to repay the loan once he received the payment.

On Wednesday 25 May 1983, during the second week of the general election campaign, the cheque for $88,270 (£57,188) arrived at the Cheapside offices of Coopers and Lybrand, Browne's accountants. Acting on the MP's instructions, they immediately delivered it to his bank, Coutts and Co., at 15 Lombard Street. That afternoon his young secretary, Carolyn Abberley, received a phone-call from Browne. 'There's a problem with a cheque that has arrived for me,' he said. 'It's for a very large amount in a foreign currency, so I need to counter-sign it on the back. This is very important so keep it safe.'[33]

Abberley then collected the cheque from Coutts and took the train to Winchester, where Browne was campaigning. The reason for the MP's urgency soon became clear. The money, due to be paid into the Falcon Finance Management account, was instead deposited into Browne's personal Coutts dollar account. Browne then set up another company, Falcon Finance Services Ltd, and a week later transferred $88,000 into that new firm's Coutts dollar deposit account. A fortnight later Browne used this money to buy 30,000 shares, worth $50,000, in Cybermedic Inc., an American computer company. He spent $1,260 on a painting from the Galerie la Chèvre d'Or in France for his office. The rest paid off loans, travel expenses or remained in various Coutts bank accounts.

It was not until 5 September 1983, three months after the Saudi Arabian Monetary Agency cheque had been cashed, that Elizabeth

Browne discovered what had happened. She had by then left the MP, but remained a director and shareholder of Falcon Finance Management. She immediately sued him for her £20,000 loan to be repaid, plus interest. In the High Court, the judge was not impressed by John Browne's evidence. Mr Justice Gibson 'found the affidavit of Mr Browne lamentably inadequate and was gravely troubled by it as it cast doubt on anything Mr Browne had said'.[34] The MP was ordered to pay his ex-wife £25,600.

Browne's case was that he diverted the cheque 'because I apprehended the misuse of the funds by my wife'.[35] But it was impossible for Elizabeth Browne to draw on Falcon Finance Management funds. She never had a company chequebook and had been removed from the firm's bank mandate on 6 May – nineteen days before the cheque arrived. This was done without a board resolution or meeting.

Working for the Yankee dollar

The Saudi Arabia episode inadvertently involved another of Browne's foreign clients. This was Emmet A. Stephenson Junior, an American merchant banker who had advised the MP to buy the Cybermedic shares from the proceeds of the agency's cheque.[36]

Browne had known Stephenson since 1969 when they were classmates at the Harvard Business School. After graduation Stephenson moved to Denver, Colorado, while Browne went to New York to learn investment banking. In 1977 Stephenson became senior partner of his private investment management firm and began to meet Browne regularly. The talk was always about business, even over dinner or at Annabel's, the exclusive nightclub. Stephenson had a vast range of commercial interests. He was chairman of General Communications Inc., Charter Bank and Trust and Circle Energy Inc. He was also a director of Satellink Corporation, a cable TV company, and ten other oil and gas companies. Like Browne, he was an underwriting member of Lloyd's of London, the insurance market.

In 1980 Stephenson founded his own private merchant-banking firm, based in Denver, Colorado. He immediately hired Browne on a commission basis. The MP's task was to persuade individuals and banks to invest in projects managed by Stephenson Merchant Banking. Browne spent some time visiting investors in Paris and the Swiss cities of Basle, Geneva and Zurich. A typical approach was a letter to Jacques Rossier, vice-president of the Swiss Bank Corporation. Browne suggested:

> A pilot scheme could be established with Emmet Stephenson and an investor of your size could effectively write their own ticket with regard to the structure of the vehicle and the investment criteria to be followed.
>
> P.S. I enclose herewith a copy of a recent speech I made in the House of Commons.[37]

Many such letters were written on House of Commons note-paper. This was in breach of parliamentary rules, which state that 'such circulars must not be used for correspondence of a business or commercial nature'.[38]

Stephenson was particularly keen on investing in real estate in his home town. Browne lobbied firms and banks on his behalf. 'I believe that Emmet Stephenson represents an outstanding opportunity of investing in what must be one of the great growth areas of the next quarter of the century,' he wrote to Crédit Suisse of Zurich.[39] Another potential investor was told: 'For the first time in my adult life, we in England are now free of foreign exchange controls and I am advising all my clients to have between 25 and 50 per cent of their free assets in the United States ... Denver and Colorado in particular represent opportunities to invest.'[40] The same message was conveyed to Banque Worms, the French merchant bank. Browne was at the time a director of their London subsidiary, Worms Investment Ltd, at an annual fee of £2,000.

Browne's target was to raise $10 million for Stephenson. If successful, his placement fee was 1 per cent. However, by 1984 the MP had secured only $4 million and his commission was reduced to 0.2 per cent. This meant Browne received $64,000, which was paid in eight annual instalments. The first $8,000 remittance was channelled through a private Bermudan Trust set up by the MP as a tax avoidance scheme.[41]

In July 1984 Stephenson wrote to Browne and confirmed the payments. He added:

> There is no change in our agreement for splitting fees 50/50 for mergers, acquisitions and private placements if one of us finds the deal and the other one finds the money. Although the $4 million raised for Stephenson Merchant Banking is the only business we have accomplished thus far, let us hope that the future will enable us to do business in these other areas as well.[42]

The MP took full advantage of Stephenson's commercial hospitality. He opened a representative office of his company, Falcon Finance Management, in Denver and began to contact investors. After meeting Iqbal Mamdani, president of the Trans Arabian Investment Bank, in Washington, Browne wrote to him: 'We may be able to do some very interesting business together in the field of identifying investment opportunities for your clients. The areas that I specialise in are: energy, particularly oil and gas; local real estate; high technology; and publishing.'[43]

It was Browne's energy interests that attracted another US investment firm – Dallas-based Natural Resource Management Inc. The MP worked for them on a commission basis, introducing senior executives to potential investors. In 1985, he was hired to arrange entertainment for clients, bankers and brokers as a 'thank-you present' for the money raised that year. On 1 July he took sixty-two clients to lunch at the Guards Polo Club at Windsor, where some of them were introduced to Prince Charles. A week later Browne laid on a special dinner for the group at Goldsmiths Hall. The MP spent a total of four days with the Natural Resource Management clients and was paid a fee of $9,200.

Despite receiving fees from them since 1983 ($2,100 in November of that year), Browne did not declare the client until 1988. The $64,000 from Stephenson was also not disclosed to Parliament. This was despite the Commons rule that 'any payments . . . received from or on behalf of foreign governments, organisations or persons' should be divulged. Instead, from 1980 until 1987, he merely declared Falcon Finance Management, with no mention of clients. When pressed about details of his foreign earnings, Browne's standard reply was: 'All financial implications are reflected in the accounts of Falcon Finance Management.' But this was incorrect. An examination of the company accounts produces no information about clients or income. Instead, there is this statement: 'The Directors consider any disclosure of the geographical breakdown of turnover prejudicial to the interests of the company.'[44]

Abroad on business

One of the main grievances held by voters against MPs with foreign commercial interests is the amount of time spent away from their constituencies. It is not just consultancies and directorships that keep MPs abroad. Well-organised, all-expenses-paid foreign visits to exotic locations are also a useful lobbying tactic by companies and governments.

In recent years the number of privately funded trips has increased substantially – 425 declared in 1990, compared with 283 in 1989. Known as 'jollies' in the Commons because of the lavish travel and hotel expenses, the invitations can range from an inaugural British Airways flight to Rio to a visit to a Bavarian brewery.

Official 'fact-finding' missions (or fee-finding expeditions according to street-wise lobbyists) are paid for by the public purse. But they are organised in a remarkably private, club-like way. The excursions are arranged by the MPs themselves. What is more, the Commons Liaison Committee, which approves funding for these foreign trips, is made up of chairmen of select committees – the very same people who are asking for the cash to go abroad. 'Not surprisingly, they all scratch each other's backs and decide their trips are absolutely essential', according to the Labour MP and former Industry Minister Bob Cryer, a member of the Liaison Committee. 'I am not aware of any trip they have refused. They all just vote for each other's junkets.'[45]

In 1989 this committee awarded £360,000 to their colleagues for such trips, almost every application having been accepted. The Foreign Affairs Select Committee was given £25,000 to visit Bonn, Paris, Madrid, Strasbourg and Brussels. The Energy and Agriculture Committees both received over £30,000. Even the Home Affairs Committee was handed £12,000 to go to Amsterdam and Rome. Ironically, the biggest money-spinner was the Select Committee on Members' Interests, which received £24,000 for a single visit to study lobbying in Canada. Bob Cryer, also a member of the Members' Interests Committee, boycotted the Canadian trip in protest:

Some of these committees spend almost more time abroad than they do on British soil. Some have genuine reasons for going abroad. But others are little more than trips to watch trees grow in America or New Zealand. It is now seen as a perk of committee membership.

A lot of the trips are entirely unnecessary. I am tired of the interminable discussions over whether the MPs should travel first, club or economy class. It [the Liaison Committee] is more like a travel agency than a Commons committee.[46]

One organisation that could not be accused of taking MPs off to glamorous pleasure resorts is the import-export company Rindalbourne Ltd, which specialises in trade with Eastern Europe. But they have arranged trips to corrupt Communist dictatorships. In March and October 1985 they paid for Labour MPs Frank Haynes and Harold Walker, Deputy Speaker of the Commons, and Tory MPs Andrew Hunter and Richard Alexander to visit Romania.[47] Hunter, unlike his fellow MPs, failed to declare the excursions. 'It was a bad, but genuine mistake on my part,' he reflected. 'They were jolly good trips, and we tried to increase UK commercial interests.'[48]

The delegations, led by former Labour Prime Minister Lord Wilson, a director of Rindalbourne, met and presented gifts to President Ceauşescu. After the March 1985 visit, the company was awarded a £100 million trade concordat with Romania. According to Philip McKearney, the British ambassador in Bucharest at the time:

> It seemed that the idea behind the trip was to build up Rindalbourne's position *vis-à-vis* the authorities. Any back-up they could receive from British politicians would have been very helpful. I thought that they were all a bit naïve. They hadn't examined the motives of the firm and the use that the Romanians would make of the visit. From the point of view of the British government, it was not helpful, desirable or useful.[49]

McKearney's analysis proved correct. After those trips both Hunter and Alexander asked the DTI questions which provided detailed information about Anglo-Romanian trade.[50] Alexander has been a consultant to Rindalbourne since 1985.[51]

Puppets on a southern African string

In recent years one of the most controversial lobbying campaigns has been conducted by the South African backed government of Bophuthatswana. The country is very much the child of the Pretoria regime – 'born out of the womb of the obnoxious policy of apartheid,' as Tory MP Tim Rathbone described it after one visit.[52]

On the creation of Bophuthatswana in 1977 as part of the homelands policy, the black Tswana people were given six scattered, fragmented regions with no common border. The country remains economically dependent on South Africa (24 per cent of its budget comes from Pretoria) and its police force has a brutal human rights record. It also provides a pool of black labour for industry around Johannesburg and Pretoria.

Bophuthatswana is perhaps best known for 'Sun City', a vast leisure complex similar to Las Vegas. Ostensibly a tourist resort, it is used to host celebrity musical and sporting events, providing useful international publicity. Stars like Frank Sinatra are paid enormous fees to perform although many artists have boycotted it in protest. 'Sin City', just two and a half hours' drive from Johannesburg, is also a haven for gambling, vice and prostitution. Their best customers are wealthy white South African businessmen, grateful to escape the puritanical restraints of their fatherland.

Despite 'Sun City', only South Africa acknowledges Bophuthatswana as an independent state. Every other country, including the United Nations, has disowned the homeland as a mere appendage of apartheid. For the Bophuthatswana government, political and diplomatic recognition is the primary motivation behind their lobbying activities.

In the summer of 1980 Peter Emery, the Tory MP for Honiton in East Devon, was visiting South Africa when he met an old business friend, Leon Tamman, chairman of International Generics. Tamman, who was trying to secure a deal to build hotels in Bophuthatswana, introduced Emery to the country's President, Leon Mangope. The MP and the President got on well and Emery became a confidante. Within eighteen months Emery and his company, Shenley Trust Services, were hired to advise and promote Bophuthatswana in their bid for international acceptance.

Emergy was an astute choice. As a young MP in the early 1960s, he entertained the Ghana nationalists Mboyo and Nkrumah at his flat in Paddington and later formed the Anglo-Ghanaian parliamentary group. But he also led an active commercial life and once described himself as 'a businessman rather than a politician'.[53] His commercial career began in 1955 when, while a parliamentary candidate and a Hornsey borough councillor, he set up, with his wife Elizabeth, his own private import-export consultancy company, Emery and Emery Ltd. In 1959, at the third attempt, he became a Conservative MP. During the 1964–70 Labour government he was an Opposition spokesman on Trade and Treasury matters while on the board of several companies, notably Phillips Petroleum International UK. In April 1972 he resigned these directorships when he joined the Department of Industry as a junior minister. He was later given extra responsibility for Trade and Consumer Affairs. He also had a short spell at the Department of Energy, which ended with the fall of the Heath government in 1974.

After the election defeat Emery returned to the back-benches – and to the business world. He immediately restructured his consultancy firm, which became Energy and Environment Engineering Ltd – 'project managers on enterprises relating to the environment or energy resources'. He also joined Shenley Trust, a small private bank, with the job of building up a 'corporate and industrial finance division'.[54] As a consultant, Emery's brief was to raise private capital on behalf of company clients. But Shenley was not a success and collapsed after less than three years in operation.

In April 1976, Emery made another fresh start. This time his firm was remodelled as Shenley Trust Services Ltd and given a wider remit as 'project managers, advisers and consultants'. Emery was its chairman and chief executive, and owned 95 per cent of the shares. For the first four years the MP drew an annual salary of £12,000. But from 1981 the directors' fees increased substantially, and by 1984 Emery and Jamie Guise, his business partner, were being paid £35,000 a year each. Most of their earnings came from overseas – £117,100 in 1983 alone.[55]

Shenley act as project managers and consultants for British and foreign companies, specialising in raising corporate finance for joint industrial ventures overseas. Their clients have included British companies trying to do business in the Soviet Union, Romania, Yugoslavia, the Arab states, Kenya, Nigeria, Zimbabwe and Ghana. However, when Emery agreed to represent the government of Bophuthatswana in 1981, it was a different kind of client relationship. Unlike other countries, the homeland needed more than commercial counselling. They required political muscle.

At first the MP was given low-level instructions. 'It is best at this stage,' said the Foreign Affairs Minister, 'to pursue our objective of political recognition via the fields of commerce, trade and tourism and by proving the positiveness of our independence to the rest of the world.'[56] Emery and his firm agreed with this strategy. But first a UK base or 'Embassy' was needed to co-ordinate the lobbying. Emery advised President Mangope that by forming a company and securing a controlling interest, the Bophuthatswana government could buy a property in London. Mangope was delighted, and in November 1981 the Bophuthatswana National Commercial Corporation Ltd was formed. The directors were Mangope, the Foreign Minister Molatlhwa and Jamie Guise, representing Shenley Trust Services.

On their behalf, Emery bought a large, elegant Victorian mansion at 60 Holland Park, west London. He then arranged for the house to be decorated, furnished and equipped with telex and telephone lines. The total cost, including the purchase, was £865,000.

On 1 January 1982, Emery and his company were officially hired as Bophuthatswana's consultants in the UK. The fee was £84,000 a year (plus expenses), paid in instalments of £14,000 every two months. There was also a secrecy clause in the contract: 'The advisers [Shenley Trust Services] undertake not to disclose to any third party, either during the performance of this agreement or after termination, any confidential information acquired, unless the government consents in writing.'[57] The consultancy was to last nearly three years, but Emery did not declare it to Parliament – either as a client of Shenley or as a foreign payment.[58]

Emery and Shenley's remit was to sponsor Bophuthatswana's case for political and diplomatic recognition. This meant being more than just advisers. Lobbying and public relations were also required. The African government called on the firm 'to promote' their interests through lectures, meetings, social functions, circulating information to the media and organising trips to Bophuthatswana.[59]

Emery later denied his company was a lobbying organisation for the homeland: 'Shenley does not act, nor has it at any time acted, as a public relations company either for the government of Bophuthatswana or for any other organisation.'[60] He also denied being 'a provider of publicity' for his clients. However, Emery's own personal assistant at Shenley Trust Services, Gillian Craig, sent out a large bundle of glossy publicity brochures which consisted of glowing government booklets promoting the homeland. Craig, who spent nearly all her time on the Bophuthatswana account, wrote a covering letter on Shenley note-paper: 'I am enclosing some literature on the Republic of Bophuthatswana which I hope will be of some use.'[61]

Shenley also employed a public-relations consultant, Ruth Rees, who worked on the Bophuthatswana account from the company's offices at Sackville Street, off Piccadilly. Rees was hired by Langford Letlhaku, the director of Tourism, who told her: 'As we have just appointed an MP to handle our interests in England, he [Emery] will need to approve your appointment and it will make sense for you to use his facilities.' Emery's view of Shenley's role was revealed when he told Rees that her job included 'building up diplomatic links in order to "*Spread the Gospel*" about Bophuthatswana' (my emphasis). He also wrote a 700-word feature article in *The Times* praising his clients – 'The Acceptable Face of the Homelands'.[62] Readers of the 'Top People's Paper' were not told that the MP was a paid consultant to the country whose cause he was promoting.

By the autumn of 1982 the renovation of 'Bophuthatswana House' in Holland Park was complete. On 7 September, Emery hosted its opening reception with a seminar on tourism and a cocktail party. Despite a picket of 200 anti-apartheid demonstrators, several Tory MPs and VIPs attended and were introduced to Bophuthatswana ministers.

One of the main lobbying tactics was to take British MPs out to the South African homeland on all-expenses trips. According to Bophuthatswana's former PR consultant Ruth Rees, many of these visits were organised by Sir Peter Emery (he had been knighted in January 1982 for 'political services').

However, Sir Peter's responsibility was more than just promotional. He was also the sole signatory to Bophuthatswana's Coutts current bank account at their Mayfair branch at 10 Mount Street. This placed the MP in the position of authorising all UK expenditure.

Sir Peter's consultancy with Bophuthatswana ended in a prolonged period of controversy. In July 1984, the Bophuthatswana government terminated the business arrangement on friendly terms. 'It is trusted,' said the Secretary for Foreign Affairs, 'that our valuable friendship will continue to grow and prosper in the future.'[63] Sir Peter's company, Shenley Trust Services, was given four months' notice and paid £70,000 in outstanding fees and expenses. The row started after Sir Peter withdrew £75,902 from the Bophuthatswana bank account. This took place on 14 September 1984 – ten weeks before the end of the MP's consultancy. A week later, when Sir Peter was on business in Geneva, Switzerland, he opened a new bank account at Crédit Suisse and deposited the £75,902 cheque.

In April 1986, eighteen months later, Bophuthatswana government accountants inquired about the £75,902 and confronted Sir Peter. He replied that the money had been held in trust in a secret deposit account for President Mangope's personal use. The President angrily denied this and issued a High Court writ alleging that the

MP had 'wrongfully converted' the funds 'to his own use by transferring it to a third party for collection'.

Sir Peter was equally adamant about the ownership of the cash:

> The President of Bophuthatswana gave instructions that certain money held in London be transferred to Shenley Trust Services. As chairman of that company, I was given specific authority to receive this money and, on the President's instructions, this was originally deposited in a company of which the President was a director. At all times this money has been properly invested. It has never belonged to Shenley Trust Services or myself, neither has it ever been suggested that it did.[64]

A month later, on 11 June 1986, the writ was withdrawn when Sir Peter repaid the money plus interest (a total of £89,255). This was done, said Sir Peter, on the instructions of President Mangope.

Again the President took issue with the MP. On 22 August 1986, he asked the City of London police to investigate 'Sir Peter's . . . actions in respect of his illegal removal of funds'.[65] By the end of the twenty-month police inquiry, Bophuthatswana's lawyers, the City firm Norton, Rose, reported on the prospects of the DPP recommending any charges under the 1968 Theft Act.[66] However, the Crown Prosecution Service replied: 'There would only be sufficient evidence to justify criminal proceedings if the Director of Public Prosecutions received an undertaking that President Mangope will give evidence in this country.'[67]

The President declined to give evidence, claiming that Bophuthatswana's constitution prevented him from giving evidence in a foreign court.[68] No criminal proceedings were ever brought, and in April 1988 the City of London police investigation was terminated.

There was a final twist to this saga. In January 1990 a *World In Action* investigation into MPs' business interests included this story. Transcripts of the programme were requested by the press and one reached Sir Peter's local paper, the *Exmouth Herald*. André Gibbons, the paper's most experienced news reporter, followed up the story and made his own inquiries.

In the early evening of Thursday 15 March, the day before publication, Gibbons was in the news-room polishing his report when he looked up and saw a familiar face. This was PC Kim Chapman, a local police officer Gibbons had known for six years. 'André, I don't know what it's about but I've been sent round on higher authority,' said Chapman. 'I understand you're working on an article about Sir Peter Emery. Can I have a copy of it?'

Gibbons was surprised at such a request, but was unperturbed as his story had already gone to press. A copy was printed out and taken away by the police officer. But an hour later a stunned Gibbons was told by his editor that the story would not be published. The decision had been taken by the paper's owners, Eastern Counties Newspapers.

The next morning the article was returned by 'the higher authority' – the Devon and Cornwall Police headquarters at Middlemoor in Exeter. Gibbons's detailed report about Sir Peter never reached the public domain.

The bitter dispute with Sir Peter Emery in the summer of 1986 produced a new era in the lobbying strategy by the Bophuthatswana government. In December 1986, Ian Findlay was appointed chief executive of their London operation.

A white administrator who had worked for the Zimbabwe government, Findlay believed the best way to achieve political recognition was to court and cultivate MPs. He entertained them to lunch and dinner – either at the expensive L'Amico restaurant near the Commons or at the Holland Park residence. In September 1987 a British Bophuthatswana Group was formed in the Commons.

It was from this period that the use of controversial free trips to the South African homeland was intensified. The ten-day visits began by flying the MPs and their wives business class to Johannesburg and then on to Bophuthatswana. The tickets are open so the couples can return at their own discretion. The tour is a combination of reception cocktails, visits to the platinum mines, excursions to 'Sun City', meetings with government ministers and tours of schools and hospitals.[69]

Bophuthatswana officials in London are convinced these trips are a worthwhile investment in their bid for political recognition. When giving evidence to a Select Committee inquiry into lobbying, Ian Findlay was asked: 'Are you satisfied that your government is getting good value for money out of British Members of Parliament?'

'Very much so,' replied Findlay. 'There is not the slightest doubt in my mind that we get a tremendous return in the dedication of these people.'[70]

However, Bophuthatswana's own public-relations consultant for six years, Ruth Rees, has a completely opposite view. She disapproved of the way the 'freebies' were organised because, she said, the MPs 'were only showed the good parts'. She told me:

> The freebie method was causing a lot of harm, particularly as wives were asked along as well. The MPs are bound to be influenced by the hospitality, an all-expenses paid, five-star luxury trip to a country which has beautiful weather and lovely places to visit. But what they are not told are the realities of the ordinary daily life of the Tswana people who have no means of voicing their disapproval because there is no opposition party.

Rees, an experienced travel writer, had extensive knowledge of southern Africa, having lived there for nine years. She began working for Bophuthatswana in 1982 and developed a great fondness and empathy for the Tswana people. Visiting journalists recall her as being a vigorous and staunch defender of the regime. Her disaffection started in early 1987 when the free trips escalated. She had always been opposed to them and clashed with Findlay. 'I must tell you,' she said, 'that your policy of taking MPs out with their wives is counterproductive because the media see it as a perk.' Findlay was unmoved. 'You don't understand,' he replied. 'Their wives are also influential in their own way through groups like the Women's Institutes.'

Rees's main objection was that the Tswana people were 'being misled' into believing that the MPs' trips would result in political recognition. But Findlay declined to listen to her anxieties and excluded her from key decisions about lobbying tactics. The final catalyst for her disillusionment came in June 1987, when *Africa Confidential*, a specialist independent magazine, published a detailed article about an alleged corrupt relationship between an Israeli businessman and the Bophuthatswana government. Rees was horrified and immediately negotiated a right of reply. She then went into Findlay's office, showed him the article and suggested a response.

'Don't you think these allegations should be investigated?' she asked. 'They are very serious.'

'No, just say no comment if anyone rings up. Just forget about it,' replied Findlay.

Despite being promoted to public-relations executive, Rees was now constantly in conflict with Findlay's lobbying policies. In November 1988 she was summoned to the European head office in Paris and sacked.

Rees's demise coincided with the rising influence of Andrew Hunter, the right-wing Conservative MP for Basingstoke. A consistent opponent of sanctions and sporting bans against South Africa, Hunter was the first chairman of the Bophuthatswana Parliamentary Group. He has been a frequent visitor to the homeland. At a farewell dinner during one visit he outlined his lobbying strategy: 'Every conceivable means of presenting Bophuthatswana's case has and will be used through formal debates, oral and written questions, correspondence with ministers and the Prime Minister and informal lobbying on a personal basis with ministers.'[71]

Hunter was more specific in his private dealings with the London office. On 25 March 1988, he wrote a confidential five-page memorandum on Commons note-paper. Entitled 'A Foreign Policy for Bophuthatswana – a view from Westminster', it argued that 'the highest priority' must be given to lobbying: 'Nothing will be achieved without first affecting a revolution in media-handling and public relations.' One of his main proposals was for the reunification of Botswana and Bophuthatswana by maximising economic contacts. Hunter was not a paid consultant to the Bophuthatswana government, but his advocacy of closer economic links with Botswana placed him in a potentially delicate situation. For the following year he was a founding director of and later shareholder in Maestro Trading Ltd, a subsidiary of the import-export company Rindalbourne Ltd.

For its first six months this firm specialised in business in southern Africa, including Botswana. The MP resigned as a director in June 1990. Two months later he joined the board of its parent company, Maestro Properties (Botswana) Ltd, where he was also a shareholder.

After eight years, despite Hunter's enthusiastic promotion of Bophuthatswana, their lobbying campaign has not worked. The Foreign Office continues to refuse to recognise Bophuthatswana 'or any of the "independent" homelands'.[72] It is also clear that hiring an ex-minister (Sir Peter Emery) as a consultant failed, as did entertaining groups of MPs and their wives to what amounted to free holidays. Bophuthatswana's London office believe otherwise. But the stigma of being a child of apartheid is an almost impossible obstacle to overcome. It seems the only real solution will come when the political map of southern Africa changes.

Being paid by foreign bankers, clients and governments encapsulates all the problems of MPs for hire – secrecy clauses, huge fees, expensive travel and discreet lobbying of ministers. But equally serious are the major flaws in the rules governing foreign business interests.

Both Sir Peter Emery and John Browne have relied upon rule seven. This states that payments received from 'foreign governments, organisations or persons' should be declared. The escape route is that this seems to apply only when it 'affects his conduct as a Member'. This means that in theory an MP could be paid hundreds of thousands of pounds by a foreign agency and not be obliged to declare it.

Sir Peter and Browne were also able to avoid public scrutiny by setting up their own effectively one-man consultancy companies. This enabled them merely to declare the directorship and shareholding of their firm but not, crucially, the identity of their clients.

However, as John Biffen, Conservative MP and former Cabinet minister and Leader of the House of Commons, said: 'It is questionable whether MPs should be allowed to be hired by foreign governments or organisations at all.'[73]

CHAPTER 3

In the City

'A loaf of bread,' the Walrus said,
  'Is what we chiefly need:
Pepper and vinegar besides
  Are very good indeed –
Now if you're ready, Oysters dear,
  We can begin to feed.'
Lewis Carroll, *Alice in Wonderland*

In the summer of 1965, James (now Lord) Callaghan, then Chancellor of the Exchequer and later Prime Minister, delivered a speech which turned out to be one of the most controversial of his career. It was a reflective appraisal of MPs' conduct after observing them in the House of Commons. The Finance Bill was passing through Parliament and Callaghan was clearly outraged. He told his Swansea audience:

> I do not think of them as the Honourable Member for X, or Y or Z constituency. I look at them and say Investment Trusts, Capital speculators or 'That is the fellow who is the Stock Exchange man who makes profit on Gilt Edge.' I have almost forgotten their constituencies, but I shall never forget their interests. I wonder sometimes whom they represent. The constituents or their own or friends' particular interests.[1]

It was an uncharacteristically radical speech from a minister of life-long moderate views. But his fellow MPs were incensed by his allegations. Sir Robert Cary, the Conservative Member for Manchester Withington, complained to the Commons Privileges Committee. Callaghan was then called upon to explain himself. He backed down:

> I did not have in mind in my speech either to state or imply that hon. members who possess interests are acting or were acting improperly in taking part in discussions on the Finance Bill . . . I submit to the Committee that

47

if political speeches calling attention to such interests are to be regarded as a breach of privilege, then legitimate comment and rights of free speech will be seriously impaired.[2]

The Chancellor was cleared of contempt of the House on the grounds that his speech was 'ambiguous'. But his observations are as valid today as they were twenty-six years ago – if not more so.

The uninterrupted period of Conservative government since 1979 has resulted in an unprecedented expansion in business activity. Whilst legislation was passed to control the restrictive practices of trade unions, the City was left to self-regulation. This generated a frenzy of speculative take-overs and mergers in the City and industry which, together with legislation to break up state and private monopolies, has created lucrative clients for merchant banks, stockbrokers, lobbyists, insurance companies and accountants. The maxim, expressed by the banker Jack Hambro, that the City was like the British Empire ('there's nothing more to gain and quite a lot to lose') no longer held.[3] Big Business was profit-hungry again.

To help them take advantage of these new opportunities, companies have hired MPs as consultants. Some are used as their 'eyes and ears' in Westminster, some as lobbyists. Others are paid commission fees to introduce new clients. The City-friendly atmosphere has also seen MPs prepared to play the stock market, particularly when a state-owned industry is being privatised.

A share of the market

To Anthony Beaumont-Dark, Conservative MP for Birmingham Selly Oak, speculating in the stock market has been as familiar as his often controversial political comments are to the public. An investment analyst since the early 1960s, he is quite open about his activities: 'In the investment business we are a bit like fishermen. It's the good ones that get away that most get you. And while I have had plenty of successes, I have had many that have got away . . . There have been cases when I have bought when I should have sold. Too often you reinforce failure and sell success.'[4]

Most of Beaumont-Dark's buying and selling has been with the stockbrokers Smith, Keen and Cutler. In 1979 he became an MP and continued as the firm's senior partner for six years when he was made a consultant. A member of the Treasury and Civil Service Select Committee since his election, he began expanding his business interests in 1983. That year he became a director of the construction company Birmid-Qualcast PLC and held 10,000 shares. In November 1989, Beaumont-Dark resigned from Birmid-Qualcast and joined the board of stockbrokers J. Saville Gordon, where he holds 16,000 ordinary 10p shares. He also became a director of TR High Income Trust PLC.

The extent of Beaumont-Dark's activities was shown by his reaction to 'Black Monday', the day of the stock-market crash in October 1987. When asked how much he had lost, he replied: 'I've lost too much to laugh about and not enough to cry about.'[5] In fact, it was a six-figure sum, which the MP dismissed as 'only paper money'.[6]

In 1990 Beaumont-Dark was being paid £30,000 a year for his three outside jobs and, to his credit, disclosed this amount. 'I'm quite happy to say what I get, though others would hate it,' he remarked.[7]

Another MP to have grown wealthy from his shares is Sir Peter Hordern, the Conservative MP for Horsham since 1964. A stockbroker since the age of 23, Sir Peter's business career took off in 1975 when he became a director of the investment firm TR Technology PLC. As of 1990 he held 31,320 ordinary and preference shares, worth £28,962. In 1977 he joined the board of another investment company, Foreign and Commonwealth Smaller Companies PLC, and has been chairman since 1986. He owns 48,000 shares, worth £34,080. A Lloyd's underwriter, Sir Peter has been a director of Petrofina UK, parent company of the Italian oil giant, since 1973. He has also been a consultant to Fisons, the chemical firm, and House of Fraser PLC since 1982.

Other MPs have been more reticent about their shareholdings. Jonathan Aitken, the Tory MP for Thanet South and great-nephew of Lord Beaverbrook, has combined a flair for the City with intimate Middle East interests. He is a director of Al Bilhad (UK) Ltd, the chairman of which is Prince Mohammed Fahd Abdulaziz, son of King Fahd of Saudi Arabia. Al Bilhad (UK) Ltd receives payments from contracts with Saudi Arabian royal family interests and government agencies.[8]

Aitken was also chairman of Aitken Hume International PLC, his mini-conglomerate financial services group, when it secretly channelled £2.1 million of Saudi royal funds to buy a stake in TV-am PLC at a time when the station's future was in jeopardy. After this was disclosed in 1988, the MP promptly resigned as a director of TV-am.[9] He remains deputy chairman and a director of Aitken Hume International, which numbers among its clients the investment firm Eagle Trust. These interests have been registered.

However, Aitken has been a shareholder in a company which he has not declared to Parliament. On 27 October 1979, he joined the board of Fadace Ltd, an investment and research company, along with two Saudi Arabians, Said M. Ayas and Fahad Al Athel. Three months later the MP bought a 32 per cent stake in the firm, later increased to 34 per cent. According to company accounts filed in June 1989, Aitken retains that shareholding. Yet he has not declared it in the Register.

Shareholdings are particularly important to disclose, because they often provide an accurate measurement of an MP's interest in a company and its activities. Sir Gerard Vaughan, Minister for Health and then Consumer Affairs from 1979 until 1983, failed to do just that. On 18 April 1985, the MP became a director of Chingbury Ltd, the family consultancy firm, and took a 10 per cent stake. This was not declared in the 1986 Register, appearing only in January 1987.

Other MPs who did not declare major shareholdings have included the spy author Rupert Allason (76 per cent in his publishing firm Westintel Research Ltd), Jack Aspinwall (50 per cent in Sacrum Investments Ltd), John Wilkinson (98 per cent in EMC Communications Ltd) and David Ashby (26 per cent in his family firm Drimount Ltd).[10] They were not registered until 1991.

Share-ownership by MPs in privatised industries, has been more transparent, but sometimes acquired in iniquitous ways. For example, Keith Best, a former army captain, was on the verge of a glittering political career when British Telecom's shares were floated on the Stock Exchange. Then the Conservative MP for Anglesey, he had been an enthusiastic advocate of privatisation in Parliament.[11] He had already cashed in by buying shares in four other denationalised concerns – Enterprise Oil, Cable and Wireless, British Aerospace and Britoil. But British Telecom was in a different league. It was the government's first major privatisation, with 2 million people purchasing a stake, including ninety-four Tory MPs.

In an attempt to discourage the speculators and spread share-ownership, restrictions were imposed on the number of shares that could be bought by one individual. Before the flotation, lawyers advised Kleinwort Benson, the government's advisers, that multiple share applications could be illegal under the 1968 Theft Act. Investors were then told (in the British Telecom prospectus) when they signed the application form: 'You should apply only once. Any multiple applications or suspected multiple applications are liable to be rejected.' As a barrister since 1971 and an experienced politician, Best should have been fully aware of the implications of these conditions. But he wanted more shares for himself than the maximum of 800 per person and used three variations of his name and four different addresses to obtain a total of 4,800 shares (six times the limit). This extra allocation secured a profit of £4,680.

When the Labour Research Department, a trade union-funded research unit, exposed Best's duplicity in April 1987, the MP confessed to the deed: 'I accept that I made six separate applications for British Telecom shares in my name, each one of which was accompanied by a cheque drawn on an account in my name and signed by me. At the time of making the applications I did not consider that I was acting improperly.'[12]

Conservative MPs and even some party officers were incredulous at his assertion that he was unaware of the fraud. One member of his constituency association said: 'I too bought shares in British Telecom and like everyone else I knew the legal limit. Mr Best is an intelligent man. He doesn't need the money and, frankly, his explanation so far doesn't wash.'[13] A fellow north Wales Tory back-bencher, Sir Antony Meyer, said: 'As a lawyer, he should have realised what he was doing was illegal.'[14]

Although there were immediate calls for Best's resignation and prosecution, he refused to admit the offence, assuring his constituency party that he would provide 'a full and frank explanation' and that 'examination of other privatisation issues will not yield any further embarrassments about my share dealings'.[15] This, however, turned out to be another deception when the *Observer* revealed that the MP had used four variations of his name and address to purchase shares in the privatised car company Jaguar. Best had bought four batches of 250 shares, paying £16,500, but failed to inform his constituency association of this share dealing.[16]

Eventually Best relented and declared that he was standing down from his Anglesey seat at the next general election. By not resigning immediately, he saved his party an embarrassing by-election. But he could not escape the law.

In October 1987, Keith Best was prosecuted and found guilty of dishonestly procuring more shares than his entitlement. He received a four-month jail sentence and a £3,000 fine and was ordered to pay £1,500 in costs. 'You engaged in carefully calculated acts of dishonesty, designed to provide a substantial profit,' Judge Butler told him. 'Nor have you expressed one word of regret.'[17]

After a weekend spent in Brixton prison, Best returned to court on 5 October 1987 in order to attend his Appeal hearing. Lord Lane, the Lord Chief Justice, revoked the jail term but increased the fine to £4,500. 'It is only by the skin of his teeth this appellant escapes jail,' said Lord Lane.[18]

Two days later, on the morning of the Tory Party Conference debate on law and order, another Conservative MP, David Evans, was interviewed. Evans, a millionaire who had profited from privatisation of local authority services, was asked by the BBC whether he considered Keith Best to be a criminal. 'Oh, I think Keith Best was just somebody who got caught,' replied the MP. 'I think most people are at it. I don't think he is a criminal in any way.'[19]

The Lloyd's syndicate

To be an underwriting member of the Lloyd's insurance syndicate you need to be very wealthy. Aspiring members, known as 'names', are required to show they have unencumbered assets of £250,000. Part of this wealth, known as 'means', must be deposited at Lloyd's and maintained at all times.

As of 1991, there are sixty-two MPs, including seven ministers, who are underwriting members of Lloyd's. So whenever the affairs of the world's largest insurance market are debated in the Commons, the back-benches are soon filled.

The Society of Lloyd's is one of the most traditional and powerful institutions in the City of London. Incorporated in 1871, it is a highly specialised insurance market. Underwriting members band together in a series of clubs called syndicates. Each syndicate hands over the management of its business to an agent. Acting through an underwriting company, the agent then commits individual 'names' to participate in selected insurance projects.

Members of Lloyd's make their money by assessing commercial contracts of insurance. These are in three main markets – shipping, aviation and the motor industry. Members analyse the risks associated with the project and then charge premiums for placing their assets as liabilities. However, in the late 1970s Lloyd's was beset by fraud and a series of scandals. This left many underwriting members liable for huge amounts and they began to sue the Lloyd's governing committee for negligence for failing to spot the fraud. By 1980 the gentlemanly style of running Lloyd's made legislation inevitable. But the Society of Lloyd's pre-empted this by introducing their own private bill. This established self-regulation by setting up disciplinary committees to investigate 'suspected malpractice' and, where necessary, to discipline members. In addition, members of these internal committees were given immunity against being sued for negligence and incompetence.

The bill was sponsored by Sir Graham Page, solicitor and Conservative MP. He was not a Lloyd's member. His briefing document summed up its purpose: 'Lloyd's needs powers which can tackle abuses which in recent times have received publicity. There is, therefore, an argument for providing some immunity for the Council.' Sir Graham was supported by fellow MP Sir Anthony Royle, a Lloyd's member and insurance broker since 1950. He was also a director of a major insurance broking firm at Lloyd's. After declaring his interest, Sir Anthony made a speech 'to underline the wholehearted support that the community of Lloyd's gives to the bill'.[20] He concluded: 'It is vital to our future and crucial to the City that Lloyd's is able to function well . . . It is right that, where possible, our major institutions should police themselves and not involve the government.'[21]

The bill created a massive conflict of interests for the House of Commons. There were at that time fifty-four MPs who were members of Lloyd's. Some, like Sir Nicholas Bonsor, had interests in two syndicates and moved amendments on the bill.[22] Other Lloyd's members included Michael Jopling, then Government Chief Whip and a Cabinet minister, Bernard Weatherill, then Deputy Speaker and Chairman of Ways and Means, and Francis Pym, then Leader of the Commons. All three were responsible for the arrangements for guiding private bills through Parliament. However, the three did withdraw their active involvement in the Lloyd's bill.

Usually such a controversial bill is talked out. And its fate seemed sealed when the Speaker ruled that MPs who were members of Lloyd's should consider not voting for it because it was a privately sponsored bill, as opposed to government legislation. But the Speaker's ruling was later ignored as twenty-one MPs with a Lloyd's interest, including Michael Jopling, backed the bill.[23] This ensured a successful passage and the bill reached the statute book in 1982.

Another advantage of being a Lloyd's member comes from the investment opportunities. This involves investment management of insurance premiums received before claims are paid. So it was a matter of political controversy when the 1986 Financial Services Bill excluded Lloyd's from regulation.

As the minister in the Department of Trade and Industry responsible for the bill, Michael Howard found himself with an unenviable conflict of interests. He had been a member of five Lloyd's syndicates since 1981. Although he ceased his underwriting activities in September 1985, he remained a non-underwriting member and retained an interest in 'the pre-existing contracts into which I entered until they expire'.[24] He was accused by the Opposition of not totally divesting his Lloyd's interests, and they demanded that a different minister should sponsor the Financial Services Bill. Austin Mitchell said: 'The minister told us that he has a continuing income from contracts agreed at Lloyd's before he became a minister. We need to know whether the continuation of that income depends on the regulation or the non-regulation of Lloyd's under this bill.'[25]

'I have no idea what the contracts are worth,' replied Howard. 'I cannot renege on any debts that arise or bring those liabilities to an end in any other way.'[26]

Howard declined either to stand aside as the responsible minister or to bring Lloyd's within the scope of the bill. So the Labour MP Bryan Gould raised the matter with the Prime Minister: 'The size of the cheques from Lloyd's which will land on Michael Howard's doormat over the next three years will depend crucially on whether Lloyd's is subject to the same rules as to compensation provisions as will apply to other financial institutions. That is a question to which the minister himself will provide the answer.'[27]

Mrs Thatcher replied: 'Michael Howard has an interest in the inclusion or exclusion of Lloyd's from the bill to the same very limited extent as members of the standing committee of an area of investment in which they might engage – for example unit trusts or life assurance.'[28]

Banking on MPs

For generations merchant banks have viewed government and parliamentary affairs with a lofty mercurial air. But the commercial opportunities created by government policy in the 1980s required that investment banking enter the political arena. Privatisation meant merchant banks were needed to act as advisers and underwriters to the share issues. And legislation to deregulate the City made it easier to acquire new clients.

It was a good time to be alive for the money men, and for none more so than Morgan Grenfell. Between 1980 and 1985 the bank doubled in size and profits increased by 400 per cent. This was almost entirely due to its increased involvement in take-over bids, mergers, privatisation, overseas project financing and investment banking. As 1986 dawned Morgan Grenfell looked forward to a year of unprecedented expansion and success. In October came the long-awaited 'Big Bang' (the reform of the Stock Exchange's restrictive practices, which opened up new markets and clients). Suddenly, for almost the first time in its 150-year history, Morgan Grenfell decided their political and public profile was important.

In January 1986 a Corporate Affairs Department was set up. Its founding director was Byron Ousey, an affable former journalist and finance director of the South African mining giant De Beers. His first act was to introduce a glossy new company logo, together with literature on the theme 'Corporate Visual Identity', something that left the austere merchant bankers feeling rather bemused. 'Time was when no director of Morgan Grenfell would have met a public-relations man,' reflected Dominic Hobson, a former employee, 'let alone succumbed to his blandishments.'[29]

The key appointment in the Corporate Affairs Department was Desmond Harney, an urbane former diplomat who had served in Iran during the final years of the Shah. He joined the bank's international division in 1980 and then ran the private office of Bill Mackworth-Young, the chairman. Harney knew the bank intimately and was ideally suited to his new job of 'liaising with Parliament and government'. One of his main duties was to work closely with the bank's paid parliamentary consultant, Andrew MacKay, Conservative MP for East Berkshire since 1983. MacKay had been appointed by the board in 1984 because 'the bank needed a friend in the House'. Harney strenuously denies that the MP was used as a lobbyist: 'His job was to keep the bank informed about the business of the Commons and for us to get to know MPs and ministers. He was our Ambassador and Envoy. He was not used to push our case in Parliament but for general advice.' But Byron Ousey saw MacKay in a more active light: 'He was an excellent guy and very useful. He was an eyes and ears operator. He would give a view as to what the government was thinking and was particularly active in the "Big Bang" period.'

MacKay visited the Morgan Grenfell head office in Great Winchester Street once a month for briefing sessions. He also organised discreet lunches, cocktail parties and dinners for MPs at the bank's private flat at Whitehall Court, off Parliament Square. 'For security reasons,' said MacKay, 'merchant bankers do not like entertaining in public restaurants because people can see who they are talking to.'[30] Dinner at the flat ('used for general entertainment') was usually for six (three MPs and three Morgan Grenfell directors) and would finish just in time for the back-benchers to scamper across Parliament Square for the division bell.

In the spring of 1986, when the Financial Services Bill was being debated, the lobbying exercise was stepped up. MacKay invited all six Tory members of the Commons committee examining the bill for a champagne dinner to meet George Law, Morgan Grenfell's compliance director. Law's job was directly concerned with Stock Exchange regulations affected by the proposed legislation. Not every MP accepted the invitation, but MacKay acknowledged his own role: 'It was my idea so that the Conservative members on the committee could meet Morgan Grenfell directors. I should emphasise that no documents were given to MPs nor did we ask them to act on any particular clause.'[31]

Morgan Grenfell did very well out of the Financial Services Bill and 'Big Bang'. Deregulation enabled merchant banks to swallow up new markets and provide more services to clients. Combined with the highly successful flotation of its shares in June, this allowed the bank to approach 1987 with some optimism.

However, in place of the expected good cheer the New Year produced calamity and embarrassment. In January, the chief executive, Christopher Reeves, and corporate finance director, Graham Walsh, resigned after disclosures that Morgan Grenfell had got involved in keeping Guinness shares artificially high in their take-over of Distillers PLC. The bank had been chief advisers to the acquisitive drinks conglomerate. Further disaster struck when Geoffrey Collier, a senior Morgan Grenfell director, was convicted of insider dealing; although he escaped prison, he was fined £25,000. Then another executive, Roger Seelig, the bank's chief advocate of the take-over market, was charged with twelve criminal offences, including theft, over the Guinness affair. By the end of the year no fewer than twenty-one of Morgan Grenfell's forty-eight directors had resigned or been sacked.[32]

Behind the scenes the Corporate Affairs Department was in a constant state of anxiety. They mounted an intense damage-limitation exercise, one tactic of which was to call in their consultant, Andrew MacKay. This was revealed in an internal memorandum by David Douglas-Home, a Morgan Grenfell director, chairman of its Scottish company and son of the former Prime Minister Lord Home. Written in March 1988, the document was sent to all London directors:

> As you are all aware, Andrew MacKay, MP, advises us on our political strategy and it is no small credit to him that we have recovered our political acceptability in Westminster and Whitehall following the problems of early last year. I do not believe that we are using his considerable talents sufficiently as far as our clients are concerned, many of whom are extremely naïve as to how to work with and use their MPs and government to advantage.
>
> Many companies under-estimate how much their MP can do for them and many companies don't even know who their MP is. I think we all ought to give some thought, and discuss with our clients, as to how Andrew can assist us.

Clearly, Morgan Grenfell wanted 'their MP' to do more than provide a monthly briefing of 'general advice' and host dinner parties. The intention was to represent and lobby for clients. This was why Quintin Davies became a consultant to the bank after being elected the MP for Stamford and Spalding in 1987. A former diplomat, Davies had previously, since 1974, worked for Morgan Grenfell. From 1981 he was an executive director in the Corporate Finance Department, responsible for marketing services to Europe.

Davies had been very much the financial consultant, providing strategic advice to clients, although he is also a director of Dewe Rogerson International, the lobbying firm specialising in privatisation.

Whether MacKay has been able to 'recover' the bank's 'political acceptability' is unclear (as this book goes to press a former Morgan Grenfell executive still faces criminal charges over the Guinness scandal). But what his consultancy does reflect is how MPs may be used by their paymasters in times of crisis and controversy.

Help with the accounts

Accountancy firms have also benefited from the short-lived prosperity of the Square Mile. Like merchant bankers, they benefited from the 1980s craze for service conglomerates by merger and take-over. No longer mere auditors, City accountants increasingly act as management consultants, investment counsellors, tax advisers and corporate financiers.[33]

The 'Big Six' accountancy companies have done well out of such diversification. In 1990 they reported £140 million in revenue just from insolvency work.[34] Arthur Andersen and Co., which includes a former Prime Minister, Edward Heath, on its review board, now has 2,200 partners and fees from clients amounting to $3.2 billion. Price Waterhouse has done better than most. Between 1986 and 1990 total fee income has more than doubled[35] and it now audits the accounts of twenty-two of the top hundred UK firms. One area of specialisation has been management and computer consultancies. A major source of such business is contracts with government departments.

Since 1986 Price Waterhouse's paid parliamentary consultant has been Tim Smith, the Conservative MP for Beaconsfield and member of the Public Accounts Committee. On 18 February 1987, Smith asked eighteen government departments for detailed information on management consultancy contracts. The motive behind these parliamentary questions surfaced a year later. This time the MP put down the remarkable total of fifty-eight questions on the same issue – disclosing the contracts, the successful firms, their assignments and the government expenditure involved.

These were extremely useful commercial data, but they were not asked for on behalf of Smith's constituents or the public. They were acquired on behalf of Price Waterhouse, who were preparing a marketing and business plan for their clients. Smith did not declare his interest when asking the questions (which cost the taxpayer £3,500 to answer), as he is not obliged to do so. He remained unrepentant:

I am entitled to ask whatever questions I want of the government. I do not think there is any principle involved. Although it obviously costs government departments about £60 each to answer written questions, I think in the long run it is of benefit to government to have a business sector in management computer consultancy which is well-informed about the markets that they are dealing with. It won't just be Price Waterhouse which benefits, it will be everybody because this information is widely available.[36]

Smith's lobbying for Price Waterhouse has become an annual parliamentary event. In April 1989 the MP obtained more details on computer consultancy contracts from twenty-seven government departments. In March 1990, he asked the same ministries about the numbers and cost of internal auditors, and whether any work was sub-contracted to private firms. Three weeks later answers to a further thirty-two questions – again on computer and management consultancy contracts – adorned several pages of *Hansard*. 'This is commercial information which is of interest to them [Price Waterhouse],' acknowledged Smith, 'as it is to anybody who is competing in this market.' But the MP admitted that he would not have asked the questions if he had not been a consultant to Price Waterhouse.[37]

Despite repeated protests to the Speaker that MPs 'should not ask parliamentary questions in return for payment', such lobbying is allowed to continue.[38] Smith remains adamant: 'I'm perfectly prepared to defend this. It's not against the rules of the House. My interest is quite clearly declared. I don't have a problem.'[39]

Monopolising the airways

Lobbyists and MPs are never so busy as when governments try to break up long-standing monopolies. This is particularly the case in the aviation industry.

In the spring of 1984 the Civil Aviation Authority (CAA) produced a report which found that the then state-owned British Airways (BA) had a near-monopoly on air routes. The CAA called for a large-scale mandatory transfer of some of BA's most profitable routes to the leading private sector airline, British Caledonian. The aim was to increase competition in the industry.

To the political ears of Nicholas Ridley, then Transport Secretary, the report was sweet music. He welcomed its recommendations unreservedly and set about implementing them. But Lord King, the resourceful B A chairman and confidante of Mrs Thatcher, had other ideas. He was furious with the report and bitterly opposed the proposals. He even 'let it be known' in Whitehall that the B A board 'would defy orders to hand over the routes selected by the C A A, insisting that the government would have to sack them first'.[40] He also authorised an intense lobbying campaign. At the time, B A retained the services of Shandwick P L C, the public-relations firm owned by Peter Gummer, brother of the Tory Cabinet minister John Selwyn Gummer. The Shandwick executive dealing with the B A account had singled out the well-connected Conservative M P Michael Grylls as a key figure. Grylls, chairman of the Tory Trade and Industry Committee since 1980, had a special interest in aviation, and so Shandwick introduced him to B A executives.

In July 1984, just three days before publication of the C A A report, B A changed lobbyists and turned to Ian Greer Associates. What happened next was a stark illustration of the way MPs use their influence. Grylls had met B A chairman Lord King privately and told him: 'If you have a problem and you're not very satisfied, why don't you approach Ian Greer Associates and see if they would be happy to work with you and prove to you they would do a better job.'[41] Lord King agreed and, after a brief meeting with Greer, promptly hired the lobbyist. Greer was delighted with the £100,000-plus account and 'grateful' to Grylls for the recommendation. In return for this introduction Greer paid the M P a 'one-off fee' which was received on 1 November 1985.[42] This 'thank-you payment' was never declared by Grylls and his commercial relationship with the lobbyist was not properly registered until October 1989 (see chapter 6 for details). Greer and Grylls have both refused to disclose the amount.

Armed with a new aggressive lobbying outfit, B A set out to defeat the C A A plan and change the government's mind. The chief strategy was to use its 'friends in the House'. Heavy briefing sessions of back-benchers took place. Just before the Commons debate on the C A A report, on the night of 24 July 1984, Greer arranged for eighteen selected MPs privately to meet Lord King and other B A directors.[43]

The B A lobby was a combination of moderate inducements (free lunches and dinners, trips to exotic locations), power politicking in Whitehall and marshalling the troops in the Commons. And it worked. Nicholas Ridley reluctantly backed down and agreed to compromise. BA surrendered their lucrative Gulf routes to British Caledonian, but only in part-exchange for British Caledonian's less profitable South American business. Ridley had wanted to implement the CAA recommendations but admitted privately that 'the BA lobby would not have allowed it'.[44]

BA's next political battle was in 1987, and it was fought over their take-over of British Caledonian. Once again the government was concerned over the competition implications. The bid was referred to the Monopolies and Mergers Commission (MMC) and the lobbying began. Michael Colvin, Tory MP for Romsey and Waterside, chairman of the back-bench Conservative Aviation Committee and a supporter of the merger, recalled: 'British Airways piled in down here in droves, seeing committees, writing letters and pouring champagne down people's throats. The BA lobby was extremely professional – but then again, there were an awful lot of them.'[45]

BA's chief and most vocal supporter was Michael Grylls, who campaigned for the take-over inside and outside Parliament. He implored the Trade and Industry Minister Kenneth Clarke: 'Will my right hon. friend bear in mind that British Airways is not all that large in international terms ... An airline must be large enough to compete overseas. Perhaps British Caledonian is not big enough to compete on the international routes and that may be a very good reason for allowing the merger to go ahead.'[46]

It was not long before Lord King and his parliamentary cohorts won the day, and the merger went through.

BA have only occasionally resorted to hiring MPs directly – Michael Portillo was a consultant between July 1985 and July 1986. Instead, their most controversial lobbying tactic is arranging free air tickets and overseas trips for MPs. These excursions ('facility trips' to BA, 'junkets' and 'freebies' to its critics) are funded from a worldwide public-relations budget of £5 million. Up to seventy Conservative and Labour MPs are targeted and no expense is spared.[47]

In January 1984, BA was campaigning for a fifth terminal at Heathrow. One of its most persistent critics was the Conservative MP Toby Jessel, whose Twickenham constituents are constantly concerned with aircraft noise from Britain's biggest airport. Jessel was an assiduous constituency MP, and in February repeated his hostility to a fifth terminal. Shortly afterwards he happened to be talking to Don Perry, then head of BA public relations, and mentioned that he was planning a holiday with his wife Eira in the Caribbean that summer. According to Jessel: 'I think I was talking to them [BA] about something else. Then they just offered to provide two tickets to the Caribbean. I refused of course. I couldn't possibly have accepted the offer. I feel it would have compromised the stand that I have taken against the fifth terminal.'[48]

This was denied by Perry: 'No offers of free holidays in the Caribbean or elsewhere in the world were made by me or by my public affairs staff . . . When the airline has carried MPs on facility trips this has been in order for them to experience BA services and study civil aviation. In an industry which is so closely controlled and supervised by governments around the world, this is right and proper.'[49]

But BA 'facility trips' did not always match up to Perry's austere portrait. A typical example of their often more sumptious nature was the special inaugural flight in May 1985 to promote BA's new route to South America. Accompanied by Lord King, five MPs, two Fleet Street editors and a senior Department of Transport official were flown first-class to Rio de Janeiro. The MPs included Michael Grylls and his wife Sarah, Alan Haselhurst, then chairman of the Tory Aviation Committee, and Angela Rumbold, then parliamentary private secretary to the Transport Secretary, Nicholas Ridley. The senior civil servant was David Holmes, a deputy secretary and principal finance officer in the department, who took his wife Ann.

The 34-strong party stayed at the luxury five-star Rio Sheraton for five days, and BA paid all expenses. According to the *Sunday Times*:

> The hotel has tennis courts, three pools, a sauna, massage, three bars and a poolside restaurant. During their stay, many of the party sunbathed and sipped Cachaca cocktails – fermented sugar cane with fresh fruit at £2 a glass. The airline laid on a series of sight-seeing tours, including trips to Sugar Loaf mountain, a schooner around Paradise Island, a visit to Iguacu waterfalls and a night out at a topless cabaret club called the Oba Oba.[50]

When they returned home, two of the MPs, Alan Haselhurst and Trevor Skeet, declared this 'facility trip' in the Register. But their colleagues Michael Grylls and Julian Amery did not do so. Rumbold did declare the Rio visit, along with a free atlas from BA, as 'a gift'.[51]

One MP who has benefited from these trips is Michael Colvin, chairman of the Aviation Committee. Between 1986 and 1990 he accepted BA's hospitality on several occasions but failed to register any of them. Colvin said he thought this was 'an oversight'.[52] 'It's very important that we do go abroad,' he reflected. 'You cannot cover the subject and become expert on it just by sitting in Parliament. These trips certainly aren't jollies, they're bloody hard work.'[53]

Another financial perk awarded to selected MPs by BA was allowing them to fly first-class on economy-price tickets. For years MPs had telephoned friendly BA executives from Heathrow airport requesting that their seats be 'bumped-up' to luxury status – free of charge. The solicitation was nearly always granted, particularly at politically opportune times. This undeclared practice has proved a valuable benefit for MPs. For example, to travel economy-class to Tokyo costs £962, while a first-class ticket costs £4,568 – a net gain of £3,600. At its peak, BA were giving away up to 400 first-class return flights a year at the cost of economy fares. The lost revenue involved was an estimated £500,000.[54] 'Bumping-up' for MPs was eventually stopped in February 1990. BA stated: 'Our policy is still to upgrade MPs and VIPs, but only if they are on British Airways business. As a general rule we do not upgrade MPs.'[55]

BA defends the 'freebie' school of lobbying by arguing that it is in parallel with other industries. 'It seems to me it would be every bit as consistent with an MP going to a ball-bearing factory in Scunthorpe and being given lunch,' remarked David Burnside, BA's director of public affairs since 1984. 'Our business is flying people around – their business is making ball-bearings.'[56] But Burnside found himself in some difficulty when asked, at a select committee inquiry: 'What is the difference between the Ford Motor Company giving an MP the free use of a motor car and British Airways giving an MP the free use of a seat on an inaugural flight?' He replied:

> I think it is slightly – not slightly, I think it is a lot more dangerous. It would worry me if I were director of corporate affairs at Ford to be giving the use of cars to MPs. I think it would if it became public . . . it would not help the position of MPs and would not help Ford. I think that is going too far. Making a seat accessible is different in that it is showing a service.
>
> If an MP were privately given by BA twenty-five free trips a year over the next five years to do what he wanted with his wife and family, or whoever he wanted to take, that would be incorrect practice for British Airways to engage in.[57]

BA was not the only airline to engage in political lobbying. Their chief competitor, British Caledonian, retained a paid consultant from February 1984 until the merger with BA in 1987. This was Robert (now Sir) McCrindle, Conservative MP for Brentwood and Ongar, then a member of the Commons Select Committee on Trade and Industry and chairman of the All-Party Aviation Group.

The smaller independent companies have also forged connections in Parliament. Their principal backer is Anthony Steen, Tory MP for the South Hams, Devon, and a long-time aviation enthusiast. In 1983 he was approached by British Midland Airways PLC and asked: 'Would you like to act as adviser to our Board?' Steen agreed, and has been a consultant every since: 'I believe in their business and the independent airline sector. The fact that one is paid a fee does not make one's contribution less valid.'[58]

Steen's first major contribution came during the crucial debate over the CAA's report in July 1984. Ted Leadbitter, a Labour MP, was praising BA and opposing the proposed transfer of routes. Steen intervened: 'Will the hon. gentleman give a thought to the future of the many independent airlines in private ownership?'[59] He did not declare his interest, as technically he did not have to as he was asking a question. But an hour later Steen again interceded: 'Does he [the hon. gentleman] agree that other domestic private airlines flying only in and around Britain should be allowed to compete against British Airways out of Heathrow?'[60]

Steen did not disclose his consultancy with the British Midland Airways Board. He continued to speak up for and promote their case and that of other independent airlines in subsequent debates and Question Times. He usually declared his interest, but not on every occasion.[61] In 1985 Steen became a paid consultant to Manx Airlines and Logan Air, a position he held for two years. In 1986 British Island Airways PLC hired him as an adviser which he remained until 1990.

Despite the South Devon MP's best efforts for his clients, it was the BA lobby that won the battle of the airways. This is due, I suspect, to greater resources and to Lord King's friends in the highest places. However, what the BA operation demonstrated was how combined political and commercial clout can overcome political will.

Under the influence

The alcohol industry constitutes one of the most powerful concentrations of ownership in Britain today. Six companies (Bass, Grand Metropolitan, Allied Lyons, Scottish and Newcastle, Whitbread and Courage) control 74 per cent of the drinks market (beer, wine and spirits) and own 75 per cent of the pubs.[62] Four of the 'Big Six' are in the UK's top fifty companies, and their annual combined pre-tax profits are over £1.8 billion.[63]

In March 1989, the MMC produced a report which directly threatened their supremacy and profitability. The 500-page document concluded that the 'Big Six' operated 'a complex monopoly' and called for radical plans to curb their power and increase competition. After a two-and-a-half year investigation, the MMC found that the brewing giants did not only produce the beer, but also sold it, both wholesale and retail. This meant they were able to restrict the supply of drinks by competing brewers and thus ensure that only their beer was sold by their landlords on the premises. Hence the term 'tied pubs'. The 'Big Six' also effectively captured about half of the 'free houses' by offering low-interest loans, which also tie those outlets to selling the brewers' products. The MMC said this system 'restricts competition at all levels' and severely curtails the opportunities for an independent wholesaling sector to prosper.[64] They recommended that brewers be confined to owning 2,000 public houses each and that they should be compelled to sell off the rest within three years. As the 'Big Six' already owned 34,000 pubs, this meant the mandatory divestment of 22,000 houses. The Commission also advocated that a guest beer should be on sale in all tied houses and that tenants should be free to purchase other drinks wherever they liked.

As with the 1984 CAA report on BA, the government reacted positively. Lord Young, then Trade and Industry Secretary and the Cabinet's doyen of the free market, announced he was 'minded to implement the recommendations without delay'. He said: 'I believe that these proposals will preserve the good features of the present system, whilst giving the landlord and the customer a little more say about the future of their own local. It is very much about setting the pub free.'[65] The small independent brewers were delighted. At last they had the chance to compete in the industry and sell their beer to 'tied pubs'. The 'Big Six', however, angrily denounced the MMC report and launched one of the most controversial lobbying campaigns of recent years. Its aim was to change the government's mind and preserve the status quo.

The operation was conducted on a number of fronts. In public there was the £6 million advertising campaign. Within a month double-page spreads and billboards declared that if the MMC proposals were implemented, it would do more damage to our national heritage than Henry VIII during the Reformation or the Luftwaffe during the Second World War. The usually dormant House of Lords was also mobilised. During their debate on the MMC report, peer after peer rose to declare interests before echoing the brewers' line. The Bishop of Truro, married to the daughter of a brewer, said that the 'potential destruction' of the industry reminded him of Henry VIII's 'dissolution of the monasteries' – a familiar phrase.[66]

Over at the House of Commons, Conservative back-benchers were being mustered for the counter-attack. At the time there were no fewer than forty-seven MPs with declared financial interests in the alcohol industry – either as consultants or company directors, or through family connections.[67] Chief among them were Neil Hamilton and Allan Stewart, parliamentary consultants to the Brewers Society, which represents eighty-three brewers and co-ordinated the 'Big Six's' strategy. Other paid advisers were Sir Paul Dean (Grand Metropolitan), Sir Dudley Smith (Bass), Roger Gale (Scottish and Newcastle),[68] Gerry Neale (Allied Lyons) and Roger Sims (Scotch Whisky Association). Another MP, Bowen Wells, was a consultant to International Distillers and Vintners, a subsidiary of Grand Metropolitan, while Sir John Farr was a shareholder in Home Brewery Co. Ltd, owned by Scottish and Newcastle.

At first the lobbying was fairly mild stuff, consisting of the usual discreet briefings and lunches arranged by hired conduits and middlemen (Ian Greer for Whitbread, Geoffrey Tucker for the Brewers Society). Bass Charrington, for example, hosted a cosy meeting for sympathetic MPs over beer and sandwiches at a private room above the Marquis of Granby, a local Westminster pub just off Smith Square.[69] The campaign caught fire only on 9 May 1989, when ninety-three Tory MPs signed an Early Day Motion praising the brewing industry and rejecting the MMC report outright. It was signed by Neil Hamilton, consultant to the Brewers Society and deputy chairman of the Conservative back-bench Trade and Industry Committee. Other signatories included Sir Dudley Smith (management consultant for Bass) and Allan Stewart (paid adviser to the Brewers Society).

This caused some commotion in the government. The next day Lord Young attended a tense, packed meeting of the Tory Trade and Industry Committee. According to those present, the minister received a 'mauling' as one MP after another 'savaged' his support for divestment. In a parallel move, the brewers brought pressure to bear through local Conservative associations. For generations the 'Big Six' have had an intimate relationship with the Tory establishment. Many regional brewery chairmen and company directors are also chairman and president of constituency Conservative parties. For example, Sam Whitbread, chairman of the brewing giant that bears his name, is chairman of Bedfordshire Conservative Association, High Sheriff and deputy Lord Lieutenant – the epitome of the Tory squire.[70] Three of the 'Big Six' also contribute heavily to Conservative Party funds. In the financial year ending March 1989, Allied Lyons paid £92,000, Scottish and Newcastle £50,000 and Whitbread £30,000. Together with contributions from nineteen other brewing firms, the total amount swelled party coffers that year to £249,325.[71]

The beerage felt betrayed. It was now payback time. Tory backbenchers were lobbied ferociously – either directly by company directors or indirectly through constituency associations. One Conservative MP who witnessed this tactic was James Cran, a member of the Commons Trade and Industry Select Committee, former director of the CBI and a critic of the brewers' case:

> It was a very sophisticated and very aggressive campaign. If you agreed with the brewers, there was no problem and you were treated with kid gloves. If you happened to be against what they were saying, it was quite different . . . The brewers mobilised anybody in my constituency who they could find to put as much pressure on me in a way, frankly, I don't find in other issues.[72]

One chairman of a major brewing company lifted the stakes higher one day when he telephoned Cran. His message was clear – back us or we will withdraw our donation:

> One representative of a brewer made it clear to me in oblique terms that if I didn't back the brewers and the Brewers Society, then of course perhaps some money might be withdrawn from the Conservative Party at whatever level. That seemed to me to be wholly outrageous and if that

individual ever expected that I would change my vote as a result of that, he was sadly mistaken. But I could see that in some circumstances perhaps some MPs might have to think about that twice.[73]

Cran may have rejected such threats, but Lord Young was wilting under the onslaught. The Trade and Industry Secretary suggested compromises and concessions. The brewers responded by arranging for ten executive members of the 1922 Tory back-bench committee to write to the Prime Minister condemning these latest proposals.

By the first week of July 1989, less than four months after the original MMC report was published, it was clear that Lord Young had been ambushed by his own back-benchers. After being told by the Tory Chief Whip that the troops would desert in droves, he surrendered. He announced that the 'Big Six' could keep all their pubs and the proposal limiting brewers to 2,000 each was now dropped. 'I think that we must avoid too much turbulence in our society,' said Lord Young.[74]

For consumer groups and the independent brewers it was a capitulation generated by political and corporate clout. This view was shared by Sir George Young, a Tory MP and former Health minister, who said: 'It did give the impression that the brewing industry had a disproportionate pull on the Conservative Party. I just think it was caving into some fairly clumsy political pressure by the brewing industry.'[75]

For the 'Big Six', it was mission accomplished. On the day of Lord Young's climbdown their share value rose sharply by 26 per cent. A week later Bass, Whitbread and Courage increased the price of their beer by up to 10p a pint. For the lobbyists, the brewers' operation demonstrated a phenomenon that is often derided or understated. Namely, that back-bench MPs with vested interests and backed by vast resources can exercise real power and influence. That Lord Young was defeated by such a force was perhaps a measure of his political naïvety. But the awesome clout of a monopoly industry when facing reform should serve as a warning to any future government that embarks on such a hazardous course.

CHAPTER 4

The Privatisation of Power

'Any MP is entitled to take up whatever outside interests he wants.'
Sir Marcus Fox, MP for Shipley, *Bradford Telegraph and Argus*, 5 November 1983

In the spring of 1981, the Labour MP Dennis Skinner interrupted a debate to challenge the morality of MPs voting for laws to privatise state assets.

It was a typically robust intervention from the Bolsover back-bencher. But his objection was not just an ideological one. It was that the pro-privatisation MPs were voting for legislation from which they would benefit financially through their commercial interests. This was immediately dismissed by the then Deputy Speaker, Bernard Weatherill, who replied: 'That is a hypothetical question.'[1]

Over the past decade Weatherill's nonchalant response has been proved wrong. MPs have increasingly voted and lobbied for bills which have enhanced their business interests. Indeed, privatisation and deregulation have been the main factors behind MPs rushing headlong into the world of commerce. The contracts, franchises, clients and commissions arising from dismantling public corporations have proved an irresistible temptation for MPs keen on providing little pots of gold for themselves.

Companies, stockbrokers and merchant banks believe that in order to take advantage of these opportunities they need inside knowledge and intelligence of government plans and policy. Competition to win, for example, cable television franchises is intense, and firms consider that hiring an insider gives them an advantage. As MPs are the obvious candidates to play this role of agent and middleman, it has resulted in a boom in consultancies and created a 'lobbyists' paradise'.[2]

Public services, private interests

When competitive tendering for cleaning and ancillary services in the National Health Service (NHS) and local government was first introduced, private companies faced severe problems. Several local councils and regional health authorities were hostile to the policy, and potential contractors complained to Whitehall about the lack of progress.[3]

In 1981 Gerard Vaughan, then a Health minister, who later became chairman of Private Medical Centres PLC, wrote to health authorities: 'I have been disappointed to hear that some authorities have not responded constructively to approaches from commercial companies, notably from the cleaning industry.'[4] But contractors believed such ministerial pleas were not enough – they needed political muscle. By 1982 a number of MPs had been hired as consultants and directors. One of the most influential was Sir Marcus Fox, the Conservative MP for Shipley. He had recently joined Brengreen Holdings Ltd, a contract cleaning company, after a two-year stint as a minister in the Department of the Environment.

Sir Marcus was an ardent and vociferous privatiser but not always so forthcoming about his commercial interests. In December 1982, he opened an adjournment debate by opposing the closure of Shipley Hospital. Sir Marcus was angry at the official reason for the hospital shutdown – savings of £200,000 off Bradford Health Authority's £48 million budget. He urged Geoffrey Finsberg, the Health and Social Services Under-Secretary, to 'examine carefully the options that are available', and continued: 'I select one example of where savings can be made. In the budget of £48 million, the sum for domestic cleaning is £2,655,689 . . . It is known that private contractors can perform this work at an average saving of at least 20 per cent. If one third of the cleaning services were put out to such contractors, Shipley Hospital could stay open.'[5]

Sir Marcus did not disclose his consultancy with Brengreen, which at that time was preparing to bid for cleaning contracts. The MP said he did not declare an interest because 'it was not relevant to the main thrust of the debate'. He added: 'I should have thought it made excellent sense to point out any measures whereby that hospital could be saved.'[6]

During his Commons speech in December 1982, Sir Marcus implored Finsberg to 'contemplate issuing a circular giving a guidance to health authorities on their responsibilities' to appoint private contractors. Three months later a draft of such a circular was written, and on 8 September 1983 it was officially distributed. This called on all health authorities to put their cleaning, catering and laundry services out to private tender.

Three weeks later, on 1 October 1983, Sir Marcus joined the board of the Care Services Group, based in Shipley. Its main subsidiary, Hospital Hygiene Services Ltd, is the second largest hospital-cleaning company in the country and had already won the first three NHS contracts on offer. Care Services' chairman, Richard Holdsworth, made it clear his firm was bidding for more contracts – the hospital-cleaning market alone was worth £50 million a year.[7]

Ten days after his appointment, Sir Marcus went to the Tory Party Conference to make a special plea for Shipley Hospital. He was not called in the debate but a copy of his planned speech makes interesting reading: 'In the Bradford district, if only two of the nineteen hospitals were handed over to private contractors as far as cleaning is concerned – savings more than enough to keep Shipley Hospital open could be achieved.'[8]

It was clear by now that the Shipley MP was lobbying for his commercial client as well as his constituents. This was confirmed by his remarks after the Party Conference: 'I joined this group on the basis that not only do I support what they're doing, but blimey, if I could only get them in there we could keep my hospital open.'[9] He saw no conflict of interests: 'As a back-bencher, and being a Conservative MP, I'm quite free to follow any interests I've got. The point is that Care Services is in my constituency, plus the fact that I've taken an interest in privatisation from the beginning ... We agreed a certain figure to pay me for the time I put in and the expertise I've got that will help them.'[10]

The company also saw their MP in a far from passive capacity: 'He [Sir Marcus] takes no active part, but he keeps us informed of political activities which could affect the industry and obviously directly affect this group. He's not a shareholder. He's on a retainer, which is a very small one in fact.'[11]

By late 1983 some health authorities were refusing to privatise their ancillary services. The contractors were becoming anxious. They believed political clout was needed and so a special unit was set up inside the Association of British Launderers and Cleaners, their trade organisation. It was called the Common Interest Committee (CIC) and a lobbying firm headed by the Conservative MP Michael Forsyth was hired to represent them.

The Scottish MP had established Michael Forsyth Associates Ltd in 1981, at which time he was a pioneer for privatisation as a Westminster City councillor. Michael Forsyth Associates was one of the first lobbying agencies to take advantage of the desire of cleaning and catering firms for political influence in the battle for contracts. One of its first acts was to sign up the Conservative MP Michael Brown as a director on a monthly fee of £235. He was then retained as a consultant until 1983.[12] The multi-national Pritchards Services Group, which dominated the cleaning market, was engaged as a client.

Michael Forsyth Associates soon realised the awarding of contracts was an intensely political operation. According to a former director, Kevin Bell, this was useful to clients because of the 'labyrinthic nature of the corridors of power'. He stated:

> The political PR adviser should certainly be able to point clients in the right direction. Better still, he will have had past dealings with officials in many departments, and may be able to bring matters to their attention on an informal basis. While many matters can be settled through the intervention of one or two sympathetic MPs, or discussions with the right officials, effective lobbying on important or contentious issues usually requires much more substantial and widespread effort.[13]

This strategy became apparent in January 1984 when Michael Forsyth Associates hosted a lunch between potential NHS contractors and John Patten, the Junior Health Minister. According to a confidential report by Michael Forsyth Associates, this lunch was one of the 'political PR highlights' of the year. 'As a result,' the report stated, 'it is understood that an internal department inquiry looked at problem district health authorities as outlined at that meeting.'[14]

The 'problem authorities' were the ones holding out against privatisation. For Michael Forsyth Associates, 'political pressure nationally on the NHS through parliamentary PR' was needed to overcome this obstacle. This should be 'based on direct consideration of the commercial interests of member companies'.

Subsequently, a series of Commons receptions, private lunches and briefings were held where up to thirty MPs at a time were entertained. 'In total,' the report concluded, 'we judge this effort to be a valuable investment in identifying MPs and political peers sympathetic to privatisation.'[15]

But MPs did more than take advantage of expensive lunches and free champagne. Many became consultants, directors and shareholders in the companies seeking contracts in the NHS and other public services. By the spring of 1984, twenty-four Conservative MPs had acquired such financial stakes. Seven of these had shares in Grand Metropolitan PLC, whose subsidiary Grand Met Catering Services has contracts in catering and refuse collection.[16] Among them was Michael Ancram, the Scottish Office Minister, who owned 1,491 shares in Grand Metropolitan PLC.

Despite this intense lobbying campaign, several health authorities continued to resist the private sector. One of them was Leeds Eastern Health Authority. On 5 March 1984, Sir Marcus Fox asked Kenneth Clarke, then Minister of State for Health, why Leeds 'has decided to ignore his circular on competitive tendering and what action he will be taking in this matter'.[17] What the minister was not told during the question was that at the time one of the frustrated contractors submitting tenders was in fact the Care Services Group.

Three weeks later Sir Marcus again pressed a Health minister in the Commons over competitive tendering. This time it was John Patten, who was asked 'if he will inquire into the reasons why Merton and Sutton Health District appointed the direct labour force despite the fact that contractors put in lower tenders against the same specification'.[18] Sir Marcus did not mention that he was a director of one of these contractors, namely Care Services (although he was not obliged to do so). But he did later confirm that his company was bidding for the business at the time of his parliamentary probing. When asked about his questioning of Ministers, he replied:

> It relates to my directorship of Care Services Group, which is based in my constituency, with whom I have had a long connection . . . We submitted tenders for every one that came up initially. It would have been very difficult for me not to have put down a question if we were putting in tenders for all the hospitals at that particular time . . . I see nothing wrong in that. It was the overall policy I supported and will continue to do so.[19]

When the Care Services Group (through Hospital Hygiene Services) did obtain contracts, their director MP was often at hand if problems arose. This occurred when Bromley Health Authority cancelled Hospital Hygiene's contract to clean Orpington Hospital because of 'repeated poor performance'. Sir Marcus promptly contacted Kenneth Clarke and complained at the contract's being terminated at short notice. The next day Clarke issued a directive to all health authorities making it much more difficult to sack private cleaning companies.[20]

Sir Marcus confirmed his intervention: 'My personal knowledge of what was happening was such that I drew it to the minister's attention. Any MP can lobby a minister about anything he wants to do. There's no secret about my involvement . . . I am not involved in the day to day running of the company [Hospital Hygiene Services]. My main job is to be a Member of Parliament.'[21]

Sir Marcus was not the only MP to lobby the government over health-authority resistance while retaining a commercial interest. As a minister in the Department of Health and Social Services (DHSS), Sir Geoffrey Finsberg was a keen advocate of privatisation of NHS ancillary services.

Sir Geoffrey left the DHSS in June 1983. Later that year he became a consultant to the Office Cleaning Services Group of Companies Ltd. Most of this firm's business had been in school cleaning. But in early 1984 a new subsidiary, OCS Hospital Services Ltd, was set up and began to bid for hospital contracts. In April 1984, Sir Geoffrey backed a Commons motion which urged that 'local authorities should be required by law to submit to competitive tender a wider range of their functions and services'.[22]

Another former minister who promoted the privatisers' cause was Sir Anthony Grant, the Tory MP for South-West Cambridgeshire. From 1978 to 1986 he was a paid consultant to the Pritchards Services Group. During that period he repeatedly called for non-medical NHS services to be run by the private sector. On one occasion, in March 1982, he lobbied Geoffrey Finsberg from the side-gallery of a packed chamber: 'Is my hon. friend aware that millions of pounds a year could be saved and used for patient care and vital medical equipment if a great deal more ancillary services in hospitals were carried out by private enterprise? Will he urge health authorities to contract out wherever possible?'

In the next three years Sir Anthony continued to urge ministers to privatise cleaning services.[23] He also co-hosted receptions for Pritchards on the terrace of the Commons. On 18 July 1985, his commercial stake went undisclosed when he sponsored a Commons motion that stated: 'Local authorities should be required by law to submit to competitive tender.'[24] At three-fifty that afternoon, Sir Anthony rose in the Commons to read out and draw attention to his motion. He then urged the Leader of the House: 'Can my right hon. friend assure us that the government have not lost their nerve on this issue, even if some local authorities have?'[25]

Sir Anthony did not have to declare his interest, as technically it was an intervention not a speech. He denied there was a conflict of interest and argued that inserting the Pritchards consultancy in the Register was sufficient: 'It is not necessary for MPs to declare interests in every question or intervention in the House. To do so would waste an inordinate amount of time.'[26]

It was not until after the 1987 general election that privatisation of many local authority services was enshrined in law. This was through Section 2 of the Local Government Act, which created contract opportunities for conglomerates like Grand Metropolitan, P and O, British and Commonwealth Holdings, Trusthouse Forte and BET. These five companies control over 50 per cent of the turnover of privatised local authority catering.

By the time of the second reading, thirty-three MPs had commercial interests directly affected by the bill through shareholdings, directorships and consultancies. Despite protests, these back-benchers were allowed to vote for the legislation to proceed. 'There is no bar to an hon. member exercising his vote in the House,' said the Deputy Speaker, Sir Paul Dean, who himself was a consultant to Grand Metropolitan, the giant catering contractor.[27]

One MP who voted for the bill was David Evans, elected to represent Welwyn and Hatfield a month earlier, in June 1987. Before entering Parliament, Evans was a wealthy businessman in contract cleaning through his company Brengreen Holdings, which he had sold to BET in September 1986. In his maiden speech, he immediately extolled the virtues of competitive tendering: 'Privatisation is the answer.'[28] He promptly declared an interest as 'a director of a company in the service sector'. This was Harefield Contract Services Ltd, then a subsidiary of BET, which holds 23 per cent of all NHS private cleaning contracts.

Evans was not only allowed to vote for the bill. He was also a member of the Commons standing committee which steered the legislation through Parliament. During the committee sessions Evans spoke up for competitive tendering and declared his directorship.

The following year the MP joined the board of Initial PLC, another major cleaning contractor.

The privatisation provisions of the Local Government Bill which became law in December 1987 was the culmination of a six-year campaign for many contractors. Lobbying was a crucial tactic, because the guidelines on competitive tendering issued by the government in the early 1980s did not have legal sanction. Hence some health and local authorities were able to defy privatisation. To conquer this resistance, the contractors hired lobbyists and MPs to wear down civil servants and ministers. This was done covertly rather than in the full glare of publicity. It was very much a case of private interests overcoming public services.

The electric beauty contest

Many of the major privatisations of the last decade have been long in realisation. The sale of the electricity supply industry is a case in point. At first the lobbying was political. But then came the commercial phase. And it was when these two worlds merged that the role of MPs with financial interests became controversial.

One of the most ardent champions of privatisation was Tim Eggar, the Conservative MP for Enfield North. In 1982 he became chairman of a special working party at Tory Central Office, which examined priorities for denationalisation. It was a private committee, but many of its findings appeared in 1984, in a Conservative Party pamphlet entitled 'A Policy For Denationalisation'. The principal author was Eggar, and electricity was one of the industries targeted for sale: 'The twelve Area Boards should be sold as independent regulated businesses. They would buy electricity from the national grid or generate their own ... The national grid in England and Wales would operate as a regulated monopoly, with its shares sold to the public.'[29]

Whenever there is any possibility of a shares issue of a public corporation, it is often the merchant banks that are the most assertive lobbyists. This is because of what bankers call the 'Beauty Contest'. The stockbrokers and banks present their credentials as the advisers on the sale, and government departments and companies then adjudicate on the most attractive proposition. Competition is always intense, and electricity was no exception. Despite official denials, the government had hinted at privatisation by removing restrictions on private power generation. The word in Whitehall and the City was that electricity would be the next prize. By the summer of 1985, the 'Beauty Contest' had begun.

Hill Samuel was one of the most avid participants. Founded in 1831, this merchant bank had acquired a voracious appetite for privatisation and share flotations. The financial rewards were enormous, and in the early 1980s the bank's eighty-strong Corporate Finance Department was deployed to advise the government on the sale of Sealink and Jaguar into the private sector. In 1984 Hill Samuel was commissioned to advise the Department of Transport on the share flotation of British Airways. But having failed to secure British Gas and the British Airports Authority as clients, the electricity industry became a prime target.

Knowledge is power, and Hill Samuel executives soon realised that information was the key to winning this beauty contest. For help they turned to Tim Eggar, by then a paid parliamentary consultant to Wood MacKenzie, the bank's stockbrokers. Eggar, who was also an adviser to the City lobbying firm Hill and Knowlton, had retained his enthusiasm for selling off electricity. On 11 March 1985, he urged the Energy Minister, Alastair Goodlad, in the Commons: 'Now that the miners' strike is over, will it not be necessary to think in terms of restructuring the finances of the electricity supply industry? If so, is not that yet another reason to move radically towards privatisation of the industry?'[30]

Three months later, on the morning of 27 June 1985, nine Hill Samuel executives held a special meeting on 'Privatisation Advisory Roles'. They had not brought good news. The discussion on 'Government Connections' was virtually a post-mortem on why the bank had not been short-listed for the British Airports Authority and British Gas. But one decision was made: 'Contact should be made with Eggar.'[31]

The Tory MP was invited to lunch the following week at Hill Samuel's headquarters in Wood Street, in the heart of the City. On the morning of the lunch, 2 July 1985, a note was circulated to three senior executives outlining the type of data required. Under the heading 'Electricity', this asked: 'Who to cultivate? . . . How to get an inside track on policy?'

When Tim Eggar attended the lunch he was 'pumped for information' on privatisation in general, and electricity in particular. The MP told them that 'electricity would be privatised on an area basis and the CEGB floated off separately'. He advised the bankers to 'look most carefully at the South of Scotland which is a self-contained entity and the one most ready-made for privatisation'. There was a 'good chance of getting it,' said Eggar, 'with Woodmac.' This was Wood MacKenzie – the MP's client.

The Hill Samuel directors were impressed with this guidance: 'It does appear that South of Scotland is something we should look at very closely and that we should begin to make friends with the right people there as soon as possible.'[32]

The bank's bid for the South of Scotland commission failed, but Hill Samuel did win a major award in the Electricity beauty contest. They became the financial advisers to the National Grid Company, which is one of the four successor companies to the Central Electricity Generating Board. Wood MacKenzie were taken over by County Natwest, the corporate division of which were appointed advisers to NORWEB, one of the distribution companies after privatisation. As for Tim Eggar, he severed his consultancy with Wood MacKenzie in September 1985 when he became a minister in the Foreign Office.

It was not until the summer of 1988 that the commercial opportunities created by electricity privatisation became apparent. Legislation was to be introduced in November, and the bill was scheduled to become law in 1990.

For foreign companies providing heating systems, this potential new market was an enticing prospect. In Denmark the Board of District Heating (DBDH), a business association acting for thirty Danish communal central-heating firms, became interested. The scope for increased exports was enormous.

But the DBDH needed political representation. One lobbying outfit eager to play intermediary was Grafton Interaction. Bearing the slogan 'Marketing and Motivation', Grafton shares offices with the Major Energy Users Council (MEUC), a trade group representing large industrial companies, in Cork Street, off Piccadilly in central London. In 1988 Grafton and MEUC also shared the same parliamentary consultant – Peter Rost, the Conservative MP for Erewash, Derbyshire. Rost was perhaps the most active and influential political figure in energy policy. A member of the Commons Select Committee on Energy since 1979, he had also acquired a number of commercial interests.[33] Between 1980 and 1984 he was energy consultant to Challoner Associates.

In February 1983, Rost successfully promoted an amendment in the Energy Act which imposed duties on electricity boards to adopt schemes for combined heat and power (CHP).[34] In his Commons speech in support of the bill, he said: 'This will provide a fair deal for the private generation of electricity and in doing so will offer the opportunity for competitive heat and power generation in this country ... There is one publicly quoted company which is already in the business – Associated Heat Services, a £20 million public company.' He then quoted from a letter written by that company's chairman: 'We look forward to the opportunities provided by the proposed new legislation,' concluding his speech by saying: 'That is positive evidence from someone already in the business who has achieved a great deal in providing cheaper heat and electricity.'[35] Later that year Rost became a paid consultant 'on energy matters' to Associated Heat Services PLC.

Five years on it was the ambitious Danish heating companies who sought to take advantage of the MP's enthusiasm for CHP. Rost was already known to them, having delivered seminars on CHP at the Danish Embassy.

In July 1988, Sven Perning, the DBDH's export adviser, flew to London to meet the MP and Andrew Bainbridge, Grafton's chief executive. At this meeting Rost said that the 'time has come' to implement activities which would help Danish influence on the British development of CHP/district heating. He outlined what he saw as the beneficial political circumstances, including the timetable for electricity privatisation, and suggested: 'This opens up the possibility of establishing CHP-generation via former [CEGB] Area Boards.' He was 'ready to enter into a formal co-operation' as a consultant to the Danish firms, via the DBDH.[36] Rost and Bainbridge suggested a trial period based on a fee of £2,900 a month. Perning was interested, and later compiled an aide-memoire, describing the MP's value:

The DBDH will be able to use Peter Rost's political influence, trade experience and contacts for the implementation of the first stage of Danish activities. Among other things, this will involve a meeting in the British Parliament with an exclusive circle of politicians and specialists, who shall discuss the further activities with a number of Danish politicians and specialists.[37]

Perning's colleague, DBDH chairman Lennart Larson, was more explicit in his assessment: 'We are interested in close contacts in political circles in London, hoping that they will do the lobbying for us. Therefore we have contacted, for instance, MP Peter Rost. We hope this will be a way to increase exports of district heating and energy solutions in the UK.'[38]

That the proposed consultancy was very much a joint Rost/ Grafton deal is evident from the lobbyists' formal submission. Bainbridge outlined several areas 'where our expertise, experience and influence can be of value':

Market Intelligence. We can supply regular reports of developments in the UK ... and information from leaders in the energy industry, the Combined Heat and Power Association, local authorities and industry in general.

Political Intelligence. We can supply confidential reports of political activities, discussions with UK government ministers and the thinking of the specialist groups in Parliament.

Personal Introductions. Following your clear briefing, we can arrange top level introductions to, and meetings with, potential customers and people of influence, particularly in government.

Project Appraisal. We can smooth the way with advice on customer relations and commercial procedures in individual cases.[39]

Bainbridge and Rost also made it clear that if hired they would not represent any competing company.

The potential use of Rost and Grafton to the Danish companies was demonstrated during negotiations over the consultancy. On 11 November 1988, Bainbridge wrote to the DBDH and enclosed a copy of the government's response to the report by the Commons Energy Select Committee on electricity privatisation. Grafton's chief executive explained: 'Peter [Rost] thought you might like to see the attached government response ... it is confidential information until it is formally published.'[40] The select committee's report on privatisation was not published until 22 November 1988 – eleven days later.

On 12 December 1988, Rost made a passionately pro-privatisation speech during the Electricity Bill debate. Two days later, while discussions between Grafton and DBDH continued, he was nominated to serve on the Commons Standing Committee for the Electricity Privatisation Bill. This was a key committee, as it examined the bill in some detail and perused amendments.

The next day, 15 December, the MP went to the Heathrow Penta Hotel for a meeting of the Major Energy Users Council, member firms of which were keen backers of the bill as they wanted privately to generate their own electricity. Rost was a consultant to MEUC, sponsored by Associated Heat Services PLC and Slough Estates PLC.[41] During his 'Political Commentary', Rost told the forty-four members present about the Electricity Bill. He said that the powers of the regulator would be fundamental to the effectiveness of competition after privatisation. But as he had just been elected to sit on the standing committee, he would be able 'to ensure that the major users' interests would be considered'.[42]

The potential for a conflict of interests was recognised later that day, when Rost was removed from the Electricity Bill Standing Committee after a *Guardian* article that morning disclosed the Rost/ Grafton overtures to the Danish heating companies. The afternoon brought more bad news, when Labour MPs attacked Rost in the Commons over his links with Grafton. Rost, however, was not in the chamber to answer the charges – he was at the Heathrow Penta Hotel, advising MEUC on the Electricity Bill.

Five days later Rost responded to the allegations: 'My interest in and contribution to energy efficiency for the last eighteen years are well known inside and outside the House. Where those involve commercial interests, they are declared. I deeply resent the accusation that in pursuing such interests I am motivated by personal gain.'[43] He had not, however, declared all his interests. His consultancies with MEUC and Grafton had been absent from the Register on 15 December – the day the *Guardian* story was published.

Rost's DBDH contract faded away, and the protracted negotiations were called off, but he continued to back the privatisation of the electricity industry while retaining commercial interests affected by the legislation.[44] He argued: 'If you believe in something, such as eliminating fuel poverty, increasing fuel efficiency and reducing high energy costs, and you feel there is a way you can achieve it, then you pursue certain interests.'

But what, he was asked, if you receive substantial payments for promoting those interests while remaining an MP and a member of key committees? 'A professional consultant,' he replied, 'presumably gets a consultancy fee like everyone else.'[45]

A share of the water

Like that for electricity, the beauty contest for the privatisation of the Water Authorities took place over several preliminary rounds. For merchant bankers Hill Samuel, information about the competition at an early stage was again crucial if they were to catch the judge's eye.

Hill Samuel's first approach was in early February 1985. The bank's chief executive, Richard Lloyd, sent a memorandum on water privatisation to John Moore, then Chief Secretary to the Treasury. This detailed note expressed a strong interest in being the advisers on the preliminary financial study of privatisation. Their enthusiasm was well timed as a few days later, on 7 February, the Treasury announced it was setting up a working party to investigate privatisation.

The merchant bank's memorandum was then sent to the Water Directorate of the Department of the Environment (DOE). From June 1985, Hill Samuel began lobbying civil servants for the advisory role commission on privatisation. In private meetings, executives reported to colleagues that on the water industry the bank 'acquired specific knowledge at an early stage'. However, 'the advantage was lost through lack of continuity'.[46] The solution, they decided, was 'close contact with the right people' at the Environment Ministry so that they could 'get to know its thinking'.[47]

As with electricity, Hill Samuel turned to Tim Eggar, consultant to their stockbroking subsidiary Wood MacKenzie. At a lunch at the bank's head office, Eggar told executives that he believed 'Kleinwort had the inside track with the DOE and Lazard's had Thames Water in the bag.' After the meeting a strategy was devised. Peter Greenhalgh, a director, advocated: 'We should consider asking Eggar to try and get some information on the DOE's thinking which is clearly far advanced.'[48]

In the summer months of 1985 Hill Samuel continued to lobby the DOE and the Water Authorities, particularly Roy Watts of Thames Water. This strategy met with mixed success. In February 1986 the bank entered the water privatisation beauty contest and lost out to

J. Schroder Wragg. But they did win a lucrative bonus prize. Hill Samuel were chosen to underwrite the sale of the shares. As one bank executive confided: 'The kudos comes from doing the privatisations, whereas profits come from sharing in the underwriting.'[49]

After the Water Bill had been navigated through Parliament the role of MPs became more significant. One of them was Keith Raffan, Conservative MP for the Welsh seat of Delyn. Raffan was a member of the Commons standing committee which oversaw the privatisation of the water industry.

During the committee's sessions, Raffan praised Welsh Water for increasing local access to land purchased in anticipation of denationalisation: 'Thanks to privatisation, greater public access to that part of Welsh land has been assured.'[50]

On 6 July 1989, the bill received Royal Assent and became law. This enabled the twelve water authorities to be sold off as publicly quoted companies.

In September 1989, after the announcement of the flotation but before the sale of the shares, Raffan flew to Australia. During the visit he did some consultancy work for the newly privatised company, which paid his travel and hotel expenses.

Nine months later Raffan was hired by Welsh Water PLC as its 'Special Business Adviser'. His assignment was to act as the company's liaison officer with Welsh Tory MPs, advise on parliamentary matters and promote Welsh Water PLC overseas.[51] The newly privatised firm refused to discuss the fee: 'That is a matter between us and Mr Raffan.' But Raffan was unconcerned. 'I don't see any conflict of interest at all,' he remarked. 'The two things are separated by well over a year ... It is flattering to me that the chairman of Welsh Water and his colleagues think I have a fairly considerable knowledge of the industry and that I can therefore be of help.'[52]

Selling the cable network

The shift to the private sector in the past decade has resulted in other forms of beauty contest being hosted by the government. One of the most competitive was the award of franchises for the emerging cable-television business.

In March 1981, the Home Office granted licences for five companies to take part in a pilot scheme. For the next decade the intense interest shown by companies in cable TV confirmed that commercial opportunities as well as franchises were there for the taking.

One Conservative MP who saw the business potential earlier than most was John Browne. He had spent part of 1980 lending his political weight to a consortium, Southern Counties Ltd, in their bid for the ITV South franchise. The MP was a substantial shareholder with a 12 per cent stake. But he received no return on his investment, as in December 1980 Southern Counties failed to win the franchise.

Browne had worked alongside Barry Chattington, a young film producer whom he met while appearing on Kuwaiti television. In early 1981, the MP asked Chattington whether there were any other opportunities in the television business. 'One potential area is cable and satellite TV,' he was told.[53] He immediately took soundings, writing to Home Office ministers requesting information about the government's intentions. He had lunch with David Scholey, a director of the merchant bank S. G. Warburg, to discuss 'the chances of financing a cable TV venture'. The MP told Scholey: 'If it goes ahead, I will contact you on a more serious basis in the future.'[54]

In March 1981, Browne met Brian Deutsch, a wealthy property developer whose Belgravia house at 12 Eaton Square made him a neighbour. For the next year Chattington, Browne and Deutsch held a series of informal meetings to discuss setting up an integrated communications business. The first was on 29 March 1981, over lunch in the Rib Room of the Carlton Tower Hotel, Knightsbridge. Others were usually over drinks or Sunday lunch. In September 1981, Browne interrupted a month-long business trip to spend four days with Deutsch at his house in Taos, New Mexico.

The three each had a clearly defined role. Deutsch was a sharp business operator. Browne was the political fixer, arranging discreet meetings and lunches with ministers, while Chattington had the technical knowledge. The focus of their discussions was always cable television, particularly how to take advantage of its commercial spin-offs, like new information technology systems. In October 1981, Browne had lunch at the Commons with Harry Clark, President of Transition Communications. Clark told him the next day: 'As you think through your options for participating in the expanding new technology programming market-place, please note our interest in participating in such an enterprise. If you would like to pursue a possible co-venture in new technology programming and production, please let me know.'[55]

In March 1982, Browne approached the electronics group Thorn EMI. He wrote to the chairman Sir Richard Cave about his increasing interest in the videotex and cable TV industry:

> I am writing to ask whether you would have any interest in engaging me as a consultant to Thorn EMI ... I believe that companies working in this field would find it a great benefit to have someone working for them who is close to William Whitelaw (Home Secretary), Kenneth Baker (Information Technology Minister), and to the back-bench media committee.[56]

A week later, Browne asked the Prime Minister:

> Does my right hon. friend accept that recent government action has opened truly vast opportunities in the videotext and information technology industry, both for employment and for real wealth creation? Will my right hon. friend reassure the House that such great opportunities will not be eroded by government caution or unnecessary over-regulation?[57]

Mrs Thatcher reassured him: 'We shall not tie up those opportunities with red tape, but we must consider some regulatory matters before final decisions are made on cable television.'[58]

Browne's enthusiasm was rewarded three weeks later when he was invited to lunch by Thorn EMI's chairman, Sir Richard Cave. This took place at the company head office in St Martin's Lane with two senior directors present. The four discussed cable and direct broadcasting systems and the possibility of a consultancy for the MP.

The next day Browne wrote to Sir Richard, thanking him for 'a most interesting lunch'. He added: 'I look forward to seeing you again some time in the future. In the meantime, I hope that I will be successful in being called in today's debate to put over some of the excellent points you made, particularly concerning financing.'[59]

The debate was on Satellite and Cable Broadcasting, and sitting in the Visitor's Gallery was the MP's potential business partner Brian Deutsch. During his twenty-minute speech Browne did indeed convey his own and Thorn EMI's views:

> There is little need for the control of cable television ... It is a free enterprise investment as opposed to a political investment. Investors will therefore be looking for financial returns. The people in the entertainment industry look to those in the information technology business and hope that they will finance the laying of cable.[60]

Browne then laid out his own plan for the industry. The government should license a private consortium to co-ordinate local cable firms: 'This company should be allowed to take a minority shareholding interest in the local operating companies. This would mean that a money-earning and informed think tank would co-ordinate the growth of the industry.'[61] The House was not told that for at least nine months Browne had been setting up his own 'money-earning think tank' along with Deutsch and Barry Chattington. This is despite the Commons convention that Members should declare any interest 'that they may have or *may be expecting* to have' (my emphasis).

During the debate ministers had expressed considerable enthusiasm for private sector investment in the cable industry. Browne and his two business associates believed the time was finally right to make their pitch. But the schedule was tight. Kenneth Baker, Minister for Information Technology and a cable enthusiast, had announced that submissions to the cable inquiry needed to be delivered within five weeks.

A week after the debate, on 27 April 1982, the MP had dinner with Brian Deutsch at the Ebury Wine Bar, just around the corner from their Belgravia homes. Three days later, on Friday 30 April, Browne, Deutsch and Chattington hosted a lunch at the MP's house for Kenneth Baker and Ian Deary of Wang Communications.

The following Tuesday, after nearly a year of preparation, a company was finally formed. Entitled 3 C's Ltd (Cable Communications Consultants), its directors and shareholders were Browne, his wife Elizabeth, Brian Deutsch and Barry Chattington.

The firm's purpose was to act as a consulting and co-ordinating firm for the two emerging industries – videotex and cable TV.[62] To achieve this for videotex, shares in 3 C's would be sold to major corporations involved in its hardware, like Plessey, Wang and British Telecom. For cable TV, the plan was for 3 C's to serve as both provider and co-ordinator. A local station would be owned 51 per cent by a franchised cable operator and 49 per cent by 3 C's. Funding would come from participating companies and a public shares issue.

The company's 'Business Plan' was formulated six weeks later over lunch at the Browne family home. Its aim was 'to participate in the profits of the videotex business' and 'franchise this package within the industry'.[63]

Lobbying took place on two fronts: in the executive suites of potential cable manufacturers and owners, and in private meetings with ministers. Browne and Deutsch went to Plessey's head office at Millbank to have lunch with the chairman, Sir John Clark, a constituent of the Winchester MP. Two weeks later, on 24 November 1982, Sir George Jefferson, chairman of British Telecom, was a guest at the MP's house, along with the rest of the 3 C's Board.

Another recipient of John Browne's Belgravia hospitality was John Butcher, who had just been appointed Minister for Telcommunications, in April 1982. Later that year Butcher and Kenneth Baker again met the MP and Deutsch to discuss 3 C's Ltd.

This meeting took place on 30 November 1982, at Browne's office in the Commons, just above St Stephen's entrance. It was just two days before the debate on Broadcasting and Cable Systems and the two ministers were urged to ensure that the cable industry would be free of regulation. Browne attended the debate but made only five brief interventions.

Throughout 1982 the Hampshire MP's directorship had been absent from the Register of Members' Interests. Yet Browne continued to lobby Kenneth Baker over his business plan to 'manage cable systems nationwide'.[64] This, however, as with his attempt to become a Thorn EMI consultant, was unsuccessful. On 10 January 1983, Baker told Browne: 'A single privately-financed organisation being allowed overall national control of wideband cable systems seems to have many disadvantages.'[65] That decision effectively finished off 3 C's. Two weeks later John and Elizabeth Browne resigned from the board.

In early January 1983, a week before its publication, the MP entered his directorship in the Register. But for most of 1982, while the Commons debates on cable TV and information technology raged, Parliament and the public remained unaware both of his impending commercial interest and of his executive directorship of 3 C's Ltd.

Browne maintains that it was not necessary to declare his interest until May 1982 because he had decided to set up 3 C's Ltd only *after* the cable TV debate on 20 April 1982. Therefore, according to the MP, he did not 'expect to have' a pecuniary interest during the debate. But an internal company report written by director Barry Chattington states that '3 C's was incorporated in early 1982'. Another document puts it earlier than that.[66]

Elizabeth Browne, the MP's former wife who was a 3 C's director and the company secretary, told me: 'There is no doubt that the company was being set up months before the debate in April 1982. There were numerous lunch parties and meetings planning it.' Brian Deutsch, chairman of 3 C's, who worked full-time for the company, had discussed the cable TV venture with Browne as early as 24 May 1981. He recalled: 'I certainly know that we talked about it before the debate. Whether the company existed or not I have absolutely no recollection.'[67]

Whether or not 3 C's Ltd was officially incorporated by 20 April 1982, the evidence indicates that Browne was planning some form of cable TV consultancy company from the summer of 1981. Consequently, as he was seeking to obtain a commercial benefit from the industry, he should have declared an interest during the debates.

Some time after his resignation from the cable firm Browne reflected on his decision. 'I only wish I was still involved in the company 3 C's Ltd which is potentially a very profitable enterprise,' he said. His frustration was well founded. For in the years since the transfer of his energies to other activities, the cable industry continues to be potentially lucrative. And it has been closely interlocked with government decision-making and regulation.

The road to legislation began in December 1982 with the Commons debate on Broadcasting and Cable Systems. The issue was not *whether* cable would be adapted, but *how* it would be incorporated into the broadcasting system.

Many MPs already had potential commercial stakes in the industry. Timothy Brinton, a former newscaster, was a 'broadcasting consultant' and paid adviser to Communications Strategy Ltd. Brinton declared his interests. He then urged the government 'not to delay the introduction' and declared that 'cable should be intensely and openly competitive'.[68] A fellow Conservative MP, Ray Whitney, announced: 'I should declare a putative interest in the cable industry. When the progress is achieved that we all hope will take place, I hope that a group of friends will launch into cable technology.'[69] In 1987 Whitney became a consultant to (and later chairman of) Windsor Cable Television. In January 1989 he became chairman of the Cable Corporation.

As the Cable and Broadcasting Bill was being drafted in early 1984, many of these MPs still retained their financial stakes. Several of them even became members of the crucial Commons standing committee overseeing the new law. Among the five Tory MPs who declared cable interests during the committee hearings were Timothy

Brinton, John Gorst (Ladbroke Group Ltd) and Robert Key (share-holding in Salisbury Cablevision Ltd).[70] It was a remarkable situation: 25 per cent of the committee guiding the Cable Bill through Parliament consisted of MPs with a financial interest in the industry.

Aided by a battery of lobbyists representing the cable operators, vital concessions were secured during the committee stage. Cable franchises would be extended from twelve to fifteen years, and proposals to limit advertising were eased. Many of the MPs who backed cable television later picked up shares and directorships. On 15 August 1984, three weeks after the bill received Royal Assent, Sir Gerard Vaughan owned 100 shares in Cable Health UK, a film and TV production company. For the next two years Sir Gerard retained this 20 per cent holding but did not declare it in the Register. The company did not trade that year and it was eventually dissolved in 1988.

In June 1988, the Labour MP Dennis Howell, who had been sympathetic to the industry as a member of the Cable Bill Standing Committee, became a director of Birmingham Cable Co. Ltd. The following year another committee member, the Tory MP Robert Key, joined the board of Wessex Cable Ltd. But the holder of the most cable directorships has been former diplomat Sir Peter Blaker, Conservative MP for Blackpool South and a former Defence minister. In 1985 he became chairman of Central Lancashire Television Ltd, which put in a bid for local cable franchises. Two years later Sir Peter joined the board of East Lancashire Cablevision Ltd. Since May 1989, he has been a director and chairman of Maclean Hunter Cablevision Ltd, which has six cable franchises. These three directorships have been declared.

Sir Peter has also actively lobbied ministers, Home Office officials and Parliament on behalf of his clients. In the spring of 1990, he led a delegation of ten representatives from cable companies and three MPs – Simon Coombs, Peter Viggers (chairman of Britannia Cablesystems Ltd) and Ray Whitney (chairman of the Cable Corporation and Windsor Cable Television) – to see David Mellor, Home Office Minister of State.[71] The meeting took place at the Home Office just before a crucial debate on the 1990 Broadcasting Bill. Whitney and Viggers had already spoken privately with Mellor about 'reconsidering some aspects of the bill' which might damage 'some of the investment that is ready, at long last, to carry the cable revolution forward'.[72] The ten cable firm executives represented £2 billion worth of investment. They were concerned about apparent advantages held by local licensed delivery operators when renewing cable systems. Their MPs backed their case and Sir Peter Blaker, chairman of a major cable company, was chief advocate.

Shortly after that meeting, Sir Peter moved a new clause and amendments on the Broadcasting Bill which benefited the cable industry. He declared his interest as 'chairman of a company which has six cable franchises'.[73]

It was clear from Sir Peter's speech that he was representing the cable operators:

> There is a feeling in parts of the cable industry that the government's attitude is becoming less enthusiastic . . . The industry has been dismayed by the apparent discrimination against it as compared with the licensed delivery operators in the provisions of the Bill dealing with the system of renewal . . . The industry is not asking for any privileges. It is proposing a fair and common-sense solution.[74]

David Mellor, the Home Office Minister, was convinced. He accepted an amendment on the key issue of the arrangements for renewing cable licences. 'The industry' was placated.

Who's next?

A decade of deregulation and privatisation has been as prosperous for lobbyists and MPs as it has been for merchant bankers and contract-seeking companies. Back-benchers and former ministers have run willingly into the arms of the brokers and consultants, despite the conflicts of interest.

Whether MPs have been effective commercial ambassadors is unclear. Certainly, the cleaning contractors benefited enormously from retaining MPs as the hired help. But what is indisputable is that back-benchers will be lining up for the next privatisation beauty contest.

This could be for the 'Crown Jewel' – the Post Office. Throughout the 1980s, the postal service was immune from the charms of denationalisation, many Conservative MPs from the Shires believing that any deterioration of rural services could be a serious vote-loser. The appointment of Nicholas Ridley as Trade and Industry Secretary in July 1989 gave the privateers fresh heart. But it remained a controversial proposition. The government was sceptical, anxious about creating a private duopoly and about the huge start-up costs.

The interested firms responded by launching a lobbying strategy. It was co-ordinated by the International Express Carriers Conference (IECC), a business association which campaigns for deregulation of postal services. In January 1990, IECC hired Ian Twinn, Conservative MP for Edmonton, as their consultant. 'At Westminster, there is a groundswell of support for greater competition in the Post Office,' said Twinn. 'My role is to advise the IECC on presenting its case.'[75]

The IECC represents TNT (the Australian-owned transport group), Federal Express and United Parcels. Within weeks these companies were having monthly meetings at the DTI to discuss privatising the collection of the mail. The massive initial investment remained an obstacle, but according to Kevin Bell of Westminster Strategy, the lobbying firm working for IECC alongside Twinn, the DTI were being won round.[76]

This was confirmed less than a year later, in January 1991, when a proposal to privatise the Post Office was openly welcomed by the DTI. The plan would enable private operators like TNT to compete for licences with the Royal Mail from a new regulatory body. This was described by the Trade and Industry Secretary Peter Lilley as 'the sort of proposal the government should be looking at for its next manifesto'.[77]

It appears then, that the Post Office is next for the market-place, as there seems to be ideological sympathy at the DTI. TNT has enlisted the help of Ian Twinn as a paid consultant. It will be interesting to see how many other MPs who advocate private collection of the mail also accumulate consultancies and directorships.

CHAPTER 5

Selecting Your Interests:
Select Committees and Standing Committees

> Whenever a Member of Parliament is closely connected with business circles outside, and especially with a particular concern, it cannot be disputed that there is a danger of the conflict of his political duty with his private interests being decided in favour of the latter.
>
> Karl Weber, *Rechtswissenschaftliche Beitrage* (Berlin, 1931)

Sir Geoffrey Howe, Deputy Prime Minister and Leader of the House of Commons until November 1990, is the embodiment of the British parliamentary establishment. Educated at Winchester and at Cambridge University, he was a barrister at 26 and a QC at 39. In the 1980s he became the consummate Conservative MP and Cabinet minister, famous for his extravagantly moderate language and soporific tone.

The former Chancellor of the Exchequer and Foreign Secretary was also known for his excessive caution. The last politician to make moralistic outbursts, in essence he was 'Mr Respectable' the personification of propriety. Thus it was an occasion of considerable significance when Sir Geoffrey, in December 1989, while Leader of the Commons, addressed the delicate issue of Members' interests. He was uneasy about MPs with financial stakes in areas which they were monitoring and suggested that members of select committees 'should accept an obligation going beyond the general requirement for MPs to declare their interests for the purpose of the Register'.[1]

Sir Geoffrey went further, and told MPs: 'There is a case, indeed, for considering non-participation if a Member has interests that are relevant to the work of the select committee. If he has external interests relevant to the work of the select committee itself, he might actually stand aside from it rather than simply declare an interest.'[2]

This was a remarkably forthright statement by a senior Cabinet minister. Clearly aware of the dangers to the independence and credibility of select committees presented by outside commercial concerns, he was also drawing attention to the fact that there are no strict rules governing the disclosure of interests by MPs serving on select committees. For decades, Members have relied, in true club tradition, on procedure and practice, and the traditional custom that MPs should declare their interests. However, a precedent was set in 1943 over a select committee on national expenditure. Its chairman, Sir John Wardlaw-Milne, was asked in the Commons: 'Will he give an assurance that when any investigations are carried out into the organisation or activities of any private or public company, no member of the select committee who is directly interested in that concern or in any competitive business sits as a member of the committee or sub-committee that is charged with this task?'

'Yes, sir,' replied Sir John. 'To the limited extent to which the question applies to the inquiries of the select committee, it is our practice that a Member would not so take part.'[3]

This is confirmed by Erskine May, the parliamentary bible, which asserts: 'It is not the practice for a member of a select committee to take part in any inquiry while the affairs of any body in which he may be personally interested are under investigation.'[4]

Most MPs have ignored this statement and blithely continue to participate in inquiries which could benefit them financially. The Speaker always refuses to intervene, despite the abundant potential for a conflict of interests and for MPs peddling for their paymasters. Members of select committees have privileged access to detailed and sensitive data from documents supplied to the committee by companies and government departments. Useful information is also acquired from publicly funded trips both in Britain and abroad. The opportunities for abuse are enormous.

This is particularly the case during special inquiries. Members of select committees adjudicate on the content and structure of the investigation. They can then lobby for their clients during the hearings, supply them with commercially useful information and then play a key role in drafting the final published report.

Influence of the chair

The chairmen of select committees are in a particularly influential position. According to Robert Sheldon, chair of the Public Accounts Committee: 'While members of committees have a responsibility to disclose their interests, there is an even greater obligation on chairmen of select committees, who frequently have access to information, much of which may be classified as confidential or secret or may be submitted on a "commercial-in-confidence" basis.'[5]

Some MPs argue this is an exaggerated assessment of their power. But it is a view supported by Terence Higgins, chairman of the Treasury and Civil Service Select Committee, who in May 1990 wrote to the Select Committee on Members' Interests: 'Although [the chairman] only has a casting vote he does, together with the clerk, determine the shape and to a large extent the programme of the committee and determine the report. Although he only has a casting vote when the report is debated, the initial shape of the report may be relevant to any interest which he may have.'[6]

Among committee chairmen with business connections to companies active in their area is Jerry Wiggin, the Conservative MP for Weston-super-Mare. Since 1987 he has been both chairman of the Select Committee on Agriculture, which deals with the sugar industry, and a consultant to the British Sugar Corporation. Wiggin has lobbied on his client's behalf in the Commons chamber. In November 1989 he intervened during a debate to draw the attention of the Secretary of State for Agriculture, John Gummer, to a proposed British Sugar plant that 'may need substantial contributions from the government'. The Somerset MP did not declare his interest and continued: 'Will the minister make representations to the Department of Trade and Industry in favour of that excellent British enterprise?'[7]

Wiggin denied that his British Sugar interest ever conflicted with Agriculture Committee business. He also defended the notion of MPs on select committees having related financial stakes: 'It's very difficult to get knowledgeable people if you get too fussy about what I would call general interests.'[8] But he did acknowledge there was a problem: 'If the Agriculture Committee chose to undertake an inquiry into a field where I had a financial interest, I would simply stay away from the relevant meetings.'[9]

Sir Hugh Rossi, chairman of the Select Committee on Environment since 1983, also recognises the potential for conflict, but has stopped short of leaving the chair. In May 1990, his committee began an inquiry into indoor pollution. As a consultant to Carter Commercial Developments Ltd and director of Stock Land and Estates Ltd, Sir Hugh was faced with a clash of interests. But he immediately saw the problem and declared his interests during the session of evidence.[10] Ten months later, his interests again collided with his chairmanship of the committee. On 13 March 1991, the Chemical Industries Association gave evidence as part of an inquiry into land waste. Sir Hugh declared that he was a consultant to Simmons and Simmons, a firm of enviromental lawyers who advise the Association. He is opposed to more stringent rules for committee chairmen. 'At the end of the day, it is a matter of personal integrity and honour of the individual person concerned,' he remarked.[11]

Kenneth Warren, chairman of the Select Committee on Trade and Industry since 1983, takes an equally scrupulous view: 'I have an absolute, firm principle that with any of my business interests I do not participate in any negotiations or lobbying of government under any circumstances.'[12] But his interests have twice conflicted with the topic of an inquiry. In 1988 he was a director of Datapoint UK Ltd while his committee conducted an investigation into information technology. He declared his interest at the beginning of the inquiry, describing himself as having been 'involved in the computer industry for some twenty-five years'.[13] The following year Warren withdrew from a session that was taking evidence from British Telecom, giving as his reason his directorship of a company that had contracts as a British Telecom supplier.[14] Apart from Defence, the Trade and Industry Committee is closest to the commercial world. But Warren remains defiant: 'If you can't have any interests which could be vaguely connected with the committee's work you would preclude many people from serving whose experience is invaluable.'[15]

Warren is also opposed to an extension of the rules: 'I believe that Members are right to treat each other as "Honourable Members". Our mutual trust, born of experience of working together in the committee, is of far greater value than more regulation relating to Members' interests which would not enhance the common confidence we have in each other.'[16]

A stake in their own rules

It is one of the delightful ironies of British democracy that the members of the select committee responsible for policing MPs' interests should themselves have consultancies and directorships. In 1990 the Select Committee on Members' Interests held an inquiry into the rules governing the interests of MPs on Select committees. Six of the thirteen members of that investigation held financial stakes potentially affected by its outcome.

The committee's chairman since 1979 has been Sir Geoffrey Johnson-Smith, the affable Tory MP for Wealdon. He holds five directorships, notably Taylor Alden Ltd, an industrial public-relations and marketing company, and Brands Hatch Leisure PLC. He is also on the board of London Weekend Television, which has been under threat because of legislation to auction ITV franchises. In February 1989, Sir Geoffrey declared his interest and complained that the government's plan to auction new licences would 'encourage unrealistic bids'. He also called for franchises to be awarded 'not to the highest bidder but to the bidder offering the best value for money'.[17] Ten months later he was again putting London Weekend Television's case, during the Broadcasting Bill debate. He argued, having declared his interest, that 'a requirement of the bidding process now advocated is that a quality hurdle should be linked to what they call a business credibility hurdle'.[18]

Sir Geoffrey is also a consultant to two other companies – MEL, a division of Philips Electronic and Associated Industries Ltd, and the insurance group Eagle Star. MEL is a major defence contractor with a special electronic warfare division at their Crawley HQ. As chairman of the Conservative back-bench Defence Committee, Sir Geoffrey is a strong advocate of greater defence expenditure. During the 1988 Defence Estimates debate, he opposed reductions in defence spending, claiming that the Soviet threat was 'growing stronger and more efficient'. He added:

> It would be wrong, out of respect for our allies, to undermine our current defence responsibilities in the interests of short-term financial criteria . . . Any fundamental change that we may be forced to make if we starve our defence forces of the resources that are necessary for an adequate modernisation programme will bring into question our reliability as a staunch member of the Western European Union.[19]

However, by not declaring his MEL consultancy, Sir Geoffrey appears to have broken his own committee's rules.

Another experienced member of the Select Committee on Members' Interests is Robert Adley. A Lloyd's underwriter, he holds three directorships and is marketing consultant to Commonwealth Hotels International Co. Ltd. The longest-serving member is Sir William Shelton, also a 'name' at Lloyd's. He has his own consultancy firm, Saracen Consultants Ltd, and is a consultant to McCann-Erickson Advertising Ltd. One of the committee's most recent appointments is Peter Viggers, the Conservative MP for Gosport. Since October 1989, he has been a director of Britannia Cablesystems Ltd and is chairman of five parent cable companies. Two other members of the committee, responsible for overseeing lobbying, are themselves consultants to lobbying and PR companies. Sir Michael McNair-Wilson is a paid adviser to Shandwick Public Affairs Ltd and Dame Peggy Fenner is retained by S. Western Consultants Ltd.

In defence of their interests

The Defence Select Committee is one of the most important units of government accountability, monitoring as it does the £22 billion defence budget. Members of the committee receive classified material on the progress of major defence projects, confidential briefings on the failure rates of defence equipment, data on British exports from defence attachés while on overseas trips, and information from defence contractors in the form of written and oral evidence.[20] Hence, committee members are in a privileged and potentially useful position. If they then become advisers to defence contractors, they clearly have the advantage over outside defence consultants. 'A large number of people, firms in particular and companies acting for those firms, want to meet you and explain their position,' said Neil Thorne, a Tory member of the committee. 'I'm experiencing it every week, sometimes every day. I have people approaching me because they think I am in a position to influence the outcome of a decision.'[21]

There have been many defence controversies in recent years, but few have attained the peaks of political and commercial intrigue reached by the Westland Affair. In the winter months of 1985-6, the City, Whitehall and Westminster were in the grip of a frenzied bout of infighting and chicanery. The cause was a financial crisis in a small West Country helicopter company called Westland PLC. The government was split down the middle as to how to save this defence contractor. Leon Brittan, then Trade and Industry Secretary, and Mrs Thatcher backed a large share investment by Sikorsky, an American company, allied with Fiat of Italy. But Michael Heseltine, then Defence Secretary, fervently supported a rival bid by a European consortium comprising helicopter firms from France, Germany and Italy combined with British Aerospace and GEC. The double-dealing and back-stabbing that resulted from this remarkable row later led to the resignation of Brittan, Heseltine and almost the Prime Minister herself. But, if anything, the saga was more commercial than political in nature.

It was not until 3 December 1985 that British Aerospace, which supplied millions of pounds worth of weapons and electronics for Westland helicopters, entered the fray. By this time the stakes were high and the Select Committee on Defence had just set up an inquiry into the 'Defence Implications of the Future of Westland PLC'. One of the committee's members was Michael (now Sir) Marshall, Conservative MP for Arundel. He had been on the committee since 1982 and had unsuccessfully stood for the chairmanship. From 1982 he had also been the paid parliamentary adviser to the space and communications division of British Aerospace PLC.

On 16 December 1985, in the Commons, Marshall asked Leon Brittan about the European consortium bid for Westland: 'Does he accept that GEC, as well as British Aerospace, made an offer to bring forward the European proposal? That matter causes some of us concern, as the offer was apparently rejected within twenty-four hours. Does he think that the matter should be looked at with care?'[22] Two days later the Defence Committee inquiry opened in secret session. Marshall declared his interest but continued to attend the hearings, over the next four months cross-examining witnesses in eight of the eleven sessions. He was even present when four senior British Aerospace executives, including the chairman and chief executive, appeared before the committee. Marshall wisely kept quiet during their evidence.[23]

Behind the scenes Marshall was more active on British Aerospace's behalf. By mid-January 1986, the European consortium bid was being referred to as 'The British Aerospace Solution'. As Brittan was hostile towards the Heseltine/European offer, Marshall acted as an intermediary between British Aerospace and the DTI, at one stage, on 16 January 1986, intervening during a furious row between them. The company's chief executive, Sir Raymond Lygo, suggested that Brittan had described the British Aerospace investment as 'against the national interest'. The Industry Secretary angrily denied this. That afternoon Marshall declared his interest in the Commons and suggested to Mrs Thatcher that Brittan's comment was 'a case of genuine misunderstanding'. The Prime Minister replied: 'Yes, I think that is correct.'[24] Marshall then acted to cement a reconciliation. He arranged a secret meeting that evening, at Brown's Hotel in Dover Street, between Lygo and Gerald Malone, Brittan's parliamentary private secretary. British Aerospace was anxious not to fall out with the DTI, especially as the company was at the time seeking government grants. And so a letter was drafted and published, restating there had been 'a misunderstanding' between the two parties.[25]

This incident took place in the middle of the Defence Committee's inquiry into the commercial future of Westland. Given British Aerospace's direct financial involvement in the negotiations, and amidst such a highly charged political atmosphere, Marshall should have stepped aside. Indeed, it is difficult to accept his membership of the Defence Committee at all while remaining a British Aerospace consultant.

Six months after the Defence Select Committee completed their Westland inquiry, a new chairman was elected. This was Michael Mates, the Conservative MP for East Hampshire. Mates seemed an apt choice, as he had spent twenty years in the army. He had served in the Queen's Dragoon Guards, rising to the rank of Lieutenant-Colonel, and finished his career working for the Vice-Chief of the Defence Staff. His last assignment was devising an anti-terrorist contingency plan for the Cabinet Office.[26]

In 1974 Colonel Mates entered Parliament, and it was not long before he joined the lobbying game. Two years later he became a paid adviser to Good Relations Ltd, a political and financial PR company. Among their many clients over the years was GKN, the huge defence contractor, and GEC on an *ad hoc* basis. In 1979 Mates was appointed a member of the Defence Select Committee. But it was not until 1986 that he acquired any defence-related commercial interests. That year he became a consultant to Link-Miles Ltd, a major defence contractor. Along with Rediffusion, they are the largest suppliers of hi-tech simulation equipment to the RAF.[27]

By 1990, Link-Miles had secured 106 contracts with the Ministry of Defence, worth £175 million.[28]

Mates is paid a monthly retainer plus expenses for his consultancy. He was hired to 'provide political guidance in respect of parliamentary activities on defence and related fields' as well as on marketing strategy,[29] briefing Link-Miles directors and executives at informal meetings. During one discussion the company asked Mates his advice on the future for defence contractors, given the political upheaval in Eastern Europe. He replied that their equipment would still be useful for the training of soldiers in Britain and Germany.[30]

Mates vehemently denies that he has helped Link-Miles secure Ministry of Defence business. 'If I was asked to represent their case to the MOD, I would refuse,' he said. 'If they want my advice that's fine, but I will not lobby for them or speak on their behalf.'[31] This statement, however, did not take into account the potential conflicts of interests that could arise from Mates's position as chairman of the Defence Select Committee.

The inevitable occurred in the autumn of 1989, when the committee launched an inquiry into low-flying aircraft, including the use of simulation equipment by the RAF. The relevance of simulators was apparent, as the committee had already requested and received information on simulators from the MOD.[32] Mates did not declare his Link-Miles consultancy either at the beginning of the inquiry or during any of the subsequent seven hearings. Indeed, he did not disclose this defence interest at any of the thirty-eight meetings of 1988–9, nor at the first twenty-five of 1989–90. Mates argues that he did not need to, because 'all the members of the committee have known of this association'.[33] This was only partly true. Most did know of his consultancy, but not all.[34] Equally, any ordinary member of the public inspecting the Register would not realise Link-Miles was a specialised defence contractor. It is hardly GEC-Marconi or Vickers. More important, in the context of the low-flying investigation, many committee members were unaware that Link-Miles manufactured simulator equipment.[35] The witnesses also did not know of Mates's consultancy, or of its direct relevance.[36]

The conflict of interests is well illustrated by Mates's conducting of the cross-questioning on the afternoon of 8 November 1989, when two senior RAF officers gave evidence to the committee inquiry: 'Can we turn to simulators? Your memorandum refers to the new Harrier GR5 simulator. Are there plans to introduce similarly sophisticated simulators for other aircraft, for example, the Tornado?'[37] The manufacturer of the GR5 simulator was Link-Miles Ltd, but Mates did not declare the fact that he was a paid adviser to that company until 28 March 1990, four months later, in private session immediately before the draft report was considered.

Mates's defence was that 'at no time during the inquiry was my consultancy a relevant interest'.[38] While there is no suggestion that he was promoting his business interests, the events of 8 November 1989 seem to contradict his claim. But in any case, if his consultancy was not relevant, why did he then declare it on the last day of the inquiry?

In the midst of the committee's inquiry into low flying, Mates secured another defence client, becoming consultant to a new lobbying company, SGL Defence Ltd.

The service offered by SGL was simple: in the highly competitive defence world, they would help companies obtain contracts from the MOD and abroad. This would be done by a combination of public relations, inside knowledge and expert guidance through the Whitehall bureaucracy. Its launch prospectus spelled it out:

> We will analyse a company's communications requirements and then target those clients, officials, politicians and other audiences with whom an ongoing dialogue is essential. Our experience will greatly improve a company's capacity to influence operational requirements, to win contracts in the face of national and international competition and to project its equipment and corporate image to the customer.
>
> We will provide the presentational advice and equipment to help create well written and comprehensive tender documents targeted specifically at those who assess companies' submissions.
>
> We will construct a strategy to help secure future projects by parliamentary lobbying and influential communication with Ministers and the MOD.[39]

In other words, SGL were offering brokers and middlemen to guide potential contractors through the maze of defence procurement.

SGL was the brainchild of top PR executive Christopher Shale. In the summer of 1989, he met Michael Mates informally. The two were old friends, as Shale had served as an army officer in a sister cavalry regiment to the MP's. Shale was now keen to add a defence consultancy to his network of PR outfits.

'Do you think,' he asked Mates, 'there is a niche in the defence world for an exclusively defence-orientated public-affairs company? Is there one?'

'As far as I know, there is not one in existence,' replied Mates.

'When I find the right person, and if I decide to go ahead, would you be interested in helping?'

'Certainly I am interested, all things being equal,' said Mates.[40]

Shortly afterwards Shale found 'the right person'. This was Major Mark Nicole, a mutual friend who was leaving the army that autumn. Nicole was well qualified to be managing director. He had been a serving weapons staff-officer in the Procurement Executive of the MOD, specialising in operational requirements. That meant he had up-to-date, detailed knowledge of contracts and procedures.

On 20 December 1989, Mates and SGL agreed terms, and on 9 January 1990 the MP, Shale and Nicole met to plan the launch of the company and the publication of the brochure. Later that day Mates entered his new client in the Register as SGL Ltd. The prospectus was then issued with Mates's credentials as chairman of the Defence Select Committee prominently displayed.

Mates had not declared this consultancy to the Defence Select Committee at any of their twelve meetings between his acquisition of the consultancy and the public launch. Procurement issues were discussed at some of these sessions. He argued that his SGL interest was not relevant at the time because the company had no clients and was not trading. This overlooked the long-standing rule that MPs are obliged to declare interests they 'may be expecting to have'.[41] The firm had also been officially incorporated.

Mates also denied there was a conflict of interests: 'I would not have allowed myself to get into a position where there was a conflict of interest between my duties to the Select Committee and any commercial interests.'[42] Other members of the Defence Committee took a different view. Dick Douglas, a Labour member of the committee since 1983 and its deputy chairman, was shocked by the nature of the client: 'I had no idea the chairman was involved with a consultancy which gives, as an attribute, opening doors in terms of defence contracts.'[43]

At a private session of the Defence Committee on 14 March 1990, Douglas called for Mates's resignation. When this was refused, Douglas walked out in protest, arguing that he could not attend committee meetings under Mates's chairmanship. He was adamant that witnesses appearing before the committee should be made aware of any interests and be assured that their evidence would be used only for the purposes of the inquiry. 'I take the view,' he said, 'that the interest of the chairman of the Select Committee on Defence in defence-related companies places that principle in jeopardy.'[44]

Douglas was not the only one concerned. Senior MOD civil servants were anxious that Mates's commercial interests could be a potential obstacle to the flow of confidential information to the Defence Committee.[45]

Despite his repeated denials about any conflict of interests, Mates resigned the SGL consultancy in May 1990. 'I have concluded,' he said, 'that my association with them [SGL] is not helping them to start a new enterprise in this environment.'[46]

By the time the Select Committee on Members' Interests had finished their inquiry into his consultancies with SGL and Link-Miles, Mates was an isolated figure. Their report concluded that he was 'in error' for not declaring the Link-Miles consultancy and that 'it would have been wiser' to disclose the SGL client.[47] This was a damning reprimand from a Tory-dominated committee. Even more incriminating was the comment by Sir Michael McNair-Wilson, a fellow Conservative MP and member of the Members' Interests Committee: 'Common sense should have advised him as chairman of the select committee to have made it clear to his members that he had this interest in Link-Miles. The interest was material to the inquiry and therefore one has to say it was a lapse of judgement on his behalf.'[48] He went on to say that Mates's continued position as chairman was a matter for the Defence Committee to decide. Mates remains chairman of the Defence Committee.

Some MPs believed Mates should have resigned either his defence consultancies or his membership of the Defence Committee. But there were even more moderate options available to him. He could have declared his interest at the beginning of the 1989–90 Parliament, as did two members of the committee. Or he could have taken another alternative course of action, one demonstrated by Sir Albert Costain, the respected Conservative MP for Folkestone and Hythe for twenty-four years.

In 1980 the Public Accounts Committee announced an inquiry into the construction of the Royal Hospital for Sick Children in Glasgow. The building was beset by major structural faults, resulting in the closure of all the wards. It had cost over £4 million and was falling to pieces. The principal contractor was Richard Costain (Construction) Ltd. Sir Albert had been involved with the Costain construction empire since 1933 – as a manager, shareholder and director. At the time of the inquiry he did not have a stake in the contractor but was a shareholder in two other Costain firms. Sir Albert recognised that his long association with the family represented a conflict of interests. On the first day of the investigation he told the committee of his decision not to serve. He then walked out of the room and took no further part.[49]

Selecting the standing committees

Select committees are influential. But a member of a standing committee can be even more useful, for this is the body that pilots legislation through Parliament. A standing committee of some thirty MPs and the relevant minister combs a bill in forensic detail, clause by clause, before returning it to the Commons. Hence MPs can directly alter and amend legislation in which they have a financial stake.

These committee sessions are a favourite target for political and commercial lobbyists. 'The real focus of attention for anyone wishing to influence the passage of a bill should be the standing committee,' according to Ian Greer. 'Contact with members of the standing committee considering it will . . . take place in the Palace of Westminster, more often than not in the committee corridor.'[50]

MPs on standing committees are obliged to declare their interest if it relates to the bill in question. But they can remain a serving member. Hence the opportunity for MPs to further their commercial interest by influencing legislation is enormous.

The Commons body that appoints MPs to sit on standing committees is the Selection Committee. Every Wednesday this group of eight back-benchers meet to decide which of their colleagues are to serve on committees. Their names are then placed on the Order Paper. Any objection to the appointment of an MP who has a financial stake in the legislation is not considered by the Selection Committee,[51] which is just as well, as four of the eight members of the Selection Committee have commercial interests. Sir Fergus Montgomery is a director of a television company and consultant to a PR firm; Sir Giles Shaw has three directorships and two consultancies; and Sir Michael Shaw is employed by the Costain Group PLC.

The chairman of the Selection Committee since 1984 has been Sir Marcus Fox, the Tory MP for Shipley. Sir Marcus is perhaps the most influential back-bencher in the government. From 1976 to 1979 he was vice-chairman of the Conservative Party in charge of choosing candidates. There followed a two-year ministerial spell at the Department of the Environment before Sir Marcus returned to the back-benches in 1981. As vice-chairman of the 1922 Committee, he combined the role of Parliamentary Intelligence Officer with that of sharp, loyal communicator of Thatcherite populism. As a former sales manager and company director, he also epitomised the new breed of Tory MP. He believed in combining his business and political careers, and by 1989 had acquired six directorships (including that of the lobbying company Westminister Communications) and four consultancies.

As chairman of the Selection Committee, Sir Marcus was clearly in a powerful position. He could promote those interests by placing on standing committees MPs who were sympathetic to his various clients. He has always denied any conflict of interest: 'By suggesting that I might somehow use that position to put on certain committees people who could help or are sympathetic towards clients of Westminster Communications, I do find that abhorrent. There can be no evidence of that.'[52] But one experienced lobbyist, Charles Miller, said that Sir Marcus's chairmanship of such a committee did provoke disquiet among his profession. 'There is unease,' he remarked.[53]

The potential problem that could arise out of Sir Marcus's role as Selection Committee chairman was illustrated by an episode involving one of his long-term clients, the retirement homes developer McCarthy and Stone Ltd. He had became a consultant to them in 1984, and in April 1987 joined its board of directors.

Early in 1989, McCarthy and Stone and other companies came under attack over their management agencies, which administered sheltered accommodation for the elderly. That winter several MPs received dozens of complaints. One recipient was the Labour MP Nigel Griffiths, whose Edinburgh constituency contains Britain's largest retirement home. About 120 grievances (forty of them concerning McCarthy and Stone) arrived in his postbag. An assiduous back-bencher, Griffiths took up their complaints with McCarthy and Stone's chairman John McCarthy. But McCarthy angrily rejected the allegations and even closed the correspondence with the MP.

Griffiths then embarked on a more public course of action. On 23 March 1989, he secured an adjournment debate in the Commons and went for the developers, including McCarthy and Stone: 'Elderly people have been lured in their thousands into purchasing retirement homes only to find that they have no control over the accounts or the managers. Many of them are having to suffer incompetent management and soaring costs. There is ample evidence of firms profiteering at the expense of the frail and the elderly.'[54] He announced that he planned to introduce a bill on 7 April which would give residents tough new legal rights and make the management agencies more accountable. He received a sympathetic hearing from Peter Lloyd, the Junior Social Security Minister. But McCarthy and Stone said the Scottish MP's speech contained 'a large number of inaccuracies' and released a six-page document to MPs listing the 'incorrect allegations'.[55]

A week later Griffiths was seeing off guests at the taxi rank outside the Commons at 10 p.m. when he was approached by Sir Marcus Fox.

'Hello, I'm Marcus Fox. I'm with McCarthy and Stone.'

'I know,' replied Griffiths coolly.

'We're not as bad as you're making us out to be.'

'I hear what you're saying.'

The two MPs then sat down in the lobby of the Commons and Sir Marcus began talking about his days as a local councillor in Dewsbury.

'You must know as a former local councillor that old people like to complain,' he said.

'Well, I've had people charged for gardens when they don't even own gardens,' replied Griffiths.

'That's bad. Why not come and meet John McCarthy.'

Griffiths agreed to the meeting. 'I don't mind meeting McCarthy but I'll want to bring some of the complainants.'

'Fine,' responded Sir Marcus. 'I'll arrange it, as I'm going to a board meeting in Bournemouth.'[56]

Sir Marcus had wanted to book a committee room for the meeting, but Griffiths changed his mind and met McCarthy in the Pugin Room, one of the Commons' smarter tea-rooms. The Scottish MP put his constituents' grievances and this time McCarthy was more responsive.

Sir Marcus did not attend that meeting. Instead, he arranged for John McCarthy to write a circular to dozens of MPs. The letter, written two days before Griffiths's bill was to be introduced in the Commons, accused Griffiths of using parliamentary privilege to libel the company. It also informed MPs that Sir Marcus was available to brief them on behalf of McCarthy and Stone and to arrange meetings with company executives.[57]

These briefings, notably a meeting with Tory MP Michael Jack who had been campaigning alongside Nigel Griffiths, took place, and Sir Marcus was open about his lobbying activities for McCarthy and Stone:

> In our provision of sheltered housing, of which we are the largest, we provide a service that is vital. Local authority and government will never be able to build the number of units necessary as our population ages.
>
> I take great pride in being a director of that company. There are those who would say that maybe when we apply for planning permission we have certain problems. But there are many MPs who are involved in companies in the building industry who, I would have thought, do far more difficult projects in terms of complaints from colleagues and their constituents than the provision of sheltered housing such as ours.[58]

As it happened, Griffiths's bill was published but then blocked by the government whips. But if it had proceeded and entered the standing committee stage, its members would have been chosen by the Selection Committee, the chairman of which is Sir Marcus Fox.

A licence to declare

As was seen in chapter 3, the alcohol industry is one of the most powerful lobbies in Parliament. Their influence is just as strong in standing committees.

In the spring of 1987, Allan Stewart, Tory MP for Eastwood, introduced a private members' bill which enabled magistrates to extend licensing hours. This would enable public houses to stay open between 10.30 a.m. and 11.30 p.m., choosing their own hours. During the committee stage, its supporters wanted to ensure that the bill should reach the statute book before the pending general election. And so MPs on the committee voted to double the number of hearings, including all-night sessions, to speed up its progress. Three of those MPs – James Couchman, Michael Colvin and Roger Gale – had a financial stake linked to the bill. But they did not declare their interests until the first sitting – after they had voted for the extra sessions.[59]

Couchman, parliamentary private secretary to Tony Newton, the Minister for Health, has a long history in the licensing trade. He was managing director and held a 75 per cent controlling shareholding in Chiswick Caterers Ltd. This family firm runs five pubs under three different breweries in the London area with Couchman as the licensee. 'I believe that I am the honourable member most closely involved with the operation of public houses,' he once told the House.[60]

On the first morning of the Licensing Bill's standing committee, Couchman said: 'I considered whether it was appropriate to sit as a member of the committee and on balance I felt that my experience in the licence trade might be valuable to the committee.'[61] He then repeatedly spoke up for the proposed act: 'It is important to the licensed trade. There is no shame in the licensed trade wanting the bill to make progress . . . The flexibility that the bill gives to licensing justices and to licences makes this a valuable little bill.'[62]

Michael Colvin was the paid parliamentary adviser to the National Association of Licensed Victuallers, which represents 20,000 pub tenants and freeholders. He was also, as the owner of 'The Cricketers Arms' in his home town of Tangley, Hampshire, a licensee. 'My appropriate function in the committee,' he said, 'is to marshal the troops but not to take any active part in the debate.'[63]

Of the MPs on the standing committee, Roger Gale was perhaps the most enthusiastic advocate for the liberalising of the licensing laws. He was also the parliamentary consultant to Scottish and New-castle Breweries PLC and in 1986 spent twenty-five days with the company.[64] When accused of a conflict of interests over the Licensing Bill, he responded by praising his paymasters: 'I am particularly proud, having served an Industry and Parliamentary Trust Fellow-ship with Scottish and Newcastle Breweries, to assist it further. It is a fine company which makes a major contribution to employment in Scotland and the rest of the United Kingdom through tourism.'[65]   Gale's argument was that once he had declared his interest it was then appropriate to serve on the bill's standing com-mittee. 'I have behaved entirely honourably and properly,' he said.[66]

Other MPs have even been members of both the standing *and* the select committee relating to their commercial interests. This potentially double conflict of interests occurred during the 1990 Environmental Protection Bill, when Henry Bellingham, MP for North West Norfolk, was on its standing committee and was also a member of the Select Committee on Environment. At the same time he was the paid parliamentary consultant to the National Association of Waste Disposal Contractors.

This august organisation had a lot to gain or lose by the bill and Bellingham was active on their behalf. In standing committee, he moved an amendment on 'control' of waste pollution.[67] On the floor of the Commons, he argued for and tabled an amendment which would make it easier for waste-management licences to be renewed. 'The issue was discussed in committee,' he told the House, 'and the minister said in effect that he was extremely sympathetic to my argument.'[68]

Image is all

After the Michael Mates case in 1990, the Select Committee on Members' Interests held a wider inquiry into the rules governing the interests of members of select committees. Their recommendations provide a limited blueprint for removing the abuses of recent years. A key proposal is that chairmen of select committees should be banned from retaining directorships and consultancies with companies having government contracts. Members are also called upon to resign directorships if they conflict with the business of the committee. But, in a crucial oversight, MPs are allowed to hold on to their consultancies.[69]

Other suggestions include declaring interests earlier and more regularly during committee hearings and inquiries. More important, it is recommended that whenever a select committee member 'has a pecuniary interest which is directly affected by a particular inquiry', then the MP should 'stand aside from the proceedings'.[70]

The report concludes:

> In view of the close relationship of the departmentally-related select committees . . . to the government departments they examine, it is unacceptable for any member of such a select committee to have a client

relationship with, or to seek business from, any government departments whose affairs that committee may be responsible for scrutinising.[71]

This inquiry was progressive in many ways. But loopholes have been left open. Many commercial interests are not necessarily 'departmentally-related' and so some MPs can remain on inquiries connected with their clients. There is also no reference to standing committees, although this may perhaps be intended as the subject of a separate investigation. The report has yet to be debated by the House of Commons, and so it is unclear whether these reforms will be implemented. But it reinforces the old maxim that politics is all about perception.

Membership of standing and select committees does not automatically mean that MPs are peddling for their clientele. But that is not the concern. The mere existence of a conflict of interests created by their appearance on the committee is enough to warrant suspicion by the public. Our elected representatives should surely be above that.

CHAPTER 6

The Agents of Influence:
MPs and Lobbying Companies

'Lobbyists are the touts of protected industries.'
Sir Winston Churchill

'MPs can't be expected to give us the detail as a labour of love,
can they?'
Douglas Smith, political lobbyist, *Sunday Times*, 2 October
1983

There is a little-known ritual in politics known as 'prayers'. In
government, this refers to the summoning of civil servants by
ministers for a policy meeting. But in the discreet world of lobbying,
'prayers' has an altogether different connotation.

'Prayers' take place in the small, sparsely furnished offices of political consultancy companies, usually in a Westminster side-street close
to the House of Commons. Once a month, usually late in the morning, a back-bench MP arrives to deliver a political 'briefing'. These
are informal sessions, and vary from tame parliamentary gossip to
detailed information about government plans for a specific industry.

It is, of course, not unusual for politicians to talk to lobbyists. But
at 'prayers' there is a difference. The back-benchers are financially
rewarded for their efforts at an average fee of £8,000 a year. They
are, according to one lobbyist, 'paid hacks, nothing more'.

There have always been lobbyists – pressure groups, single-issue
campaigners and charities. But the notion of MPs as paid advisers
to specialised political consultancy companies is a relatively new one.

Political lobbying is now big business. There are over fifty such
firms, with an estimated total turnover of £10 million.[1] A survey in
1985 reported that of 180 major British companies, 41 per cent

retained political consultancies for 'Government work'.[2] Fees range from £2,500 to £5,000 a month, depending on the type of service required.[3] The average annual rate is about £30,000.

Essentially, the role of the political lobbyist is to act as a conduit between commercial and consumer outfits and the government. Corporate executives are often mystified and stage-struck by Westminster and Whitehall. Fortunately for lobbyists, MPs, civil servants and ministers are equally bewildered and easily impressed by the financial and business community.

Enter the middlemen in sharp suits with a special line in smooth talk and fancy promises. They offer their clients parliamentary contacts, confidential information, meetings with ministers and officials, lunches with MPs and advice on how to alter and influence legislation. And what better way of getting on the inside track than placing a back-bencher on the payroll?

Commander Powell and the Old Guard

Specialist, professional lobbyists have been active in the political arena for decades. One of the most distinguished and controversial was Commander Christopher Powell.

Born in 1903, Powell was educated in Dartmouth and joined the Royal Navy, serving in the Mediterranean and the Far East. In 1929 he formed his first consultancy, providing a secretarial service for Tory MPs. In partnership with Charles Watney, Powell then developed a lobbying business serving a combination of causes (a life-long passion for the Channel Tunnel) and commerce (Tate and Lyle).

Commander Powell became the doyen of old-fashioned lobbyists. He was essentially a parliamentary draughtsman. He knew every rule in minute detail and was an expert in guiding private bills through the House. After the Second World War, his influence was such that he even had his own office in the Commons. He would strut around the Palace of Westminster dressed in a black jacket and striped trousers, and many visitors even mistook him for the Serjeant-at-Arms. His brilliance was tempered by a touch of arrogance. On one occasion, while striding down a Commons corridor, he was approached by a senior Cabinet minister. 'Not now, Minister, I'm busy,' said Powell brusquely, and marched on.

In the late 1940s Powell ran into trouble while full-time secretary of the British section of the Inter-Parliamentary Union (IPU). The Speaker ruled that there was a danger of a conflict of interests between his IPU post and his clients, who might promote or oppose parliamentary bills.[4] Powell was accused of 'running a lobbying agency on the American principle' amid evidence that he tried to prevent an MP from entering a standing committee.[5]

Despite his enforced resignation from the IPU, Powell's career flourished, mainly through unrivalled political contacts. He was a close personal friend of Margaret and Denis Thatcher, who used to rent a cottage on the lobbyist's estate at Hors Monsden, Kent. But in the late 1970s Powell was again the focus of controversy. While working with Tory MP Sir Gerald Nabarro on a campaign to abolish purchase tax, he secretly drafted hundreds of questions to the Chancellor of the Exchequer.

Powell died in 1989. His record is not without achievement. He revitalised the Parliamentary and Scientific Committee, making it more broadly based. His company, later to become Charles Barker, Watney and Powell, tended to lobby for causes and campaigns rather than commercial interests. But former employees have mixed feelings about him. They say he was a remarkable operator but that his expertise enabled him to influence Parliament to an 'undemocratic' extent. One claimed the Commander's power was such that he could draft, amend and virtually pass private bills through the Commons.

Powell may have over-reached himself on occasion, but he was principled on one issue. He was strongly opposed to MPs being hired guns. 'He would have been shocked by their recent activities,' said one former employee, 'because he never paid MPs anything. He totally disapproved of MPs being paid consultants.'

The grey zone and the invasion of the news-snatchers

The watershed between old- and new-style political lobbying coincided with the more direct intervention of government in the economy during the late 1950s and 1960s. Lobbyists became more than mere public-relations merchants. They acted as middlemen between the private and public sector and hired MPs to facilitate this process. In 1957 eighteen MPs were known to be retained by public-relations firms. By 1965, they numbered at least fifty.[6] The potential for corruption was first noticed by the MP Francis Noel-Baker: 'The growth of so-called "public relations" in all its aspects means that Members of Parliament have themselves become more attractive allies for business interests than they have been in the past. The door, in fact, is wide open for a new form of political corruption.'[7] He added that in the past these connections and their practitioners 'were usually well-known and identified themselves openly'. But now there was what Andrew Roth has called 'the grey zone'.[8] These consultancies involved one-off fees and retainers, needed no professional experience, no obligation to keep office hours and could be kept secret from the public.

It was this type of relationship that resulted in a major scandal. In April 1968, PR agent Maurice Fraser escorted a party of five MPs to visit one of his clients – the Colonels' regime in Greece. Fraser's firm was being paid £100,000 a year to promote the notorious new junta throughout Europe and their contract was up for renewal that September. One of the MPs on the trip was Labour's Gordon Bagier, whom Fraser had encountered while lobbying for casino interests. Four weeks later Fraser hired Bagier as a consultant at £500 a year plus commission for any new clients he was able to secure for the lobbying company.

The following month, in June 1968, Fraser Associates compiled a secret report on their activities. It boasted how the firm had 'a lobby-ist MP' working for them behind the scenes. When press and TV enquiries disclosed Bagier's association with the firm, the MP admitted the consultancy but denied lobbying for the junta.[9] A subsequent inquiry did nothing to resolve the problem – the secrecy and lack of accountability of the new lobbyists – and by the mid-1970s the situation had seriously deteriorated, even as the Poulson scandal continued to reverberate around the corridors of Westminster. It reached a nadir in the summer of 1976 when the Labour government tried to implement the Aircraft and Shipbuilding Industries Act.

As this act involved extensive nationalisation, it was bitterly opposed by private industry. One of the companies targeted for state take-over, Bristol Channel Ship Repairers Ltd, decided to take evasive action. They hired International News Service, a political PR agency, which retained a Labour MP, Ben Ford, and a Tory MP, Stephen McAdden, chairman of the bill's standing committee, as paid consultants. According to Bob Cryer, then a minister in the Department of Industry, which sponsored the legislation, the lobbyists 'ran riot'.

International News Service invaded the Palace of Westminster like a marauding army. Private dining rooms were hired for sponsored 'entertainment'. A boat, *The Lucky Dragon*, was chartered and laid on lavish drinks parties on the Thames. MPs were accosted in the lobbies before crucial votes on the bill. It was not even safe to venture on to the Commons terrace or into the Strangers Bar for a drink without being button-holed by an International News Service lobbyist. 'They treated the Palace of Westminster as if they owned it,' recalled Cryer.

The strategy of Bristol Channel Ship Repairers and International News Service was clear. The Labour government had a small majority. If just a few back-benchers could be persuaded to vote against the bill, it could be defeated. But some MPs objected to their tactics, and the Select Committee on Commons Services held an inquiry into International News Service's activities. A member of that committee during the investigation was the Labour MP Ben Ford.

Ford played down his role as consultant to International News Service: 'I merely advise this company on points of parliamentary procedure ... I am quite satisfied in my own mind that there have been no improprieties committed.'[10] The PR agency's managing director, Alan Turnbull, said that their parliamentary consultants were paid a fee so that 'we can ring them up and say: "We have a problem. What do you think?"'[11] But many MPs were shocked by his company's activities and saw it as producing a new generation of political influence-brokers. These Westminster hustlers were more aggressive, commercially orientated and were also prepared to pay MPs.

'Please don't call me a lobbyist'

Lobbyists hate being called lobbyists. A number of suitably grand epithets – 'public-affairs consultant', 'government-relations adviser', 'political communications strategist' – have been devised to provide a respectable introduction in polite company. As one American lobbyist noted: 'My mother has never introduced me to her friends as "my son, the lobbyist". My son, the Washington Representative, maybe. Or the Legislative Consultant. Or the Government Relations Counsel. But never as a Lobbyist. I can't say I blame her.'[12] Their unpopularity stems from the secrecy of their methods and the extravagance of their promises. Conservative MP Robert Adley refers to lobbyists as 'leeches'.[13] Using uncharacteristically strong language, he said: 'There is an increasing army, frankly, of spivs around this place, some of whom seem to be able to attract the services of MPs for piddling sums of money, who are responsible in my view for perverting this place.'[14]

As there is no register of lobbyists or any form of public accountability for the industry, it is difficult fully to assess Adley's tirade. But there is some evidence that sheds light on their methods.

Promises, promises

Lobbyists are adept at making convincing claims to clients about the extent of their influence. Among the keenest on marketing his product was Sir Trevor Lloyd-Hughes.

A former political correspondent, Sir Trevor was Press Secretary to Prime Minister Harold Wilson from 1964 to 1969. After a brief spell as chief information adviser to that Labour government, he set up his own 'public-affairs' consultancy. Among his fifty clients were multi-national companies and foreign governments, notably a £120,000 a year contract with the South African-backed regime of Namibia in the early 1980s. Lloyd-Hughes Associates' maxim was to smooth the 'interface between our clients and those in power': 'We prefer to be used as a fire prevention service, rather than a fire-fighting team, and to develop friendships in high places before a contact is needed to help with a definite problem.'[15]

The company was almost like a dating agency. One of Sir Trevor's favourite services for clients was to host meetings at his clubs – the Reform and Belfry – or his south London home. As he reported:

Organised lunches and receptions, some within the Houses of Parliament, attended by important people. Arranged for business leaders, including the heads of American, French and British companies, to have private meetings with eminent personalities in London, including Cabinet Ministers, former Prime Ministers, the Queen's Principal Private Secretary, former British Ambassadors, and men at the very top of the UK diplomatic and Civil Service.[16]

According to Sir Trevor, his methods have been successful:

> We have obtained important tax concessions from the British government over their legislation on North Sea oil revenues. Saved the international motor car and motor-cycle industries based in the UK millions of pounds by persuading the government to exempt them from provisions in the Trade Descriptions Acts. Won British government financial backing for a major development in Turkey.[17]

Lloyd-Hughes is often dismissed by fellow lobbyists as part of 'the old school' and not relevant to the contemporary scene. But a letter written by a budding new consultant revealed that attitudes have not changed significantly.

The author was Donald Stewart, constituency agent to Peter Brooke, Conservative MP for City of London and Westminster South and a Cabinet minister since 1987. In June 1989, while Brooke was chairman of the Tory Party, Stewart wrote to a prospective client: 'I understand that you may be interested to know about the services I could offer your company.' Among the eight services on offer were:

> Contact with ministers and civil servants in departments such as the DTI and Energy in order to enhance their understanding of the needs of your industry and company.
>
> Arrangement of luncheons and dinners for ministers, MPs and MEPs to meet and speak to company directors and managers and, if desired, their guests.
>
> Arrangement of carefully tailored social events, such as theatre, opera and sporting occasions, affording senior company personnel the opportunity to brief legislators and others on the company's needs and interests.

The letter, written on Westminster Conservative Association note-paper, concluded that it was being sent 'in a personal and entirely confidential capacity'. Stewart was unsuccessful in his bid to become a paid lobbyist while remaining Peter Brooke's agent. But it demonstrates the type of tactics employed by present-day lobbyists.

That's entertainment

An American lobbyist once quipped that: 'The way to a man's "aye" is through his stomach.'[18] This form of influence-peddling is often derided by parliamentary wags, who argue that there is indeed such a thing as a free lunch. But the use of expensive meals and evening entertainment is a common method to either extract information from or influence an MP – 'Gastronomic pimping', Aneurin Bevan called it.[19]

One company which was keen on this approach was David McDonough and Associates. Billed as 'corporate affairs consultants', the firm retained a Tory MP, Martin Stevens, as a paid adviser. Their clients included senior executives from Hambros Bank, Unigate and Thames Television.

Part of their repertoire was 'The Working Lunch Concept', which 'can be an effective weapon in your corporate communications armoury'. For prospective clients McDonough promised to:

> Generate a guest-list, supported by biographical details, to be agreed with you. What is the best number to create the desired atmosphere?
>
> Draw up a suggested menu and wine-list. Extravagant banquets may not always create a favourable impression, but a more modest meal calls, if anything, for more skill in composition.
>
> Agree a table-plan, and provide hosts and guests with (a) background notes on all present and (b) a time-table, ensuring that guests know what to expect, and when.

This is part of the soft-soak style of power-broking which involves being the facilitator for clients. It is a practice often ridiculed:

> Go to Lockets, a plush Westminster restaurant, on any weekday lunchtime and you can play 'spot the lobbyist'. It is easy: pick out a member of Parliament who looks well-fed but bored. He will be sharing a table with an earnest-looking industrialist who smiles rather too readily, and a stripey-shirt-and-spotty-tie-clad PR man who seems well intentioned but slightly vacant.
>
> The industrialist will be flattered by the MP's attentions. The MP will be pleased to prove that there is indeed such a thing as a free lunch. And the PR man will take the profit from what will often have been an expensive waste of time.[20]

Despite such well-founded criticism, companies continue to use 'hospitality' as an enticement to influence decision-making. 'It's not unknown,' said the experienced lobbyist Douglas Smith, 'for various ploys to be used to secure attendance at a bill to obtain a quorum. On one occasion, I remember a group who staged a whisky-tasting party to coincide with a very dull environment bill in which they had no interest. When the party ended, the MPs were steered into the nearby House [for their debate].'[21] Other inducements for MPs to attend certain late-night Commons debates include champagne supper parties and film shows, usually at nearby hotels.

For some lobbyists their colleagues' extravagant promises and à la carte methods are a fraud. Douglas Smith, a former chairman of the professional practices committee of the Public Relations Consultants Association, said:

> Large fees are being charged – running into six figures – based on false promises, and when the clients' funds or hopes are exhausted, the cowboy consultants move on to fresh prey. They bring Parliament and public relations into disrepute.
>
> Some of these companies are taking on every cause that moves, regardless of its chances of success. Companies and trade associations were being advised they had excellent prospects of influencing the government when, in reality, there was not a chance in a thousand of doing so.[22]

Whatever the degree of influence of lobbyists, their activities remain a serious threat to democracy. As Labour MP Bob Cryer commented: 'If the claims of certain lobbyists are true, they are alarming. If false, those who make them are charlatans. In both cases they require scrutiny so that the public is not in any way deceived.'[23]

The hidden clients

In January 1991, thirty-five MPs were paid advisers or directors to lobbying or consultancy firms.[24] They are not obliged to declare their clients in the Register. Consequently, an MP can act for any organisation or company and merely disclose the innocuous-sounding lobbying or family firm. For example, George Gardiner, Conservative MP for Reigate, was employed by T. A. Cutbill and Partners between 1985 and 1987. But his constituents remained unaware that this was a public-relations outfit whose clients included the Wines and Spirits Association and the brewers Whitbread Ltd.[25]

Clients can be traced through other sources, but most MPs prefer to keep this information secret. Michael Mates, a consultant to Good Relations Ltd since 1977, said: 'Arrangements between myself and Good Relations are a matter for me and them.'[26] His lobbying firm, which also paid two other MPs, was equally shy: 'We cannot let you have any details of the consultancy fees, of the specific clients with whom these MPs have contact because this is commercially confidential information.'[27] Timothy Brinton, consultant to Communications Strategy Ltd from 1982 until 1987, declared:

> I am available to Communications Strategy for help and advice, but I am not prepared to enter into correspondence as to which clients may be involved, or indeed what consultancy fees may be paid. Parliament makes no requirement that I should do so and I would regard this as a private matter between myself and Communications Strategy.[28]

Some MPs do identify their clients but the vast majority prefer to keep this information hidden from the public. This has caused some anxiety in Parliament. James Cran, Tory MP for Beverley, said: 'I'm not interested in being paid by lobbyists because I want to look at things dispassionately . . . But if MPs are consultants, we ought to know the clients that they personally are connected with and that should be listed in the Register of Interests.'[29]

Lobbyists also believe transparency is needed. John Russell and Charles Miller both argue that full declaration of clients should be made compulsory. Russell is particularly disturbed because of his direct experience of MPs acting as introductory agents for lobbying companies. According to him, many elected representatives spend their time recruiting clients in exchange for commission fees. Russell has found, much to his astonishment, that many of his competitors are in fact MPs – either trying to secure clients, offering their own services directly or working as lobbying firms themselves.

Return of the Fox

The lure of the lobbying firm seems particularly attractive to junior ministers leaving public office. This was the case for Conservative MPs Keith Speed and Sir Marcus Fox. After being sacked as Defence and Environment ministers, respectively, in 1981, they set up their own 'public-affairs consultancy' the following year.

Entitled Westminster Communications Ltd, the firm was dominated by Speed and Fox. According to Sir Marcus: 'We thought if we, as Members of Parliament, were actually controlling the company we could ensure we only acted for those clients who we were convinced were of good standing . . . We worked on that basis, with another two directors who joined us, in a small way.'[30]

The two MPs have built up a client list of fifty companies, ranging from the Pools Promoters Association to Suzuki cars and the InterCity division of British Rail. One of their earliest clients was the British Motor-Cycle Association. Speed, a junior Transport minister from 1972 to 1974, had been their consultant from 1975 until 1979, when he became Navy Secretary. On founding Westminster Communications in 1982, Speed regained the Motor-Cycle Association account and the lobbying began. One of his most successful operations was to persuade the government not to charge the industry £70,000 in back-dated VAT on motorbike tests. The association's chairman appreciated his efforts. At a meeting soon afterwards, he complimented the MP: 'Well, we're most grateful that you've managed to get us relieved of this awful backlog, because we haven't been charging VAT and we didn't think we should have to charge VAT. But if we had, it would be sixty to seventy thousand pounds we'd have got to find from somewhere.'

'I think it took everybody a bit by surprise,' replied Speed. 'I mean, you had to act rather swiftly and I give all the credit to the Minister for realising there was a problem.'

'And all credit to you,' said the chairman. 'This is a good example of how having a friendly man in the House of Commons can be an enormous assistance to us. I don't think we'd have ever got this settled without your help.'

'Well, I think there was a good case, you know, and we all weighed in.'[31]

Sir Marcus also worked on the Motor-Cycle Association account. On one occasion, in his capacity as a director of Westminster Communications,[32] he led a delegation from the industry to the Department of Transport. Sir Marcus arranged a private meeting with Peter Bottomley, then Minister for Roads and Traffic, to discuss the controversial issue of leg-shields for riders. The MP introduced the participants but took no part in the discussion.[33]

Sir Marcus says that his involvement in Westminster Communications is 'negligible' because of 'my other commitments'.[34] But, apart from leading delegations, he attends board meetings and monitors the client list. He also has a financial stake in the company: 'Having made an initial investment, and being a canny Yorkshireman, there is no reason why I should give up a shareholding which, because of amalgamations, has increased somewhat ... I consider this to be an investment which, hopefully, will look after me and my dear family later on in life.'[35]

Sir Marcus is an ardent defender of MPs as lobbyists: 'There is a need for a lobbying industry. That is proved by the success of companies, their growth and the fact that people are prepared to pay for this sort of information and the amount of time that is spent in often putting a good case forward.' He added that MPs 'had certain advantages by virtue of our experience'.[36]

Communicating political influence

One of the longest-standing lobbying partnerships has been between Douglas Smith and the Tory MP Peter Fry. The two met in 1961 while working at Conservative Central Office. Smith, a chatty extrovert, was a publicity officer and Tory councillor while Fry was the political education officer. They became close friends but their paths diverged when Fry left to work as an insurance broker.

In 1969 Fry became the Conservative MP for Wellingborough and resumed his partnership with Smith. Within six years they had set up their own company, Political Research and Communication International Ltd. Fry was chairman, with a seat on the board and a 30 per cent shareholding. Smith was managing director with a 50 per cent stake. The company describes itself as 'specialists in public affairs', claiming that 'our role always involves political intelligence'. Smith is the foot-soldier of the operation. Armed with a Commons pass, he roams the corridors of the Palace of Westminster, visits the library, convenes meetings of MPs and collects documents from the Vote Office. Fry is the adviser and consultant, more inclined to brief company executives behind the scenes.

Their clients are mainly in the transport arena. This has created a potential conflict of interests, as Fry has been a member of the Commons Select Committee for Transport since its foundation in 1980. The most graphic example of this was his company's consultancy with the National Bus Company (NBC).

During the 1985 Transport Bill, which deregulated the bus industry, Fry lobbied actively for his client.[37] He made speeches in the chamber and sponsored a Commons motion congratulating the Bus and Coach Council (of which NBC was a leading member) on its response to the government's White Paper on the bill. His company also helped British Aerospace secure government funds for the Airbus[38] and monitored legislation on behalf of the Scottish Transport Group.[39]

Fry was particularly active on behalf of the British Leather Federation. Clients since 1984, they view the MP as more than just an adviser: 'Certainly, he [Fry] is our spokesman in the House. There is a constituency interest because so much of the industry is centred in Northamptonshire but, yes, we retain him as well through his consultancy company.'[40] In return Fry talks to the director-general and the committee about 'the political scene'. The MP's company also provides 'an information service so that they are aware of what is happening in both Houses and, indeed, what legislation might be forthcoming to give them an opportunity to realise about any threats to them or any influence they might want to make upon legislation'.[41]

One concern for the leather industry was water privatisation, and so Fry led a deputation to the Department of the Environment to see the Minister of State.[42] A greater 'threat' was competition from the Japanese leather industry. In April 1987, Fry decided to intervene on the British Leather Federation's behalf. On two occasions during Prime Minister's Question Time he rose to put their case but was unsuccessful. Then, on Thursday 9 April 1987, Fry was called. He congratulated Mrs Thatcher on the government's 'strong line' on trade with Japan and added:

> Will she please bear in mind in the negotiations that she has announced that there are some British industries which are particularly heavily penalised? I put in a plea on behalf of the British leather manufacturing industry which, after a very small quota, has to surmount a tariff of 60 per cent to export to Japan. Will she ask our negotiators to do their best for that industry?[43]

Mrs Thatcher replied that she was 'aware of that particular industry and the problems that Japanese imports cause'. She argued that any action must be taken with 'the rest of the [European] Community'.

Fry did not declare his interest when lobbying the Prime Minister. Nor had he registered his consultancy, entering the British Leather Federation as a client only *after* his Commons intervention. According to Fry, this was because it was the first time he had been involved in parliamentary activity on behalf of his client.

Over the years Fry has prided himself on declaring the clients of his company. Indeed, when he registered seventeen clients in 1985 this caused some consternation among other MPs, clearly anxious it would create a precedent. They told him it was not necessary.[44] He did so again in 1989, 1990 and 1991. But he failed to register any clients in 1983, 1984, 1986, 1987 and 1988.

Fry is a staunch defender of his business interests:

> If MPs are going fully to understand what is happening in the country, it is very dangerous that we should cocoon ourselves and be all professional politicians ... I am there to represent my constituents, to understand the kind of problems that my constituents suffer, whether they be industrialists or employees, and so I think it is very useful to have some kind of outside business activity.[45]

But when asked by fellow Conservative MP Sir Michael McNair-Wilson: 'Why do you have to be paid to fulfil that task?' Fry declined to answer the question, except to say that other MPs are paid retainers by 'a whole host of industries'.[46]

Perhaps the answer can be found in a remark by Fry's partner Douglas Smith, who said: 'MPs can't be expected to give us the detail as a labour of love, can they?'[47]

A stake in the Chunnel

The multi-billion pound Channel Tunnel project has created a jamboree for lobbyists. There are several sources of business, ranging from construction corporations hungry for the contracts to build the tunnel and banks underwriting various consortiums, through ferry companies opposed to a fixed link, to environmentalists hostile to the scheme.

Lobbying started in earnest in October 1985 and continued over an intense 100-day campaign, necessitated by the fact that the government would make its decision in late January 1986.

The role of MPs was particularly significant, since ministers would select the type of Channel Tunnel scheme. But the final decision would be made by the Commons through a special form of legislation known as a hybrid bill. An unusual device, it enabled private operators and objectors to put their views before a special Commons committee where MPs could also pass vital amendments. Hence back-benchers were able to exert a greater influence on the bill's passage.

The consortiums sprung into action. Cabinet ministers were dined at the Garrick Club and Ritz Hotel. The lobbyists' champagne flowed. But many MPs were unhappy with the tactics. Jonathan Aitken, the Conservative MP for Thanet South, whose Kent constituents were opposed to the Tunnel, believed it was more about buying influence than informing the public: 'What worries me most is that usually lobbying is genuine in the sense that it stems from little interest groups and concerned citizens. Here we are seeing the Panzer division of big business, their heavy artillery and tanks trampling over all the small people's interests which I want to see better defended.'[48]

It was not just pro-Tunnel commercial concerns that commissioned lobbying fire-power. Flexilink, an international consortium of ferry companies and port authorities, hired the Grayling Group of PR firms to help them campaign against the fixed-link plan. Grayling was a powerful outfit for the anti-Tunnel brigade and retained David Atkinson, Tory MP for Bournemouth East, as a paid consultant. Atkinson was an assiduous lobbyist. Between 1982 and 1985 he had been a director of another parliamentary PR firm, Modus Politicus. Since 1983 he has been a partner in Exponential Parliamentary Advisers, whose clients have included Dewe Rogerson, another lobbying company. By December 1985, the lobbying for the Chunnel had reached its climax. But Atkinson had not declared his consultancy with Grayling. It was only after being challenged by BBC's *Newsnight* programme that the MP registered the client. 'I don't see there is any conflict of interests here,' he said.[49] No less embarrassing for Atkinson was the disclosure that he was also a consultant to a lobbying firm whose clients included a *pro*-Tunnel consortium. This was Good Relations, representing the Channel Tunnel Group, which consisted of four major construction companies and two clearing banks. Atkinson saw no problem in being paid by both sides, arguing that: 'A political consultancy doesn't mean backing everything their clients do.'[50]

The building firms in the Channel Tunnel Group consortium were more directly represented in Parliament. Wimpey's consultant was Den Dover, Tory MP for Chorley, who was paid £8,500 a year for his services. In an interview with *Newsnight*, he explained what he did for his client: 'I have arranged meetings with ministers. I've made sure that everything connected with the Channel Tunnel has been brought to Wimpey's attention. If they want to have a particular say at any moment, then I've made sure that their voice is heard.'[51] Dover lobbied parliamentary private secretaries and hosted lunches and afternoon teas for MPs 'to make sure they have adequate knowledge of our scheme'.[52]

Dover was also a member of the Transport Select Committee, and in December 1985 it was his vote that proved crucial in a 4:3 majority to back the Channel Tunnel Group scheme. This caused some unease among committee members but Dover insists he acted independently: 'I believe in one particular scheme and I've made sure as member of the Transport Select Committee and consultant to Wimpey that they basically came up with what I think is the right scheme . . . I don't draw much of a fee and I don't spend many hours of the week with Wimpey but what I do I'm sure they get good value for.'[53]

Another Conservative MP, Robin Squire, also had an interest in the Channel Tunnel Group option. He was financial consultant to Lombard North Central Ltd, a subsidiary of the National Westminster Bank, which was part of the Channel Tunnel Group consortium. At the same time, he was the parliamentary adviser to Sea Containers, a leading component of the rival Channel Expressway. He was hired soon after resigning as parliamentary private secretary to Lynda Chalker, then Minister of State for Transport. 'We felt he was particularly qualified,' said James Sherwood, chairman of Sea Containers, 'because he has been associated with the Ministry of Transport and therefore was one of the best available advisers.'[54]

Squire would brief and advise the company, and even fellow MPs. At one Sea Containers presentation for the Transport Select Committee he was introduced by executives as their new consultant. This caused some embarrassment for those present. 'I found it somewhat distressing,' said Liberal MP Stephen Ross. 'We were there to learn about their scheme and immediately we find that someone had been retained to boost their image within the House.'[55] Squire maintained he was acting in a merely advisory capacity. He said that when it came to the Commons, he would refuse to vote or speak on any Chunnel scheme that involved him directly.[56]

Objectors to British Rail's plans for a high-speed rail link from London to the Channel Tunnel through Kent have also resorted to lobbyists. The most active has been Channel Communications, a Kent-based firm which has represented local groups like Ashford Homeowners Association (AHA) and Sellindge Against British Rail Excesses (SABRE). In 1989 Channel Communications hired Gwyneth Dunwoody, the Labour MP for Crewe and Nantwich, as a consultant. Dunwoody, a member of the Commons Transport Select

Committee and sponsored by the National Union of Railwaymen, was used on an *ad hoc* basis by the lobbying company. According to its director, David Crowhurst, who used to work for the Grayling PR company: 'Gwyneth has acted as a political consultant as and when we have needed advice on specific campaigns and gets a consultancy fee according to the work she does.'[57] He later commented: 'We paid her for six consultancies. It was a very small amount. But it was no more than what was achieved. All Mrs Dunwoody really did was put a few questions down in the House and book a few committee rooms.'[58]

Dunwoody acted for both AHA and SABRE, but neglected to declare the consultancy in the Register. In February 1990 she admitted working for Channel Communications: 'We had a preliminary arrangement and I didn't declare it because all I did was book a couple of rooms at the Commons. I was just helping a new firm and it will not be continuing.'[59]

The key point about the lobbying for the Channel Tunnel contract was its unequal nature. Commercial interests were buying political influence – using PR outfits and MPs – while ordinary citizens were at a clear disadvantage. Hiring MPs only added to the imbalance. As Jonathan Aitken reflected: 'If you're going to be a guardian of the public interest, you can't be paid for by one side of the argument. You've got to be neutral and you've got to hold the ring between competing interest groups. I make no secret of the fact that I'm trying to stick up for my constituents.'[60]

'Mr 5 per cent'

In the boardroom of the offices of Ian Greer Associates at 19 Catherine Place is a specially commissioned oil-painting of the Palace of Westminster. On the ground floor is a division bell specially linked to the Commons for the benefit of MPs and ministers. They serve as reminders to any visiting client of the type of political consultant they are employing. For Ian Greer is the doyen of the new breed of parliamentary lobbyists.

Closely locked into the industrial and commercial as well as the political establishment of the 1980s, Greer is the embodiment of the Westminster hustler. He believes in the potential fire-power of the mobilisation of MPs:

Policy may be 'made' elsewhere (in Whitehall and increasingly in Brussels) and consultants have regular contact with ministers and officials. But once that policy is made it will then need Parliament's assent if it is to be given statutory force. Parliament has the power to throw the policy out or amend it. It is significant that Parliament has proved more willing to use that power at the same time as there has been a growth in the number of consultancies.[61]

It was some time before Greer came to this realisation. Born in 1930, he is the son of a Salvation Army couple. At the age of 24 he joined Conservative Central Office and became the youngest-ever party area agent. In 1966 he left to become director of the Mental Health Trust, where he first developed a taste for dealing with MPs. He set up a national network to campaign for greater government involvement to combat mental illness. In 1970 he launched his first political consultancy company in partnership with John Russell. At first, big business was not interested in their services, preferring to rely on the old-boy network, and early clients were as diverse as the Zambian High Commission in London and the National Federation of the Self-Employed. In 1976 Greer linked up with an American lobbying company in Washington. This experience left him with an admiration for the openness of the US system, tempered with unease about some of their sharper practices. In 1980 Russell and Greer split in bitter and acrimonious circumstances. The following January Greer launched his own company.

Ian Greer Associates was a far more politically and commercially orientated operation. Greer had retained his Tory Party connections and was a member of the influential Carlton Club. But he also forged links with the Opposition. Among Labour MPs, Doug Hoyle was a friend, as was Walter Johnson.

Johnson, MP for Derby South from 1970 until 1983, was more than just a social acquaintance. In the early 1980s he helped Greer on several campaigns including one to maintain lead in petrol. This was on behalf of Associated Octel Ltd, who were concerned about the loss of income if lead levels were reduced by law. Greer agreed to pay the Labour MP a fee for his efforts over the years. In late 1983, after retiring from Parliament, Johnson wrote in appreciation:

As you will kindly recall, you agreed to pay me a fee of £1,000 for services to your company and that this would be paid in the form of paying a bill for a holiday.

I very much regret that I have not been able to help you as much as I would have wished but, as you know, I have always been available if you wanted me, and this position still prevails.

Greer later described this as 'an ex-gratia retirement gift'.[62]

By the mid-1980s large corporations were finally persuaded that they needed lobbyists and Greer reaped the benefits. Among his new clients were British Airways, Plessey, the Al Fayed brothers through House of Fraser Holdings, the Argyll Group PLC, Babcock International, Phillips and Drew, Johnson Matthey and the National Nuclear Corporation Ltd. Together, they have made Ian Greer Associates the largest independent political consultancy in the UK, with annual earnings of over £1.8 million and a staff of 30. What is less well-known is that since 1985 Greer has been making secret payments to several MPs who have introduced clients to him.[63]

Greer's cultivation of MPs has been the key to his corporate success. An invitation list to a drinks party in December 1983 at his offices, then at Buckingham Gate, reveals that eighteen of the forty-two guests were MPs and their wives. Lunch was another favourite, with hired cars collecting MPs at the Commons and returning them afterwards. Closer links were established when two Tory MPs allowed two Ian Greer Associates employees to work as their 'research assistants', giving them access to Commons facilities and documents.[64]

Ian Greer Associates' closest parliamentary contact is Michael Grylls, Conservative MP for North West Surrey. Greer and Grylls are good friends and have known each other since 1964, when the MP was an unsuccessful candidate in Fulham. According to former executives, Grylls is more to them than just a friendly MP. He sets up meetings and has even signed letters drafted by employees. As chairman of the Conservative Trade and Industry Committee since 1980 he is in regular contact with top industrialists, and is therefore a useful MP for any lobbyist to know. That Grylls was happy to oblige was illustrated by the attendance of Ian Greer at a private meeting of the Tory Trade and Industry Committee in March 1989. Greer's interest was that the visiting speaker was Sir John Clark, chairman of Plessey, which Ian Greer Associates was representing in its epic battle to resist take-over by GEC. Greer's presence at the meeting was noted with some disdain by Conservative MPs. 'This is the first time in all my years in the House that a lobbyist has attended a back-bench meeting,' said one. 'I regard it as a disturbing commer-cial intrusion.'[65]

Ian Greer has always maintained that he does not pay MPs as consultants in return for services rendered. In October 1988, he said: 'The company does not retain any peers, MEPs, MPs or other politi-cal advisers and has never done so since its formation ... We are not taking that position from a moral point of view, it is just there is no reason to do it.'[66]

This was technically accurate but undermined by undisclosed ex-gratia fees, as well as the fee to Walter Johnson of £1,000 in 1983. The financial relationship with Michael Grylls was more complex. Since 1979 Grylls has been a paid consultant to the Unitary Tax Campaign (UTC) – a group of fifty UK companies lobbying against the way six American states tax the subsidiaries of British firms based in the USA. UTC is, in fact, also a client of Ian Greer Associates, and Grylls and Greer liaise closely on the campaign, together with American lawyer lobbyists. The MP also had the benefit of one of Ian Greer's executives, Andrew Smith, working for him on the account as his research assistant. Grylls has worked hard for the UTC client – moving amendments to the Finance Bill, leading delegations to the Treasury, tabling motions and speaking out in debates. He has proved even more useful in securing lucrative clients for Ian Greer Associates. According to Grylls:

> On three occasions, friends of mine who were chairmen of companies approached me for help as they said they needed advice. Because I knew how effective Ian Greer Associates were with the Unitary Tax Campaign, I suggested Mr Greer might be able to help them. In each instance, they decided to retain the services of Ian Greer Associates and I was subsequently offered and accepted a one-off payment for these introduc-tions by Mr Greer.[67]

These payments were made in November 1985, May 1986 and October 1989, based on a percentage of the new client's first-year fee. The first two of these fees were not declared by Grylls. He later said he had disclosed his client relationship with Ian Greer Associates by inserting it in brackets next to his UTC entry in the 1986 and 1987 Register. But on Grylls's own admission the one-off payments 'were not connected with the UTC'. Hence, both the client relation-ship and the commission fees remained hidden and disguised.

This was in breach of the Commons rules. According to Jim

Hastings, the Registrar of Members' Interests: 'As a general rule single payments, such as commissions received for introductions or other services, should be registered ... where such payments relate in any way to membership of the House.'[68] It was not until October 1989 that Grylls's commercial link with Ian Greer Associates was fully declared.

The Surrey MP was not the only one to receive such remuneration. Ian Greer has confirmed that two other MPs have been paid commission fees for introducing business – one MP in 1986 and 1988, and another in 1988. None of these payments has been declared.

MPs appear to do very little for their four-figure sums. The operation runs something like this. In the course of their routine work, MPs meet company executives and directors. During the conversation the issue of political public relations may well arise. If the businessman expresses an interest, the MP tells him: 'I happen to know Ian Greer is a good chap and runs a good company. I think he can do an able job for you. If you want to pick up the phone and arrange to meet him, why not?'[69] The MP then approaches Greer: 'Ian, I think I can introduce someone to you who may become a client.'[70] The company, usually the chairman and/or managing director, meets Ian Greer to discuss a possible contract. If the firm becomes a client, Greer contacts the MP and says: 'It was extremely kind of you [to recommend that client]. It is customary to make an introductory fee. We are very happy to do that.'[71] Some MPs refuse the pay-off, but others accept it. The amount of money involved is in some dispute but, according to lobbying sources, it would be between £4,000 and £10,000, depending on the size of the client's account.

One MP who introduces clients to Ian Greer Associates but refuses any payment is Michael Colvin, the Conservative MP for Romsey and Waterside. Colvin has known Ian Greer since 1979. He often visits the office for lunch, where he is briefed by clients. But Colvin is opposed to the introductory fee system: 'As far as Mr Greer is concerned and, you know, kickbacks for MPs, I think it would be very unwise of MPs to accept those sort of payments. I think that's really prostituting their profession.'[72]

Who are the pimps?

'Thank-you' payments are a good example of MPs making money by taking advantage of their status in Parliament. The time-worn excuse that MPs with consultancies and directorships enrich public life because they are making use of their expertise is redundant in these circumstances.

This is recognised even by MPs with substantial business interests of their own. One senior Conservative MP with several consultancies told me: 'I'm perfectly happy for MPs who have expertise and knowledge to be paid by companies. But when an MP acts as an introductory agent, almost like a marriage broker, for a PR company then I'm less happy about that. I happen to know this goes on with merchant banks and I'm very uneasy about it, I must say.'

Many lobbyists take a stronger view. They argue that MPs should not be retained in any way by political consultancy firms, and several have a deliberate policy not to do so. Indeed, there are lobbying companies with a blameless record – on the payment of MPs, promises to clients and general tactics. They act more like advisers and researchers than lobbyists.

One consultant of the old school is Arthur Butler, joint managing director of Charles Barker, Watney and Powell. He worked with the legendary Commander Powell and described why he is opposed to MPs being on the lobbyists' payroll: 'An MP is employed to support his constituency and party interests. Why should he also be paid large sums of money to speak on behalf of other companies?'[73]

CHAPTER 7

Ministers and the Money Men

Ministers must so order their affairs that no conflict arises, or appears to arise, between their private interests and their public duties.

'Questions of Procedure for Ministers', Confidential Cabinet Office rules

'I don't see why my private affairs should be anything to do with you at all.'

Nicholas Ridley, *Observer*, 13 April 1986

For the past decade, the Labour MP and former Cabinet minister Tony Benn has been valiantly trying to publish a Cabinet Office document which details the rules governing ministers' financial interests. It has been a forlorn task. Letters to the Speaker and repeated requests to the House have been met with the stubborn resistance of the parliamentary establishment. The document – 'Questions of Procedure for Ministers' – has been classified as 'Confidential'. This means, according to the official definition, that its release would be 'prejudicial to the interests of the nation'.

When Benn was asked to give evidence before a Commons Treasury and Civil Service select committee inquiry in 1986, he planned to issue the secret handbook as part of his submission. But two days before he was due to appear before the committee, its chairman, Terence Higgins, told him that the document remained 'confidential and subject to the thirty-year rule'.[1] Unperturbed, Benn appeared before the inquiry and presented 'Questions of Procedure' as part of his evidence. The committee reacted by refusing to publish the document and went into closed session, excluding the public.

Benn's campaign for publication was backed by an unlikely ally in James (now Lord) Callaghan, who was Prime Minister when the document was updated in 1976. In January 1986, Callaghan wrote to Mrs Thatcher: 'I see no reason why its contents need now be regarded as confidential.'[2] Downing Street was unimpressed and has continued to suppress its disclosure. 'It has been the practice of successive governments,' said Mrs Thatcher in 1988, 'not to make Cabinet documents public or to release them to Parliament.'[3]

The government's refusal to publish the rules is a measure of the sensitivity of ministers on the subject of their retaining any form of commercial stake. When an MP becomes a minister, even the appearance of a conflict of interests is extremely damaging. The offence is more serious and the political stakes much higher. As the former Labour Chancellor of the Exchequer, Sir Stafford Cripps, once told the House: 'It is not merely a question of whether there is a conflict, but whether anybody may think there is a conflict.'[4]

An assembly of rich men

The notion of government ministers retaining financial interests while remaining in office was born in the commercial quagmire of the period 1895–1905. It was a time of intense political activity by shipping, railway and cotton companies. Commerce was king, and this climate was reflected in Parliament. As *The Economist* reported in the summer of 1898:

> It is undeniable that during the session just ended there had been an atmosphere of money in the lobby and precincts of the House of Commons scarcely known before. All manner of 'interests' have gathered there as they gather in Washington ... More attempts to influence the votes of members have been made than has been known before.[5]

The government at the time did nothing to discourage public servants becoming what one MP memorably described as 'the decoy ducks of fraudulent finance'.[6] This was almost certainly due to their own ministers being sucked into the same murky pond. In 1895, twenty-four ministers of the new Conservative administration held between them sixty directorships in private corporations.[7] By 1905 this had increased to seventy-one in public companies alone.[8] The inevitable consequence was a saga of financial scandal and corruption. It reached such a pitch that one MP claimed the country was being 'governed by the forty thieves'.[9] The Liberal leader Herbert Asquith warned that no minister should be in a position where 'his public duty and private interest come into collision'.[10] This advice was extravagantly ignored. Lord Selborne was Under-Secretary at the Colonial Office while remaining a director of the P and O Steamship Company. Not only did P and O conduct business with the Colonial Office, they also received substantial government subsidies.[11]

Senior Cabinet ministers tried to deflate criticism of corruption. The Chancellor, Sir Michael Hicks-Beach, said: 'We all have some private affairs to which we are entitled ... The First Lord of the Treasury [Prime Minister] takes recreation at golf. I take mine by a walk along the Embankment and by a short attendance at a meeting of directors.'[12] But the agitation for reform was bolstered by allegations against the Chamberlain family.

In 1899 Joseph Chamberlain was Colonial Secretary when the government adjudicated on the amount of compensation due to shareholders of the Royal Niger Company. The firm's charter had been abolished and there was criticism over too favourable terms for the investors. Joseph Chamberlain was the responsible minister but was unable to make the decision. The reason, he told the Prime Minister, was that he had £3,000-worth of shares in a certain firm – the Royal Niger Company.[13]

The Boer War brought more charges against Joseph Chamberlain, who remained Colonial Secretary. His brother Arthur was chairman of Kynoch and Co., a Birmingham-based engineering firm. During the war Kynoch was awarded a large number of contracts to supply ammunition and explosives to the government. They were also allowed to revise earlier tenders – a privilege not granted to competitors and an unprecedented act of favouritism. Arthur Chamberlain strongly denied that he used his brother's influential position in the government to win contracts. But it then emerged that Joseph had earlier spoken out on behalf of Kynoch in a Commons debate while an MP and not declared his interest. More damning was the use of the Colonial Secretary's name in the letter of introduction used by Kynoch's sales representatives.[14]

Joseph Chamberlain angrily denied that he had any direct or indirect interest in companies receiving arms contracts for the war. Yet his family owned £140,000 worth of shares in Kynoch. More pertinent was the connection with Hoskins and Sons Ltd, which supplied fittings to the Royal Navy. This was virtually the family firm. His second son, Neville, was the company's managing director and his wife, his other son and two daughters were all major shareholders. Even more startling was a £3,000 stake held by the Colonial Secretary's brother Austen, who was at the same time the Civil Lord of the Admiralty.[15]

Joseph Chamberlain survived the subsequent debate and motion of censure as MPs voted on party lines. His final riposte to his critics was: 'Every man in every government who has saved money must invest it somewhere. It is difficult to see what form the investment, English or foreign, would not lay him open to such scandalous imputations.'[16]

Dealing with Marconi

One of Sir Henry Campbell-Bannerman's first acts on becoming Liberal Prime Minister in 1905 was to try and disinfect the stench of corruption from public life. The Premier asked his new Cabinet for details of their directorships. He did not want, he said, the government's Front Bench to become 'a sty for guinea pigs'.[17] This was a reference to the popular nickname for tame politicians acquiring easy directorships.

The government immediately announced that ministers must relinquish all directorships, except of a philanthropic nature. But legal sanction was ruled out. 'I hope that legislation will not be necessary,' said Campbell-Bannerman. 'A good example has been set.'[18] However, the failure to ban share dealing resulted in one of this century's major political scandals. It revolved around the Marconi Wireless Telegraph company and investments by senior Cabinet ministers.

In July 1912 the Liberal administration awarded a contract worth £60,000 to Marconi for a network of eighteen wireless stations, linking different parts of the British Empire. The company's shares immediately shot up in value. Four months earlier, Marconi's American parent company had announced a substantial shares issue of £1.4 million. But before the shares were offered to the public, Marconi's managing director, Godfrey Isaacs, secretly sold 1,000 each to his brother Sir Rufus Isaacs, the Attorney-General, Lord Murray, Government Chief Whip, and Lloyd George, then Chancellor of the Exchequer. The shares were bought in their own names at the pre-issue price of £2. At the end of the first day's trading on the stock market, the shares closed at £4. A few days later Lord Murray and Lloyd George sold half of their shares and then purchased another 3,000 between them.[19] Hence senior ministers had made a financial killing, using their public position for private profit. It was a case of insider dealing and, by virtue of their office, a conflict of interests. But had they also helped Marconi win the wireless contract four months later to produce a profit for their shareholdings? After all, Godfrey Isaacs was managing director of Marconi's British contractor.

Lloyd George was evasive, and blustered in the House about 'sinister rumours passed from one foul lip to another'.[20] Isaacs denied buying shares in the British Marconi company. Lord Murray fled to South America. A select committee inquiry was set up, and its Liberal majority cleared the ministers of corruption, although a minority report did criticise them for 'grave impropriety'.[21] In June 1913, Lloyd George and Rufus Isaacs made a very limited apology. But this was further diluted by the government's final act in the Marconi affair. Four months later, in October 1913, Isaacs was promoted to become Lord Chief Justice, the highest legal officer in the land.

Keeping it private

At the climax of the Marconi affair in June 1913, the Prime Minister, Herbert Asquith, made what appeared to be a definitive declaration on ministers' interests:

> Ministers ought not to enter into any transactions whereby their private pecuniary interest might, even conceivably, come into conflict with their public duty ... Ministers should scrupulously avoid speculative investments in securities in which, from their position and their special means of early or confidential information, they have or may have an advantage over other people in anticipating market changes.[22]

As this principle had been breached by Asquith's own Chancellor, Attorney-General and Chief Whip, it was hardly surprising such a ruling was ignored after the First World War – even at the highest level. During the 1926 coal dispute and general strike, Stanley Baldwin was able to combine being Prime Minister with holding 194,000 ordinary shares and 37,000 preference shares in Baldwin's Ltd – owner of several collieries.[23]

The main discrepancy in the official rules was that ministers were barred only from taking seats on the boards of publicly quoted companies. They could continue as directors of private firms. This meant that in 1926 Neville Chamberlain could retain his directorship of Hoskins Ltd when he entered the Cabinet. Hoskins was a major government contractor and in 1925–6 was awarded several Admiralty contracts.[24]

Viscount Walter Runciman was also able to take advantage of the system. From 1931 until 1937 he was President of the Board of Trade. At the same time he was a shareholder (21,000 £1 shares) and director of the shipping firm Moor Line Ltd. His other directorships included the Runciman Shipping Company, the London, Midland and Scottish Railway and three other shipping corporations. Part of Runciman's ministerial responsibility was to introduce in Parliament and then administer a £2 million subsidy to the merchant shipping industry. One of the recipients of that grant was Moor Line Ltd.[25] In 1939 Neville Chamberlain, by then Prime Minister, reluctantly responded to the outcry over the Runciman case. He closed the loophole on directorships of private companies being exempt from the rules. But it was not until 1952 that Winston Churchill issued a statement that proved to be the basis for today's rules.

The confidential 'Questions of Procedure' document is a classic British compromise. Ministers want to avoid a scandal but at the same time they are keen to preserve their financial investments. Consequently, the regulations are clear, but there are enough loopholes to keep ministers happy. The document states:

> It is a principle of public life that ministers must so order their affairs that no conflict arises, or appears to arise, between their private interests and their public duties.
>
> Such a conflict may arise if a minister takes an active part in any undertaking which may have contractual or other relations with a government department, more particularly with his own department. It may arise, not only if a minister has a financial interest in such an undertaking, but also if he is actively associated with any body ... which might have negotiations or dealings with the government.[26]

As a safeguard, ministers are required to resign *all* their directorships and divest themselves of any controlling shareholding in a company.

But the enforcement of the guidelines is weakened by secrecy and the lack of any independent arbiter, even inside Parliament. If there is a potential conflict of interests: 'Each minister should normally decide for himself how the principles apply to him ... Where there is a doubt it will almost always be better to surrender the interest but in such cases the Prime Minister of the day must be the final judge.'

There are several interests not covered by 'Questions of Procedure'. They include the use of trustees to enable a shareholding to be put aside while ministers retain a general stake in the future of a company. There is also no provision for the interests of their close family, while ministers who are lawyers and farmers are immune from the rules. Hence the presence of wealthy farmers James (now Lord) Prior (1970–72), Peter Walker (1979–83) and Michael Jopling (1983–7) in the Cabinet as Secretarys of State for Agriculture.

Thus many ministers remain judges in their own cause.

Speculating in the market

The most lucrative loophole lies in the guidelines governing shareholdings:

> Ministers cannot be expected, on assuming office, to dispose of all the investments they may hold. But if a minister holds a controlling interest in any company ... and, if there is any danger of a conflict of interest, the right course is for the minister to divest himself of his controlling interest in the company.
>
> There may also be exceptional cases where, even though no controlling interest is involved, the actual holding of particular shares in concerns closely associated with a minister's own department may create the danger of a conflict of interest. Where a minister considers this to be the case, he should divest himself of the holding.[27]

This enables ministers to buy and sell shares – either in their own name or through brokers – and then decide for themselves whether there is a problem.

Inevitably, ministers who retained their investments on taking office ran into trouble. Henry Hepburne-Scott, the tenth Lord Polwarth, became embroiled in such a row soon after becoming a minister of state at the Scottish Office in April 1972. In 1973 Lord Polwarth was given responsibility for North Sea oil developments as chairman of an interdepartmental task force. These new duties came into conflict with his private interests in the shape of oil-related investments. They were held in a series of trusts, notably the British Assets Trust and Second British Assets. The 17,000 shares were worth just under £20,000, with 8–15 per cent of the trusts' portfolios invested in oil or oil-related companies. A third trust, Atlantic Assets, had links with a corporation purchasing land for on-shore development.[28]

When these investments were disclosed the Prime Minister, Edward Heath, defended his colleague. He told the Commons that as there was no *direct* financial stake in any oil company, there was no conflict of interests. Heath argued that the Scottish minister's shareholding was too small to warrant any action: 'I do not regard Lord Polwarth's shareholdings in these trusts as rightly to come in conflict with his duties and I do not see how it could be seriously argued that they might.'[29] However, Polwarth decided to sell the shares in order to continue in office 'unhampered by a continuing campaign of unfounded innuendos'.

The Opposition took the matter more seriously. Robert Hughes, Labour MP for Aberdeen North, said: 'Anyone who believes no conflict of interest arises is incredibly naïve. The Prime Minister is saying that if a conflict of interest were to arise, Lord Polwarth would take no part in government discussions. If that is so, it negates the whole purpose of his appointment.'[30]

In Lord Polwarth's case the public were given some glimpse of what was happening. But Cecil Parkinson's investment activities were not made public.

When Parkinson, MP for South Hertfordshire, was appointed Minister of State for Trade in 1979, he handed over control of his share portfolio to his stockbrokers – Walter Walker, now known as W. I. Carr Investments. The Minister's shares were registered in Walker's nominee company name: Ferlim Nominees (named after the racehorse Millreef in an approximation of his name spelt backwards). Stock was then bought and sold at the broker's discretion.

One of Parkinson's first duties as a minister was to pass legislation making insider share dealing illegal. In October 1979 he told the Commons: 'It is essential that small shareholders develop confidence in the market and do not feel that they are at the mercy of the unscrupulous. Therefore, there is general agreement that insider dealing should now be made a criminal offence.'[31] The problem for Parkinson was that from 1979 until 1981, while he was the responsible minister, his own stockbrokers were involved in his department's first major investigation into suspected insider dealing. This was conducted under the new insider-dealing law introduced by Parkinson. Indeed, according to a documentary by Fulcrum Productions for Channel 4, some other share dealings through Walter Walker's nominee company were already under scrutiny, in a separate investigation by Trade Department inspectors.[32]

At the heart of the insider-dealing inquiry were a number of share transactions in the company Suter Electrical, including those by clients of Walter Walker. The problem was accentuated because early in 1980 Walker had bought, on Parkinson's behalf, 30,000 shares in Suter. Seven months later the stock was sold for a profit of £2,800. This share purchase – which was not part of the insider-dealing inquiry – created an apparent conflict of interests. While Parkinson held this stake, Suter was negotiating to buy Prestcold, a subsidiary of British Leyland, then a nationalised industry and the responsibility of the Trade and Industry Department.[33] Parkinson was not informed about this investment in advance of its purchase because his account was operated on a discretionary basis.

There is no suggestion of any wrongdoing by the minister. But Parkinson was, after all, the minister ultimately responsible for an inquiry which included the activities of his own stockbroker. Indeed, according to the Fulcrum Productions programme, the Stock Exchange's detailed report, which included a schedule of share dealings by clients of Walter Walker, was sent to Parkinson's department.

What should Parkinson have done to avoid the appearance of a conflict of interests? Christopher Hird, a former stockbroker and one of those who made the Fulcrum documentary, argues the minister could easily have resolved the issue. He could have changed his broker and hired an independent fund manager. But Parkinson retained Walker, and Walker continued to deal in speculative shares for his client. In May 1982 Parkinson, then in the Cabinet as the Conservative Party chairman, bought and sold 15,000 shares in Tilbury Construction for a profit of £3,500. In 1986, by now a backbencher, he purchased 50,000 shares in Newman Industries, which brought a profit of £8,000. The following year the acquisition of 40,000 shares in the transport group Mitchell Cotts resulted in an £8,000 profit.[34]

The Cabinet Office rules state that 'ministers should scrupulously avoid speculative investments'. As the minister responsible for regulating the City, and later a Cabinet minister, Parkinson needed to be particularly careful with his private holdings. He should have avoided even the slightest perception of a conflict between his public duty and private financial interests. To achieve that, he needed to do only three things: sell his shares, dismiss his broker and stop dealing. Another option was to confine himself to orthodox non-speculative investments like unit trusts. Instead, he retained Walter Walker, making at least £37,000 profit in the process.

The Parkinson example also illustrates the weakness and ineffectiveness of the regulations. As the 'Questions of Procedure' document was confidential and ministers' share deals can be hidden behind nominees, it is not easy for the circumstances to be examined by Parliament or the public. Instead, it was left to the minister to 'decide for himself' whether he had breached the rules. And, as we have seen, discretionary procedures are not the most secure systems.

If in the early 1980s Parkinson had believed his share deals created a conflict of interests, he would have been obliged to visit his long-standing friend in 10 Downing Street, Margaret Thatcher. As Prime Minister, she was the final judge and jury on the matter. Yet this would have been an occasion of some discomfort and embarrassment for Mrs Thatcher. For there is evidence that she may have contravened the spirit of the regulations for which she was responsible.

In 1971 Mrs Thatcher, then a Cabinet minister as Education Secretary, bought 348 shares for £2,142 in Broken Hill Proprietary, an Australian oil and steel conglomerate. By joining the company's dividend reinvestment scheme, her holding increased to 1,327 shares. Over the next fourteen years the stock, bought in her own name, increased in value through rights and dividend issues to £4,470.[35] She retained the shares when she became Prime Minister in 1979, and they appeared in Broken Hill's company register as 'The Hon. Mrs M. Thatcher, c/o Miss J. Robillard [her constituency secretary], 10 Downing Street, London SW1'. It was not until 1985 that the Prime Minister transferred her holding and other shares to nominee discretionary accounts, to be controlled by a firm of investment fund managers.[36] Thus for six years Mrs Thatcher held a direct stake in a company that was quoted on the London Stock Exchange. As Prime Minister and First Lord of the Treasury, she could theoretically have had access to a great deal of sensitive economic and industrial information. It was a potential conflict of interests, because she kept the shares under her own name from 1979 until 1985.

Mrs Thatcher denied that she had breached the Cabinet Office rules. 'Under those conventions,' she said, 'there is nothing which requires me, on assuming office, to dispose of my shares or to transfer them into a trust or in the name of investment managers.'[37] But 'Questions of Procedure' states: 'There may be less clear-cut cases where a minister would feel it appropriate to place his holding in the hands of trustees.'

A share of the spoils

When in 1986 the *Observer* wrote to nineteen Cabinet ministers asking them about their share dealings, the response was less than enthusiastic. Nine refused to discuss the matter and four did not even reply. Another four – Norman Tebbit, Lord Young, Kenneth Clarke and Malcolm Rifkind – said they did not own any shares. Only John Biffen, then Leader of the Commons, was forthcoming. He said he entrusted his 'depressingly small portfolio' to financial managers who administered his account without telling him the nature of the investments.[38]

However, one Cabinet minister told the paper that he had specifically ordered his stockbrokers not to buy shares in companies privatised by his government. This instruction was a measure of the sensitivity felt by some when ministers purchase stock in privatised corporations, particularly as they had promoted denationalisation in Cabinet.

Nicholas Ridley, a Cabinet minister from 1983 until 1990, arranged for his shares to be bought and controlled by his stockbroker. Hence he was unaware of any deals at the time of the transactions. But he was told after his broker bought 2,000 shares in the Jaguar car company just two months after its privatisation. Ridley was at the time the Secretary of State for Transport, having been Financial Secretary to the Treasury from 1981 until 1983. His broker had paid £4,300 for the holding at £2.15p a share on 1 October 1984. Fifteen months later Ridley's stock was sold at £4.15p a share for a profit of about £4,000.[39]

The Transport Secretary said that he was aware of the Jaguar investment only after it was made. When questioned by the *Observer*'s Paul Lashmar, he reacted angrily and said it was an unwarranted intrusion into his privacy:

> I find it extremely annoying and offensive. I don't see why my private affairs should be anything to do with you at all ... I really think it is intolerable to suggest that I should in any way be influenced by these sort of things.
>
> I didn't buy these shares and I didn't sell them – my stockbroker did. What am I supposed to do with my tiny bit of money? Am I supposed to keep it on deposit in the bank in case you ask questions?[40]

Ridley did disclose that he asked his broker to sell all his shares to 'give me some cash' as he was buying a property. But he maintained that he could not control what investments his stockbroker procured: 'There are certain shares I'm not allowed to buy, but I can't actually stop him buying them ... Supposing there is a privatisation issue and I told him not to buy it and then he went ahead and bought it, I can't stop him.'

That is debatable. A fellow Cabinet minister avoided this problem by instructing his broker not to buy stock in any privatised company. But perhaps a significant issue is why the Transport Secretary did not sell his Jaguar shares as soon as he was informed of their existence.

Three months after the Jaguar flotation, the shares of British Telecom were also offered to the public. Like the Jaguar sale, the BT stock was offered at the remarkably low price of £1.30p. Among the 2.3 million who took advantage were five government ministers, including one member of the Cabinet. None of them was in a department involved in negotiating the privatisation, and so there was no direct conflict of interests. But the nature of Cabinet, with its burden of collective responsibility, must at least raise questions of ministers making money out of government policy.

The most senior minister of the five was Nicholas Edwards, the Secretary of State for Wales, who received 800 shares. 'Like all Cabinet ministers,' he later said, 'all my investments are made without reference to me and at the complete discretion of my investment advisers.'[41] The Foreign Office minister Timothy Renton bought, through his stockbroker, 800 shares when British Telecom was privatised and another 1,700 later on the open market.[42] David Hunt, then a junior Energy minister, secured 800 shares before selling them in June 1986. Two government whips also bought the maximum 800. They were Peter Lloyd and Robert Boscawen.[43]

In 1986 another four ministers played the stock market, this time for the British Gas privatisation. They included John Lee, parliamentary under-secretary at Employment, who owned 2,300 shares;

Rhodes Boyson, a junior Environment minister, with 1,200; John Gummer at Agriculture, who bought 1,400; and two government whips, Tony Durant (with his wife Audrey) and Wyn Roberts, who picked up 300 and 800 respectively.[44]

The problem with ministerial shareholdings is that they are speculative investments – either to make some easy money or for long-term profit. This accentuates any conflict of interests that arises. Ministers argue that they hand over their investments to outside fund managers. This is not always the case, but where it is true it fails to resolve the issue of the *perception* of a conflict of interests. The ministerial rules state: 'Ministers cannot be expected, on assuming office, to dispose of all the investments they may hold.'[45]

One may reasonably ask: Why not?

Your company needs you, minister

When one experienced Cabinet minister left the government in 1990, a fellow Tory MP wryly referred to his resignation letter as akin to a 'Situations Wanted' advertisement.[46] The jibe was made only half-jokingly, as that year was dominated by a trail of Cabinet ministers leaving Whitehall for a clutch of lucrative directorships. Suddenly the explanation of 'spending more time with the family' was being greeted with raised eyebrows.

The concern about the exodus from the Cabinet room to the boardroom is based on three premises. First, that ministers are enriching themselves in the private sector as a result of their public duties on behalf of the voter and taxpayer. Second, that they are joining companies with which they had direct dealings as a minister, either awarding them contracts or through privatisation. Third, that corporations are hiring ex-ministers to exploit their inside information and contacts in their bid for government-related business.

For many years it has been the recruitment of Ministry of Defence civil servants by defence contractors which has caused concern. Certain MOD officials possess confidential commercial information and expertise which is invaluable in the competitive world of defence procurement. Consequently, the potential for corruption is immense – either by favouring the contractor just before leaving Whitehall or by exerting influence after joining the company.

In Britain, this is known as 'The Revolving Door' (in one side as a civil servant, out the other as a businessman). The Japanese expression for it is 'amakudari', or 'descent from Heaven', while in France the defection from the public to the private sector is known as 'pantouflage', or 'parachuting'.[47]

In recent times British ministers who have fastened on Golden Parachutes have landed in lush and prosperous pastures. A survey of thirty-one former Cabinet ministers who held office at some point between 1979 and 1990 reveals that nineteen secured a total of fifty-nine company directorships – an average of three each.[48]

The politics of the pork barrel

The aim of privatisation and deregulation policies in recent years has been to roll back the bureaucratic frontiers of the state and lay to rest the active role of government in commerce. However, the medium-term consequence of this process has created a new business–government complex. The dismantling of the industrial public sector has, ironically, generated fresh regulatory powers and responsibilities.

In these circumstances the inside knowledge, contacts and potential influence of a recently departed minister is invaluable to any ambitious corporation. An ideal recruit would be from the Department of Trade and Industry, which is at the sharp end of negotiations.

One of the DTI's most important roles is to review contentious take-over bids. From 1983 until 1985 Sir Alex Fletcher was the DTI Minister for Corporate Affairs, responsible for scrutinising take-overs. In September 1985, the Argyll Group launched a £1.2 billion bid for the drinks company Distillers. That month Sir Alex left the DTI as part of the autumn reshuffle. Despite reservations by the City's Take-Over Panel, the Argyll bid was given the green light in early December 1985 and the lobbying began. Two weeks later Sir Alex was hired by Argyll as its 'political adviser' – just three months after leaving the DTI. David Webster, the company's finance director, denied there was a conflict of interests. He said the former minister was assisting 'in a general advisory role. I would not want to comment on the length of the appointment.'[49]

Sir Alex's Secretary of State at the DTI was Norman Tebbit, MP for Chingford, who also left the DTI in September 1985, but remained in the Cabinet as the Conservative Party chairman and Chancellor of the Duchy of Lancaster.

In June 1987 Tebbit left the Cabinet, and four months later joined the board of the employment agency Blue Arrow PLC (now known as Manpower). He was paid £17,500 a year, held 8,800 shares and was also entitled to an all-expenses-paid chauffeur-driven Jaguar, secretarial support and membership of the company's private health plan.[50] Tebbit was by no means a passive, non-executive director. He was a key figure in a boardroom coup which unseated the chairman Tony Berry.

On 2 November 1987, Tebbit also joined the board of the industrial conglomerate BET PLC. His salary is at least £10,000, with 2,000 shares worth £5,000. In January 1990 this directorship created problems for Tebbit when BET bought an employment agency called Hestair. As Hestair was a direct competitor to Manpower in America, this produced a conflict of interests – the MP being on the board of both BET and Manpower at the same time. The situation was exacerbated, as Manpower was planning to shift their corporate base to the United States, and Tebbit eventually resigned in July 1990, citing the 'potential conflict with his board position in another company with parallel interests'.[51]

In November 1987 Tebbit also became a director of the retail company Sears PLC, replacing Cecil Parkinson. He was paid at least £10,000 a year and held 3,500 shares worth £5,000. Two months later he joined the board of J. C. Bamford Excavators Ltd, the earth-moving equipment manufacturer. In November 1990 he acquired a fifth directorship as chairman of the Onix Construction Group, the north-east leisure, construction and manufacturing company.

Tebbit's most controversial appointment was his directorship of British Telecom. He joined the company on 3 November 1987 and acquired an annual salary of £16,500 plus 2,000 shares worth £6,000. It was Tebbit who, as Trade and Industry Secretary, privatised BT in November 1984. The former Cabinet minister responded in characteristically venomous fashion to criticism that he was being rewarded for past services: 'If anyone believes I denationalised British Telecom and three years later gave up a £50,000-a-year Cabinet post just to get a £16,500-a-year job as a non-executive director, he must be either daft or too full of political spite, malice, spleen and envy to be rational.'[52] This missed the point, as the concern was the choice of company, not his salary. But even if we apply the cash test, Tebbit's argument is flawed. A conservative estimate of his directors' fees since leaving the Cabinet is that he has been earning at least £80,000 a year. Together with his MP's wages of £28,970, he has more than doubled his minister's salary. He also owns £20,000 worth of shares.

British Telecom's chief commercial competitor is Cable and Wireless (C & W), the ambitious international telecommunications group. In recent years C & W have gradually nibbled away at BT's monopoly. The strategy has been to invest profits from its Hong Kong operation into its wholly-owned subsidiary, Mercury Communications, and steadily gnaw away at BT's share of the market. However, in such a tightly regulated industry, C & W is increasingly reliant on the good will of the DTI. Licences are awarded and competition policy is monitored by that department. Consequently, as the stakes are higher, the lobbying is more intense. In these circumstances the appointment in 1990 of Lord Young, Secretary of State for the DTI from 1987 to 1989, as executive chairman of C & W was bound to cause controversy.

Young, a former property developer, had been a devoted disciple of Mrs Thatcher's government. For two years he was an unpaid special adviser to Keith (now Lord) Joseph, then Trade and Industry Secretary. In 1981, with Young at his elbow, Joseph initiated and authorised the privatisation of C & W. Five years later Joseph left the Cabinet and became a consultant to the company.

It was not until after the 1987 general election that Lord Young returned to the DTI as Secretary of State. For the next two years he was directly involved in negotiations with C & W, its subsidiary Mercury, BT and other cable companies like Racal.

One of the most competitive markets at the time was mobile telephones. In June 1989, Lord Young awarded Mercury a licence to act as Personal Communications Network (PCN) operators. The PCN was the new generation of personal and mobile phones. It was a major coup for Mercury and bitterly opposed by BT who complained of 'favouritism'.

The decision to grant the licence was made on the recommendation of Sir Bryan Carsberg, director-general of OFTEL, the industry's regulators. A month later, on 24 July 1989, Lord Young resigned from the government. Within four weeks the Mercury licence was confirmed and authorised by his successor Nicholas Ridley.[53]

Six months after leaving the Cabinet, Young became a director of Salomon Inc., the American merchant bank, and chairman of its international executive committee. But it was his public appointment as C & W executive chairman on 13 June 1990 – barely eleven months after his departure from the DTI – that caused a political row.

At a salary of at least £400,000 a year, Young's post involved the day-to-day running of the company. From 1 October 1990, the first day in his new job, he would be negotiating with the government department he had left the previous summer. 'His experience of negotiating at the highest level is a rare talent,' said Lord Sharp, C & W's outgoing chairman.[54]

The potential for a conflict of interests was raised almost immediately. A month later, in November 1990, the government launched its review of telecommunications policy. According to the *Financial Times*: 'The main item on the agenda will be whether Mercury Communications, C & W's subsidiary, should be allowed to maintain its position as the only mainstream rival to British Telecom or whether new competitors should be licensed.'[55]

As the former Cabinet minister recently responsible for telecommunications policy, Lord Young was a unique asset for C & W. He had extensive detailed knowledge not just of the DTI but also of C & W's competitors. But Young angrily denied there was any impropriety in his appointment: 'It is total British hypocrisy when people say I should have waited more than fifteen months before taking my first full-time job. It is not a question of going on to a board as non-executive to peddle any information I might have. I am going to steer the whole company.'[56]

Young was indignant that Ted Short, now Lord Glenamara, had become chairman of C & W in 1976, just six months after retiring as Labour's Deputy Prime Minister. Short was also a former Postmaster-General. But this is a weak argument. First of all, Short had been moved from Postmaster-General in 1968 – eight years before joining C & W. Second, C & W was a nationalised industry. Consequently, Short's knowledge and expertise were being used on behalf of the taxpayer. This contrasts with the potential use of privileged, contemporary information for the benefit of a relatively small band of private shareholders.

Banking on the Chancellor

There is a little doubt that a minister in Her Majesty's Treasury is privy to commercially useful information, ranging from up-to-date data on interest and currency rate policy to detailed knowledge on privatisations. The recruitment of a resigning Treasury minister gives merchant and clearing banks a potentially critical edge over competitors.

The pilgrimage of ministers to the City is not a new development. Anthony (now Lord) Barber, Chancellor of the Exchequer in the Heath government of 1970–74, became chairman of the merchant-banking group Standard Chartered soon after the Conservatives lost the election. Peter (now Lord) Rees was Chief Secretary to the Treasury with a seat in the Cabinet from 1983 until 1985. The following year he became deputy chairman of the merchant bank Leopold Joseph Holdings PLC and a consultant to the investment fund managers Touche Ross. He also joined the board of international financiers James Finlay PLC.

Rees's Chancellor was Nigel Lawson, who resigned on 26 October 1989, the longest-serving Chancellor of the Exchequer since Lloyd George. He left the Treasury with an incomparable contacts book, particularly in the overseas financial scene. His close working relationship with, for example, Alan Greenspan, chairman of the US Federal Reserve Board, made him a valuable commodity. Equally beneficial was his intimate and contemporary knowledge of the mechanics of the UK and international economies, based on six years as Chancellor.

It was not long before Lawson attached himself to the Golden Parachute and jumped in the direction of the Square Mile. Three months later he landed in the opulent surroundings of Ebbgate House, Swan Lane, with an office overlooking the Thames. This was the headquarters of Barclays De Zoete Wedd, the investment banking and securities subsidiary of Barclays Bank PLC.

Lawson had been hired as a non-executive director of Barclays Bank, working two days a week primarily for De Zoete Wedd. He was paid at least £100,000 a year (£1,000 a day). A month after his appointment the former Chancellor bought 715 shares at £5.76p each – a total investment of £4,118.[57] Apart from attending board meetings on the first Thursday of every month, Lawson's main responsibility is to advise De Zoete Wedd's clients. 'We think he'll give us the benefit of his advice on how Barclays is affected both in the UK and overseas,' said a bank spokesperson. 'He will be able to help us identify new business opportunities. It's bringing extra expertise to the board.'[58] Lawson said: 'This part-time job with a leading

British financial house, which I am delighted to join, fits in well with my plans to write a book and remain in politics.'[59]

The reaction of the City indicated the benefit of recruiting the former Chancellor. On the afternoon his appointment was announced, Barclays' stock-market value rose by nearly £90 million. Not everyone was so delighted with his directorship, however. According to Paddy Ashdown, leader of the Liberal Democrats: 'It is a corruption of the ideals on which Parliament ought to be based ... for ministers to march out of office and straight into fat, salaried jobs, often short-changing constituents by taking days off while drawing an MP's salary.'[60]

Lawson was attacked from all sides. The Queen's Chaplain, the Reverend John Grimwade, criticised his salary as excessive.[61] Reg Hales, leader of the Conservative group on Birmingham City Council, withdrew his account from Barclays in protest. He described the former Chancellor's salary as 'almost obscene'.[62] More significantly, a number of Barclays' own shareholders were unhappy with the appointment. At the bank's annual general meeting on 26 April 1990, some twenty investors raised their hands to object to Lawson's re-election to the board.

'Has Barclays' board become a rest home for discredited chancellors?' asked one shareholder.

'The Barclays board has never been a rest home for anyone,' replied Sir Martin Jacomb, the bank's deputy chairman.

The platform then faced a barrage of questions. Why was he appointed, how much work did he actually do and why was he paid so much?

'Mr Lawson does not receive an extravagant salary, nor does he expect one,' responded Sir Martin. The deputy chairman added that Barclays was 'tossing Mr Lawson a thin crust' because it was only what he was used to after ten years of public service.[63]

Lawson, sitting impassively on the rostrum during these exchanges, may have reflected that his fee was, in fact, four times what he was used to as a Cabinet minister. But he had no cause for concern. He was re-elected to the board. In April 1991 Lawson resigned as a consultant to Barclays De Zoete Wedd but retained his directorship of Barclays.

The former Chancellor did indeed seem immune to criticism. The day after he started work at Barclays, Tuesday 6 February 1990, he joined the board of Guinness Peat Aviation, the world's largest aircraft leasing company. He also became chairman of GPA Financial, a new subsidiary which plans to sell interests in the aircraft industry direct to investors and which originally approached Lawson in December 1989. 'Mr Lawson is one of the world's foremost economic and financial thinkers. His experience will contribute enormously to the development of GPA,' said the chairman.[64] Lawson works a minimum two days a month on a daily rate of £1,000.

Seven months later, in September 1990, the former Chancellor became executive chairman and a shareholder in the Central Europe Trust Company, a London-based firm of management consultants which had just been set up to advise clients on investing in newly liberated Eastern Europe. Central Europe Trust Company has among its clients GEC. It is also part of a consortium which will receive Treasury funding to help Poland with its privatisation programme. According to Lawson: 'CET provides a valuable link between the newly emerging market economies of Eastern Europe and successful corporate investors in the West.'[65]

Like his fellow former Cabinet colleagues leaving Whitehall for the City, Nigel Lawson reacted angrily to the criticism of his directorships. He described it as 'the politics of envy', 'sanctimonious humbug' and 'a nauseating form of demagoguery', and concluded:

> I obviously am now earning a substantial amount but I sacrificed far more financially during those ten years with the government. Now, it would be a terrible thing if people went into politics, as they do in some countries where corruption is rife, for what they could get out of it. But there's quite a large gap between that state of affairs and what we have in Britain today.[66]

Selling the gas

After British Telecom, the next major sale of a nationalised industry was British Gas in 1986. The Secretary of State for Energy who authorised and made all the key decisions for this share flotation was Peter Walker.

After he resigned from the Cabinet in March 1990, Walker acquired a chain of three directorships which were linked to the British Gas privatisation. On 11 May 1990, just twelve days after leaving the government as Welsh Secretary, Walker joined the board of Smith New Court PLC. The annual salary was £15,000. A City-based securities firm, Smith New Court has been anxious to build up its client list as corporate finance advisers. The appointment was secured through its chairman, Sir Michael Richardson, a long-standing associate of the minister and a veteran broker on the interface between government and business. 'I would rather have him [Walker] as a businessman than any other Cabinet minister,' said Sir Michael. 'If Peter brought in a stunning piece of business, I'm not saying we wouldn't pay him a bonus.'[67]

Sir Michael had also worked for the merchant bank that handled the British Gas share flotation for the government – N. M. Rothschild and Sons. Three weeks after the Smith New Court appointment, Peter Walker became a director of the Welsh board of Rothschild (NMR), which also owns 30 per cent of Smith New Court. Having been the Secretary of State for Wales and Energy, he was seen as a useful asset. 'He has an unparalleled knowledge of the Welsh economy and we will be able to draw on his many skills and accumulated knowledge in banking and industrial development,' said Glynne Clay, managing director of NMR Wales.[68] The perceived potential for a conflict of interests occurred within months of his appointment. As Welsh Secretary Walker had encouraged Rothschild to open an office in Wales. 'I persuaded them to come,' he said. During that period Rothschild's Welsh parent company was selected by the government as the financial advisers to the Cardiff Bay Development Corporation. In late 1990, the role of the Corporation became controversial because of its plan to dam up Cardiff bay as a 'scenic waterscape' for a property development. Now Walker was on the board of the company that would profit from the scheme, but he denied helping Rothschild as Welsh Secretary. 'I had nothing to do with the Cardiff bay appointment of Rothschild,' he said. 'I was not involved in any way.'[69]

The final link in the British Gas/privatisation chain was connected on the day Walker took his seat on the board of Rothschild. That morning, 1 June 1990, the former Energy Secretary became a director of British Gas PLC – the company he had privatised with Rothschild's help.

There was an immediate outcry. Political opponents recalled that Walker had been criticised at the time of the British Gas sale for not breaking up its monopoly or replacing the management team.[70] Walker, who was paid a £10,000 annual fee and held 10,000 shares worth £22,000, accused his critics of 'talking a load of nonsense'. He said British Gas had been a private company for four years and that he was hired for his knowledge of international oil and gas markets.[71]

Walker's third directorship on 1 June 1990 was the Worcester Group PLC, the central-heating specialists. He is also a substantial shareholder and has had a long association with the company. Other directorships picked up by Walker since leaving the Cabinet include Dalgety PLC, Thornton and Co., DC Gardner Group PLC, CBC UK Ltd, Tate and Lyle PLC and the chairmanship of Maxwell Communication Corporation.

Judges of their own propriety

In the midst of the furore over former Cabinet ministers joining privatised companies in 1990, a cartoon was published in the London *Evening Standard*, a paper not known for its radical outlook. The cartoon depicted a board of a company waiting to start a meeting. One of the directors was shown on his feet saying: 'I am very sorry. We have just had a telephone message from the chairman. He has not yet quite resigned from the government.'[72]

It was an indication of the wide-ranging, if cynical, concern about ministers accepting 'golden handshakes' from private companies they helped to create while in Cabinet. Sir Geoffrey Howe, then leader of the Commons, responded that 'it has never been the practice, under successive governments of either party, to prevent former ministers from accepting appointments in areas where they have expertise'. He said it was 'difficult to see the distinction in principle' between the appointments to privatised companies and top jobs awarded to ex-Labour ministers in public-sector corporations.[73]

There is a difference between moving sideways to a nationalised industry and joining the board of several private companies while remaining in Parliament, but Sir Geoffrey's argument does have some validity. For example, from 1976 to 1978 Edmund (now Lord) Dell was Secretary of State for Trade in the Labour government. A year after his resignation, Dell became chairman and chief executive of the Guinness Peat Group, the merchant bank and financial services conglomerate. That year, 1979, he also joined the board of Shell. Another Labour Cabinet minister was Eric (now Lord) Varley, Secretary of State for Energy and then Industry from 1974 to 1979. In 1984 he became chairman and chief executive of the Coalite Group, the coal and fuel distribution company.

The real issue is that there are no rules whatsoever for ministers joining private companies they dealt with whilst in public office. In 1962 Harold Macmillan, then Prime Minister, was asked to introduce a law preventing ministers moving to executive positions in such firms. 'I do not think that such legislation would be wise or necessary,' he replied. 'It is desirable and beneficial to the country that men of considerable experience should be available, when they leave the government, to the service of industry and commerce.'[74] This has remained the position. In 1975, Sir John (now Lord) Hunt, then Cabinet Secretary, said 'it has generally been thought to be impracticable to apply rules to former ministers'.[75]

In 1990 Mrs Thatcher stated:

> Formal rules have never been applied to former ministers considering whether to accept appointments in industry or commerce, whether in the public or private sector. They are public figures and both they and the companies have a powerful motivation to protect their good name.
>
> It is valuable for this country to have people of experience in public affairs putting their talents at the service of industry and commerce when they leave government.[76]

Nobody would argue against a greater cross-fertilisation between business and government. But senior Tory and Labour MPs maintain there is a need for accountability and regulation, pointing to the fact that civil servants joining companies with whom they had dealings are subject to stringent rules. According to Cabinet Office guidelines, officials can be banned from accepting private jobs for up to two years after leaving Whitehall. For Elizabeth Symons, general secretary of the First Division Association, 'there is one rule for civil servants and another for ministers'.[77]

This was recognised by, of all people, Norman Tebbit. The former Tory Cabinet minister said: 'I think it is right that former ministers, like civil servants, should leave a decent interval – say two years – between holding responsibilities which affect particular businesses and taking up posts with them.'[78] His former Cabinet colleague John Biffen, a one-time Chief Secretary to the Treasury, agreed: 'In these matters, where you have a relationship between government and industry, you need to be particularly cautious and careful to dispel any suggestion of an underhand pay-off situation.'[79]

Senior Labour figures took the same view. In 1990 John Cunningham, Shadow Leader of the Commons, wrote to Mrs Thatcher calling for the civil service guidelines to be applied to ministers. He also argued that privatisation had made tougher rules even more necessary:

> In the case of your former ministers, the relationship between them and the companies which now pay them was far more substantial. These former ministers took responsibility in Cabinet and in Parliament for the entirety of the creation, legal existence, financial status and trading position of these companies . . . That responsibility was unique to privatisation.

The Prime Minister replied: 'I do not believe it would be appropriate to extend the business appointment rules which apply to civil servants to former ministers. Their positions are not analogous.'[80] She referred back to Sir John Hunt's 1975 assertion that it was 'impracticable' to implement any guidelines and quoted with approval a comment by a predecessor, Harold (now Lord) Wilson. With just one remark the former Labour Prime Minister was able to capture the attitude of the parliamentary establishment on the whole issue of ministers' commercial interests. 'I think,' he reflected, 'that these matters are better left to the discretion and good sense of the individuals concerned.'[81]

CHAPTER 8

Conclusion:
Whom does your MP Serve?

'We can all think of examples of colleagues who over the years
have always espoused a particular cause for which they have
been paid, and the fact is that what they have been saying has
been rather marked down, if you like, because of that.'[1]
  Peter Fry, Conservative MP for Wellingborough and political
                                                        lobbyist

'The public do not have an automatic right to know what Members of Parliament get up to.'[2]
  Sir Patrick McNair-Wilson, Conservative MP for New Forest

I n the heart of Westminster's lobby land, just 600 yards from the
House of Commons, are the offices of one of Britain's most
flourishing management consultancies. Based at 35 Old Queen Street,
Saxton Bampfylde International PLC specialise in securing highly
paid executive positions and directorships. Some of their most enthusiastic clients are companies looking for Members of Parliament.

Saxton Bampfylde is just one of several headhunters advising firms
looking for political 'ambassadors'. As the average annual fee is
£15,000 plus perks, the demand within Westminster for such jobs is
high. Some even ask for a variety of clientele. 'A chap might have five
such directorships,' said Stephen Bampfylde, the managing director,
'each offering something different, so he could put together a
package.'[3] They represent companies, not MPs, and yet nothing
encapsulates the notion of 'MPs for hire' more than this form of
political importuning. What kind of service do MPs provide in return
for their retainer?

The scope of influence and level of activity generated by MPs
varies. At the bare minimum, director/MPs attend a monthly board

meeting and possibly a company committee. Back-bencher/consultants prefer reporting informally on an *ad hoc* basis and are available on call. They also write strategic briefing documents for clients.

Bampfylde sees an MP on the board almost like a well-polished ornament. 'Good non-executive directors are a bit like the constitutional monarchy,' he said. 'Their role is to guide, warn, advise and occasionally say no – to blow the whistle.'[4] However, other executive search consultants argue that MPs exert more power. 'There is no doubt that having an MP on the board enormously enhances a company's access to ministers who might affect their business,' said Ian Ashworth. 'The amount of political lobbying done by companies is now huge. And that is the primary reason for putting an MP on your board.'[5]

As the lobbying activities of hired MPs are conducted in great secrecy, it is difficult to assess the extent of their influence. But Lord Rees-Mogg, on the board of GEC, M & G and J. Rothschild Holdings, has provided an insight into the functions of the non-executive director. According to Rees-Mogg, the 'part-time' director is a far from semi-detached observer:

> The outside [non-executive] director shares all the legal responsibilities of the board as a whole. All directors have a collective duty to use their best efforts to run the business successfully and profitably . . . It is essential that part-time directors should have the same psychological commitment to the success of the business as the full-time directors.[6]

As nearly all MPs on company boards are non-executive directors (NED), Rees-Mogg's analysis is extremely apt. He argues that NEDs are primarily watchdogs for the shareholder and come into their own during take-over battles. 'In a bid the outside directors should be an additional resource for management,' said Rees-Mogg, who outlined their role:

> At the crisis of a company's life, when events are being decided which will settle its future for ever, outside directors ought to be willing to drop everything if they are needed . . . An outside director ought to have a sufficiently flexible life to be able to concentrate all his energy and attention on the business which needs it most. In the crisis of a business, many plans have to be made and remade under pressure. In that process, the outside director, partly because he does come from the outside, can play a helpful part.[7]

As a contentious take-over bid is often politically controversial and involves government adjudication, an MP sitting on the board is placed in an invidious position. Faced with his responsibilities as a director, conflicts of interest are almost inevitable. But there is a more fundamental point to be made about MPs on the payroll. There is no doubt, as Ian Ashworth and other headhunters testify, that most back-benchers are recruited by companies purely because of their status in Parliament. As *The Economist* noted:

> Notoriously, men are often placed upon boards of directors simply and solely because they are Members of Parliament and are, therefore, believed to be able to exercise a useful influence. It would be well if the constituencies would take the matter up and let their Members understand that they do not confer the honour of membership of Parliament merely in order to raise a man's value in the guinea-pig market.[8]

This was published in 1896, but its message is just as pertinent today, for MPs are selling themselves in the market-place as never before.

Many voters are unaware that MPs spend much of their time helping companies in return for undisclosed payments. Some, understandably, do not even know the Register of Members' Interests exists. William Miller, a Conservative voter from Shrewsbury, was so shocked by the news that he wrote to the *Sunday Telegraph*:

> I had thought an MP represented only his constituents. I consider it improper in the extreme that, having reached Parliament on their votes, he should spend his time there lining his pocket by serving interests of which they may know nothing and which may even be contrary to their own. Far from being accepted as a matter of course, this practice should be regarded as a public scandal.[9]

The secrecy surrounding MPs' paid interests is recognised by objective observers. 'It is not something which is very widely ventilated or publicised,' said Graham Zellick, Professor of Public Law at London University. 'I think the public would be nothing less than appalled if they knew the extent to which their Members of Parliament were in the pockets of those able to buy them.'[10] MPs counter-argue that they can act for their constituents as well as retain their business interests. They also maintain that it is highly unlikely that the two will ever directly clash. But this is not always the case.

In 1990, the normally placid citizens of Hove, Sussex, were loudly campaigning against a plan by the supermarket chain Sainsbury to build a new store and leisure centre in their town. They were concerned about the damage to the environment, as the store, occupying 79,000 square feet, was to be built in the Benfield Valley, Hove's last green valley. The complaints grew more vociferous when a government inspector rejected the Conservative-controlled council's objection to the store. The angry Hove people refused to give up, forming action groups and enlisting the help of their constituency MP to lobby the government on their behalf.

It was at this point that the danger of MPs retaining commercial concerns was clearly demonstrated. The MP in question was the Hon. Timothy Sainsbury, the parliamentary under-secretary at the Foreign Office. His shareholding in the family company of J. Sainsbury PLC is worth an estimated £120 million, and he had been a director from 1962 until 1983, when he joined the government.[11]

This was a clear conflict of interests, and was recognised as such. Sainsbury refused to get involved in the controversy. He would only say: 'I ceased having executive involvement with J. Sainsbury PLC fourteen years ago and have not had non-executive involvement for six years.'[12] Many of his constituents were unhappy with the situation. 'We were disenfranchised,' Jack Arscott, a local campaigner told me. 'He has let down the people he is there to represent,' said Bob Bailey, a local Liberal Democrat councillor. 'He must now decide whether his primary duty is to his constituents or his family superstore.'[13] The local paper concurred: 'The only hope is an appeal to local MP Tim Sainsbury to put his constituents before family interest. It's a vain hope, given that previous cries for help have fallen on deaf ears.'[14]

Justifying the system

MPs defend their being paid by outside interests on two grounds. The first is that they need to supplement their income. This is an unconvincing argument. An MP's basic annual salary is currently £28,970 – more than twice the national average wage and far more than most of their constituents receive. In addition, they receive £25,000 a year for running their office and £10,000 for living expenses if the constituency is outside London. MPs are also entitled to free travel between their homes and Parliament.

It is true that this compares unfavourably with the situation in other democracies, notably the United States. But it is hardly poverty wages. More significantly, some 230 MPs manage perfectly adequately without resorting to consultancy and directors' fees. If those back-benchers are satisfied with £28,970 plus allowances, the low-pay argument loses credibility. However, there is a strong case for increasing a back-bencher's secretarial and research allowances and improving office facilities.

It is also highly unlikely that a substantial salary increase would solve the problem. Most MPs with commercial interests are raking in an extra £40,000 minimum. Some, particularly former Cabinet ministers, are receiving £75,000-plus. Even if an MP's wages were doubled, it is unlikely the pursuit of the golden calf would stop.

The second line of defence is that it is of great benefit to the country to have MPs with outside interests. The conventional wisdom is that Parliament would be a sterile place if populated by Members with no experience of the real world. 'The job of a back-bencher is not intended to be a full-time one,' said Dudley Fishburn, Conservative MP for Kensington. 'A back-bencher is best who brings the outside bustle and business of the world with him to the House of Commons.'[15]

There is, of course, nothing wrong with MPs having outside interests. But politicians do not need to be on the board of several companies to have experience of the real world. And it does not explain why they need to be paid jobs, when many of their colleagues lobby for their constituents, pressure groups and the public for free.

More fundamentally, there is a strong argument for the back-bencher representing *all* interests on an equal and full-time basis. Apart from the ethical factor, there has been a massive rise in both the complexity and quantity of legislation passing through the Commons. To examine and peruse these laws is a full-time job. According to Douglas Smith, a Westminster lobbyist and Tory councillor for over twenty years:

Politicians in this day and age would be better off being full-time politicians. The public interest would be better protected if they spent their time totally on looking at political affairs, because government is now so complex. A hundred years ago you could be a land-owner as well as a politician because there wasn't as much government. But now there's the European Community as well as increased government here, so I think it's a full-time professional job.[16]

Reforming the system

To persuade MPs to work full-time for the public is a difficult enough job. But the task is impeded by the very rules that are supposed to protect and preserve the public interest.

In the Commons chamber an MP is obliged to declare an interest only when making a speech during a debate or committee proceeding. These declarations are often couched in the most nebulous terms: 'I have an interest in the banking industry.' The type of interest and name of the company are not always specified. The complacency surrounding the implementation of this resolution was noted by the Registrar of Members' Interests, James Hastings. On 19 January 1988, he wrote to Lord James Douglas-Hamilton, a Conservative MP and Scottish Office Minister: 'I suspect that its terms are not always as fully recalled by Members as they might be and are probably not always observed.'[17]

There are several escape-routes for the commercially active back-bencher, looking for a secret way to lobby for clients without breaking the rules. Here are the occasions when an MP does *not* have to disclose his consultancy, directorship or shareholding:

1 when asking oral questions;
2 when submitting written questions;
3 when making 'brief' interventions during debates;
4 when sponsoring Commons motions.

Despite these discrepancies, it seems Parliament's only real concern is that a pecuniary interest should be declared – not the conflict that it can create between private and public duties. This serves to legitimise and provide a seal of approval for MPs who continue to lobby for outside bodies in exchange for payment.

The problem is exacerbated by the fact that the Register of Members' Interests is inadequate in both its structure and its application. An ordinary constituent inspecting the Register at the local library or House of Commons will find it a baffling document. Declarations are vague and incomplete and the voter will see only a blurred vision of their MP's interests. Here are some items missing from the Register:

1 description of the type of declared company;
2 amount of money received by the Member;

3 shareholdings of less than 1 per cent;
4 value and size of the declared shareholdings;
5 clients of consultancy/PR and lobbying companies;
6 nature of services provided by MP to the client;
7 length of stay and purpose of overseas trips;
8 fees received from companies for services not directly related to parliamentary duties;
9 date of appointment and departure from company.

The Register also does nothing to prevent an MP speaking, asking
questions, lobbying, sponsoring motions and voting for private interests in return for payment. Indeed, the regulations effectively sanction
such activity.

Whenever the Select Committee on Members' Interests has examined the issue, the loopholes have been neatly overlooked. Their 1985
inquiry concluded: 'There is no requirement to disclose amounts [of
money]. The original decision to limit registration generally in this
way was come to by the House after a careful balance of advantage
between public disclosure and the right to privacy ... Identifying
interests is more important than quantifying them.'[18] Instead the
committee concentrated on relatively inconsequential malpractices
such as lobbyists masquerading as MPs' research assistants and
moonlighting lobby journalists.

The 'privacy' argument is a smoke-screen. According to Paddy
Ashdown, leader of the Liberal Democrats, MPs are supposed to be
publicly accountable:

> When a person joins this House he is involved in the business of public
> affairs and must therefore relinquish some of that privacy ... Privacy
> often leads to secrecy, and secrecy is the blanket behind which corruption
> can take place. I therefore believe that there is a need to declare all
> sources [of cash] over and above parliamentary salaries ... There is only
> one loyalty that Members of this House have, and that loyalty is derived
> from the vote cast in the ballot box.[19]

Conservative MP James Cran agreed, although for a different
reason:

> I'm very much in favour of extending the rules and asking those MPs
> who receive money from consultancies to tell us how much they're get-
> ting. The advantage that would have is to let us know those MPs who
> aren't paid at all. We might therefore listen to them rather more than we
> do to those who are paid.[20]

The refusal to grant the public information concerning how much their MP is paid by outside organisations hides important information about the nature of the declared interest. As the *Observer* commented: 'There is a world of difference between a £1,000 retainer paid to an MP by a commercial company for occasional guidance and a £20,000 "sweetener" offered, perhaps, for a much more specific purpose.'[21]

In recent years radical attempts to reform the system have been quashed. In November 1987, Graham Allen, Labour MP for Nottingham North, briefly refused to sign the Register in protest at 'its partial and inadequate nature'.[22] During his membership of the Select Committee on Members' Interests, he suggested five changes to the Register. They included more detailed information about remuneration received by MPs, declaration of clients of lobbying firms and the listing of all shareholdings.

In March 1988 the select committee rejected Allen's proposals. That month another radical blueprint was considered. Drafted by Labour MPs Dale Campbell-Savours and Tom Pendry, this plan advocated that the assets of MPs' wives should be declared, the threshold of 1 per cent on shares be lowered or all shareholdings in public companies worth over £100,000 be registered, and capital gains on a particular share exceeding £25,000 be recorded. These reforms were also rejected, although only on the casting vote of the chairman, Sir Geoffrey Johnson-Smith. The committee responded by diverting attention away from Members' interests and launching another inquiry into the activities of lobbying companies.

One argument used to discourage further disclosure is that Members are already aware of those who transgress. One of them sent an anonymous note to the *Observer*'s political editor Adam Raphael saying: 'Those MPs who are bought are discounted by the rest of us. Yours sincerely, A Tory.'[23] This ignores the fact that voters would remain ignorant of their MP's interests without disclosure.

By far the major flaw with the Register is that it is voluntary, based on custom and courtesy rather than rule and resolution. It is not legally binding, and only suspension or expulsion from the House of Commons can make it effective.

One attempt to make the Register compulsory was roundly defeated by MPs. In 1985 Dale Campbell-Savours proposed that a newly-elected Member be required to make a declaration in the Register before being allowed to take his seat in the House. John

Biffen, then leader of the Commons, opposed the motion. He argued that it would create 'the most formidable problems of definition'.[24] Some thirty Conservative MPs disagreed and voted for a mandatory Register, but they were defeated by 174 to 128, a majority of 46.

The Register's lack of credibility was starkly illustrated by the absence of any action taken against Enoch Powell. Between 1975 and 1987 Powell steadfastly refused to comply with the requirement to declare his interests in the Register. The Ulster MP admitted he was in 'clear contempt' of the House but believed that the resolution was 'unconstitutional'. The Select Committee on Members' Interests repeatedly recommended that disciplinary action be taken against Powell. But the Commons refused to enforce its own rules.

Powell's argument was that it required an act of Parliament, not a resolution of the House, to impose such conditions. 'The qualifications to be an MP, or disqualifications to be an MP, are a matter of law and can only be increased or altered by altering the law,' he said. 'No resolution of either House by itself can do that to the law.'[25]

No more inquiries, please

Powell was right — but for a different reason from the one he gave. It can be argued that many of the cases involving MPs helping companies in return for payment verge on the criminal. To expect a voluntary, restricted Register and a self-regulating Select Committee on Members' Interests to police the system is naïve and short-sighted.

As the select committee is not a judicial body, it is severely handicapped, regardless of the quality of its members. The committee of thirteen busy MPs meets only fortnightly, or weekly when reports are in preparation. It has no research or investigative staff, apart from an over-worked Registrar, and no expert advisers from the business, political or legal world. Its shortcomings are exposed during special inquiries into breaches of the rules. A thorough and independent investigation into complex and sensitive allegations is difficult enough for a court of law. Hundreds of documents need to be sought and scrutinised and witnesses cross-examined. For a part-time select committee, meeting sporadically with meagre resources, it is even more formidable.

The committee's credibility also suffers because it is not independent. The members are all MPs with an in-built majority for the government of the day. Some of them even have commercial interests themselves (see chapter 5). Hence MPs are investigating other MPs, policing themselves often in secret session. They are judges in their own cause.

For the ordinary voter, following the select committee's complaints procedure can be a frustrating experience. There is no doubt at all that its rules serve to discourage inquiries against MPs. The committee will launch an investigation *only* after a complaint by a member of the public or an MP. There is also a requirement that there must be 'prima-facie evidence as to the accuracy of the allegation'[26] before the procedure can be invoked. Naturally, an ordinary constituent is unlikely to possess such evidence. Consequently, inquiries in recent years have all been the result of media disclosures – John Browne (*World In Action*), Michael Grylls (Andrew Roth's *Parliamentary Profiles*) and Michael Mates (*Independent on Sunday*).

A case in point was that of John Browne, the Conservative MP for Winchester. For over two years Browne's activities were under the journalistic periscope because of his controversial divorce proceedings. He had been awarded a £270,000 cash settlement against his ex-wife Elizabeth and when she fell short by £49,000 the MP was prepared to see her jailed. This resulted in highly critical press comment of Browne's conduct during the case.

In December 1986, Elizabeth Browne gave the author access to hundreds of documents. The dossier detailed the MP's legal and business affairs (she had been a director, shareholder and employee of his consultancy company). Some of the material was broadcast and published, notably in a TVS documentary. But it was not until April 1989 that the full extent of Browne's mainly overseas commercial interests were revealed. He was trying to introduce a 'Protection of Privacy' bill. This included a clause which could have prevented journalists investigating the 'personal financial affairs' of individuals. There was a 'public interest' provision but this depended on reporters convincing a single judge that their inquiries could be so justified.

As Browne was one of the people who had most to gain from his legislation, *World In Action* conducted an investigation into the potential effects of the bill on the sponsor's own business activities. Based on the author's documents, the programme pulled together the known evidence and made new disclosures – on the lobbying of the Prime Minister on the subject of a lucrative Saudi Arabian commission, on the existence of a secret off-shore Bermudan Trust and on speaking out on cable TV without declaring an interest.[27]

Several of Browne's Winchester constituents were concerned about these revelations. One of them, Mrs Betty Cleary, an active and experienced Conservative Party member, was so disturbed that she wrote to the Registrar to complain. However, because of the select committee's bizarre procedure, she was unable to take it further. She believed it was unreasonable to expect her not only to provide all the documentary evidence but also to pursue the complaint on her own without possessing detailed knowledge of the allegations.

It was only when David Leigh, the top investigative journalist then working for the *Observer*, made an official complaint that the Browne inquiry was launched. Leigh had written some articles with the author on the MP's commercial activities and knew about the case. And so, after being supplied with all the documentation, he was able skilfully to present and explain the evidence before the select committee.

As it happened, the Browne inquiry was conducted with scrupulous attention to detail and objectivity. But only one witness was called and avenues of inquiry were not pursued because of lack of time and resources.

Thus the odds are stacked against the complainant. The Registrar will refer a case to the select committee only if documentary proof is handed to him personally. As a committee of inquiry is usually the arena where such evidence is obtained — often through testimony — this ensures that few cases are examined.

An example of the difficulties the public face involved allegations about the Labour MP Gwyneth Dunwoody. In July 1990, one of her constituents, Mrs Cecilia Darlington, wrote to the Registrar claiming that Dunwoody had not declared consultancy fees from an anti-Channel Tunnel lobbying company (see chapter 6). Mrs Darlington attached newspaper articles to her letter and concluded: 'I hope you will investigate this complaint.' James Hastings, the Registrar, responded by sending her a copy of the complaints procedure. As both Dunwoody and the lobbying company declined to reply to letters on the issue, nothing was done.

Mrs Darlington then enlisted the help of her local Conservative councillor, Brian Silvester. He raised the matter with Tory MP Peter Viggers, a member of the Select Committee on Members' Interests. Viggers spoke to Hastings, but the Registrar told him that he did 'not consider press reports to represent sufficient evidence' for him to refer the case to the committee.[28]

This was a remarkable response, given that most complaints had originally been based on TV and press reports. But Hastings was applying the strict letter of the rules. This enraged Silvester. 'It is virtually impossible for the average citizen to get a complaint against an MP investigated by the select committee,' he told me. 'The whole thing is a sham and a façade.'

Outside the law

Another remedy and form of accountability that MPs seem to have eluded is the criminal law. Officially, MPs are immune from prosecution for corruption if the offences are committed in Parliament.

The benchmark for the application of the corruption law to MPs was the 1976 Royal Commission on Standards of Conduct in Public Life. Their report stated that:

> Neither the statutory nor the common law applies to the bribery or attempted bribery of a Member of Parliament in respect of his parliamentary activities.
> It is clear to us that an MP cannot, in that capacity, be deemed an 'agent' for the purposes of the Prevention of Corruption Act 1906. It is equally clear that Parliament could not be deemed to be a 'public body' for the purposes of the Public Bodies Corrupt Practices Act 1889. Nor does membership of Parliament, as such, constitute public office for the purposes of the common law.[29]

The legal loophole was confirmed at the time by the Labour Prime Minister James (now Lord) Callaghan, who said: 'A Member who accepts a bribe in return for some action which is a proceeding in Parliament cannot be the subject of criminal proceedings.'[30]

In more recent years the Conservative government has also refused to apply the criminal law to MPs. 'The House itself has remedies available to it in the event of bribery of a Member of Parliament,' said John Wakeham, then Leader of the Commons, in 1987.[31] Three years later, in April 1990, this was reaffirmed by the then Prime Minister, Margaret Thatcher: 'We would consider bringing forward legislation to make the corruption of Members a criminal offence only if there was clear evidence that the present arrangements were ineffective and the House agreed.'[32]

However, there is evidence that the criminal law could be applied to MPs. According to Graham Zellick, Professor of Public Law at London University, the House of Commons could be deemed a 'public body' for the purposes of the Public Bodies Corrupt Practices Act 1889.[33] Section 1 states that any person who corruptly solicits or receives a fee as an inducement 'to do anything in respect of any transaction whatsoever, actual or proposed, in which the public body is concerned, shall be guilty of an offence.' As the 'public body' is defined as an entity which 'carries out its transactions for the benefit of the public and not for private profit', there is little doubt that the Commons falls into this category and hence within the scope of the Act.[34]

MPs also appear to enjoy immunity from prosecution under the Common Law. The 1976 Royal Commission justified this by quoting Criminal Law Commissioners who asserted that the expression 'public officer' does 'not include' MPs.[35]

However, Professor Zellick discovered countless legal definitions which established that a 'public officer' is someone who is paid out of national and public funds and serves the public.[36] 'There is certainly nothing in the English authorities,' said Zellick, 'which compels the conclusion that an MP is not a public officer.' So again it is difficult to see how MPs' status can give them legal indemnity.

This is compounded by the issue of liability and the spurious distinction between corruption outside and inside Parliament. A precedent was set in 1923 in the High Court of Australia where the judge ruled that regardless of where the (lobbying) pressure was exerted:

> It operates as an incentive to the recipient to serve the interest of his paymaster regardless of the public interest, and to use his right to sit and vote in Parliament as a means to bring about the result which he is paid to achieve. It impairs his capacity to exercise a disinterested judgement on the merits of the transaction from the point of view of the public interest, and makes him a servant of the person who pays him, instead of a representative of the people.[37]

Professor Zellick quotes Isaacs and Rich from the same case:

> He [the MP] has expressly abandoned and effectually impaired . . . his official liberty in return for personal reward. He has placed himself in a

situation embarrassing and inconsistent with that independence to criticise or censure which he is bound to preserve. He has fastened upon
himself golden fetters which preclude his freedom of action.[38]

Zellick concluded that MPs do not enjoy *general* immunity from
criminal prosecution if the existing statute law is applied. And yet
the government maintains that MPs are exempt from the law if the
offence is committed in Parliament.

The essence of the loophole is that the political and judicial establishment do not accept that an MP lobbying for outside bodies in
exchange for payment at Westminster is corrupt. According to Lord
Orr-Ewing, a member of the 1976 Royal Commission on Standards
of Conduct in Public Life and a former MP: 'It is easy to condemn
a bribe, but I do not believe that we have paid enough attention to
the difference between a fee for services rendered and a bribe.'[39]

From the point of view of the voter, I would suggest it is difficult
to see the difference.

Despite Lord Orr-Ewing's anxieties, the 1976 Royal Commission
recommended that 'Parliament should consider bringing corruption,
bribery and attempted bribery of an MP acting in his parliamentary
capacity within the ambit of the criminal law.'[40] This proposal has
never been debated in the Commons, let alone implemented.

In Canada, where members of the Federal Parliament and provin-
cial legislatures are bracketed together with judges, the issue is taken
more seriously. An MP can be jailed for fourteen years if he corruptly
accepts 'any money, office or employment . . . in respect of anything
done by him in his official capacity'.[41] Canadian MPs are also barred
from voting on any bill in which they have a pecuniary interest.[42]

Imprisonment is also the sanction in the United States. A member
of Congress can be fined $10,000 or jailed for two years, plus dis-
qualification from public office, if he or she 'directly or indirectly
receives . . . any compensation for any services rendered'.[43] There is
also a tough regulatory code which is constantly being amended.
The 1989 Ethics Reform Act requires a complete annual financial
disclosure listing all sources of income, including the amounts. In
addition, Members may not:

1 earn more than 15 per cent of their annual salary in outside income;
2 receive fees of more than $2,000 for a speech, public appearance or
   article;
3 use their official position for personal gain;

4 receive payment for services rendered;
5 accept any form of compensation from a foreign government;
6 contract directly or indirectly with the Federal Government;
7 vote on any matter in which he or she has a pecuniary interest;
8 accept gifts aggregating more than $300 in value, apart from a relative.[44]

These North American safeguards are matched by some Western European democracies. Members of the French National Assembly are prohibited from simultaneously retaining paid positions – in the private or public sector. They are also banned from continuing to act as professional lawyers. In Spain new measures have been proposed making it illegal for legislators to do any outside jobs – apart from the one for which they were elected.

The amateurish gentlemanly British Register of Members' Interests and Select Committee pales by comparison. Even when the Register is breached, as with Enoch Powell, it is not enforced.

Defenders of the UK system believe mutual trust and self-regulation to be the only feasible remedy. They argue that the criminal law and tougher rules are not required to counter conflicts of interests and corruption.

I would submit that this is precisely what is required. At the very least, there needs to be a mandatory Register and proper investigatory powers for an independent judicial tribunal. Legislation is also required preventing MPs from voting, speaking and lobbying for laws in which they have a financial interest. At the most, MPs should be barred from retaining any *paid* directorships or consultancies. They should also be obliged to submit their annual tax returns for public inspection.

One rule for MPs, another law for councillors

The government refuses to apply the criminal law to MPs, but councillors are treated rather differently. In local authorities the pecuniary interests of elected representatives are governed by tough legal sanctions.

Councillors are required by law to disclose direct and indirect financial interests in a statutory register. They are also compelled to declare an interest in any matter that comes before the council, a committee or sub-committee. They are then barred from voting or speaking on the issue. After declaring the interest, the councillor must leave the room and take no further part in the proceedings.

Any breach of these rules is a criminal offence and councillors can be jailed or fined by a court of law. This is a sharp contrast to the voluntary guidelines in Parliament. MPs are immune from the law, investigate themselves, are not obliged to declare all their interests and can lobby for their clients without fear of punishment.

The House of Commons really is the best club in town.

The colour of money

Readers of this book may wonder why relatively few Labour MPs feature in it. The answer is simple. Out of the 227 Labour MPs, only sixteen have paid directorships, consultancies, shareholdings or some form of commercial interest.[45] Another seventeen are paid advisers to trade unions and professional associations. Of the 372 Conservative MPs, 256 have business concerns – and that excludes sixty-one ministers, who are not allowed to retain consultancies and directorships.

The only Labour MP to have faced a potential conflict of interests is Dr John Cunningham, MP for Copeland in Cumbria. Between 1983 and 1989 Cunningham was Shadow Environment Secretary. Part of his portfolio was responsibility for Labour's policy on chemical food additives. In 1986 the Labour Party stated:

> It is now recognised that many additives can be harmful. Many children suffer allergic reactions to common colours, anti-oxidants and preservatives. Food workers have experienced ill-health from handling certain additives. The UK controls on additives lag behind those of many European countries.[46]

Cunningham was at that time a paid adviser on industrial policy to Albright and Wilson (UK) Ltd, manufacturers of chemical food additives. Since 1985 he has also declared a consultancy with Leather Chemicals and Dow Ltd.

Most of Cunningham's Labour colleagues are sponsored by trade unions. While this is a declarable interest, it is wholly different from the situation of MPs with shares, consultancies and directorships.

There has been some concern about such Members acting as chairmen of select committees. For example, the Labour MP David Marshall is sponsored by the transport workers' union while being chairman of the Commons Transport Select Committee. However, sponsored MPs are not paid by the trade union in question. The £600 a year is remitted to the constituency Labour Party, usually for election expenses. Consequently, as union sponsorship is not a 'pecuniary interest' or of 'material benefit' to an MP, there is virtually no comparison.

Democracy for sale

Some critics of political lobbying and of MPs acting as hired guns do so from a world-weary, cynical perspective. A favourite reference point is the former Labour Cabinet minister Richard Crossman, who famously dismissed the importance of back-benchers. MPs, he quipped, 'run nothing, decide nothing and usually know nothing'.[47]

Essentially, their argument is that lobbyists and corporations are wasting their cash and luncheon vouchers. MPs do not have power and influence. According to Labour MP Austin Mitchell:

> Lobbying [is] self-inflating and feeding on itself. Yet under our elective dictatorship, the legislature is still basically a rubber stamp in the hands of the executive . . . So lobby as we might, set procedural traps as we might, work as we might, at the end of the day we are largely impotent . . . We have all the intellectual satisfaction of heckling a steam roller.[48]

There is, of course, some truth here. Lobbyists and MPs are notorious for making brash and rash promises about their political clout to unsuspecting business clients. In a party-based system, it is also the case that the power of MPs has been exaggerated.

However, there is substantial evidence that MPs can exert considerable influence. Examples in this book include lobbying campaigns by the brewers (see chapter 3), private cleaning contractors (chapter 4) and the Channel Tunnel (chapter 6). Other cases where back-bench pressure has been successful are the Shops Bill, when seventy-two Tory MPs voted with the Opposition, and the Port Employers campaign to abolish the Dock Labour Scheme.

At the very least back-benchers can set the public agenda for their clients, largely by providing free media coverage. They can also obtain confidential information, lobby ministers, civil servants and other MPs privately and propose amendments to bills.

To what extent a hired MP can directly initiate, change or repeal legislation is very difficult to evaluate. That is part of the problem. So much lobbying is conducted in secret. But the question of whether MPs are effective is not the point of this book. The real issue is that many MPs have placed 'For Sale' signs against their names. By accepting payments from outside bodies, they are subverting democracy when they are supposed to be its custodians.

There is nothing intrinsically wrong with lobbying. It is just a stage name for campaigning. But when companies, foreign governments, PR firms and merchant banks can buy political influence, then lobbying becomes a dirty word.

Most important of all are the people an MP is supposed to serve. Many constituents will be shocked to discover that their elected representative is working for and being paid thousands of pounds by companies of which they may never have heard. MPs need to do more than prove that this arrangement is ethical. They must be completely above suspicion. Only then will democracy remain untainted by corruption.

Appendix One

The following bill has been proposed by Bob Cryer, Labour MP for Bradford South and a member of the Commons Select Committee on Members' Interests. It has twice been placed before the House, in 1982 and 1988, but never implemented.

Registration of commercial lobbying interests

A bill to provide a public register of organisations that carry out the lobbying of Parliament for commercial gain and the disclosure of expenditure by such organisations and for connected purposes.

1 The House of Commons (Administration) Act 1978 shall be amended by the addition of the following sub-sections:

> 'The Commission shall
>
> (a) ensure that a register of all organisations having as their sole, major or subsidiary aim the lobbying of Parliament for commercial gain, is drawn up and placed in the House of Commons library;
>
> (b) ensure that the register is reviewed every three months and that such alterations as are made are attached to the Register placed in the House of Commons library;
>
> (c) require each registered organisation to provide a list of meetings arranged on behalf of clients with Members of Parliament and government ministers, fees paid to MPs by registered organisations and a statement of such expenses paid on behalf of clients every three months. Such information shall be included in the Register; and
>
> (d) have power to remove from the Register any organisation failing to provide such information or for any breach of guidelines issued below.
>
> The Commission may from time to time issue guidelines for registered organisations.'

2   To Section 1 (3) of the Prevention of Corruption Act 1906 there shall be added: 'A Member of Parliament is an agent within the meaning of this Act.'

3   This Act may be cited as the Registration of Commercial Lobbying Interests Act 1988.

This Act shall come into force on the expiration of one month beginning on the day on which it is passed.

This Act applies to the United Kingdom.

Appendix Two

The following Labour MPs are directors and shareholders of companies and/or consultants and advisers to firms and trade associations:*

1   Tony Banks – parliamentary adviser to Issue Communications Ltd

2   Stuart Bell – parliamentary adviser to Merck, Sharp and Dohme

3   David Clark – director of Homeowners Friendly Society

4   Stan Crowther – parliamentary adviser to the National Licensed Victuallers' Association

5   John Cunningham – parliamentary adviser to:
    Albright and Wilson (UK) Ltd
    Leather Chemicals
    Dow Ltd

6   Dick Douglas – economic consultant on oil-related matters. Clients are not declared in the Register. Labour MP from 1979 until March 1990. Now a Scottish Nationalist.

7   John Garrett – freelance associate of P. E. Inbucon Ltd

8   Ted Garrett – parliamentary adviser to:
    B. A. T. Industries
    Machine Tool Trades Association

9   John Gilbert – director of:
    John Gilbert Associates (also chairman)
    Edmund Nuttall Ltd
    Kyle Stewart Ltd
    Member of international advisory board of Royal Jordanian Airways

10 Kate Hoey – member of advisory board of London Weekend Television

* Register of Members' Interests, 14 January 1991.

11   Dennis Howell – director of:
        Wembley Stadium Co. Ltd
        Birmingham Cable Co. Ltd
        principal in Denis Howell Consultants

12   Greville Janner – director of:
        Ladbroke PLC
        JSB Group

13   Gordon Oakes – public affairs consultant to
        3M United Kingdom Ltd
        Royal Pharmaceutical Society

14   Merlyn Rees – director of:
        Trustee Municipal Mutual Insurance Co.
        Municipal General Insurance Company

15   George Robertson – adviser to Halton-Gill Associates

16   Geoffrey Robinson – director of Agie UK Ltd, shareholder in Latchuser Ltd, the family-owned firm. He also has holdings held in trust on his behalf in Transfer Technology Ltd and Saarclad International Ltd

17   Brian Wilson – director of West Highland Publishing Co. Ltd (also a shareholder)

Notes and References

The following abbreviations have been used for documents produced by the Select Committee on Members' Interests:

HC 57: Select Committee on Members' Interests (Declaration) Report: 4 December 1969, HC 57

HC 490: Select Committee on Members' Interests, 1976–7: 13 July 1977, HC 490

HC 408: Select Committee on Members' Interests, First Report, 1984–5: 21 May 1985, HC 408

HC 110: Select Committee on Members' Interests, 1986–7: 12 January 1987, HC 110

HC 518: Select Committee on Members' Interests, 'Parliamentary Lobbying', 1987–8: 7 June 1988 [HC 518-i], 25 October 1988 [HC 518-vi]

HC 44: Select Committee on Members' Interests, 1988–9, 'Parliamentary Lobbying': 14 February 1989 [HC 44-v], 4 April 1989 [HC 44-vii], 25 April 1989 [HC 44-viii], 23 May 1989 [HC 44-x]

HC 135: Select Committee on Members' Interests, First Report, 1989–90: 19 February 1990, HC 135

HC 506: Select Committee on Members' Interests, Second Report, 1989–90: 25 July 1990, HC 506

HC 561: Select Committee on Members' Interests, Third Report, 1989–90: 25 July 1990, HC 561

HC 389-i: Select Committee on Members' Interests, First Report, 1990–91: 3 April 1990, HC 389-i

HC 108: Select Committee on Members' Interests, Second Report, 1990–91, 16 May 1990, HC 108

1: If the Price if Right

1 Dudley Fishburn, *International Herald Tribune*, 12 June 1989.
2 Ibid.

3 Register of Members' Interests, HC 140.

4 Alan Doig, *Corruption and Misconduct in Contemporary British Politics* (Penguin, London, 1984), p. 43.

5 Quoted in memorandum by Sir Barnett Cocks, Clerk to the House of Commons, in report by Select Committee on Members' Interests, HC 57, p. 3, para. 8.

6 Alan Doig, *Corruption and Misconduct*, p. 54.

7 Resolution by the House of Commons, 2 May 1695.

8 Select Committee on Members' Interests, HC 57, p. 5, para. 16.

9 Richard S. Lambert, *The Railway King* (Allen & Unwin, London, 1934), p. 22. Quoted in Alan Doig, *Westminster Babylon* (Allison & Busby, London, 1990), p. 37.

10 Simon Haxey, *Tory MP* (Victor Gollancz, London, 1939), p. 33.

11 Resolution of the House of Commons, 22 June 1858.

12 G. R. Searle, *Corruption in British Politics 1895–1930* (Clarendon Press, Oxford, 1987), p. 41.

13 John Grigg, *Young Lloyd George* (London, 1973), p. 43. Quoted in G. R. Searle, op. cit., p. 43.

14 G. R. Searle, *Corruption in British Politics* p. 37.

15 Ibid., p. 44.

16 Simon Haxey, *Tory MP*, p. 62.

17 House of Commons, *Hansard*, 18 March 1914.

18 Lord Henry Bentinck, *Tory Democracy* (London, 1918), p. 78. Quoted in G. R. Searle, *Corruption in British Politics*, p. 291.

19 Lecture to the Parliamentary Public Relations Association, 24 April 1980.

20 M. R. Hely-Hutchinson, MP, *Capitalism?* (London, 1933), p. 41.

21 Select Committee on the Conduct of a Member, May 1940.

22 House of Commons Privileges Committee, 14 June 1944.

23 Ibid., 17 June 1947.

24 Alan Doig, *Corruption and Misconduct*, pp. 115–17.

25 Special Report of the Committee of Privileges Committee, 1946–7, nos. 137–8, 142.

26 Anthony Courtney, *Sailor In a Russian Frame* (Johnson, London, 1968), p. 63.

27 Report by the Select Committee on Members' Interests, HC 57.

28 Alan Doig, *Corruption and Misconduct*, p. 199.

29 House of Commons, *Hansard*, 3 February 1972, col. 747.

30 *Guardian*, 11 May 1974.

31 *Labour Weekly*, 26 April 1974.

32 Ibid.
33 The three MPs were Albert Roberts (Labour), John Cordle (Conservative) and Reginald Maudling (Conservative).
34 House of Commons, *Hansard*, 7 March 1990.
35 Ibid., 22 May 1974.
36 Ibid.
37 Ibid., Speech by Labour MP Raymond Fletcher.
38 Ibid., 12 June 1975.
39 Ibid.
40 Ibid., 3 July 1978.
41 Grant Jordan, ed., *The Commercial Lobbyists –Politics for Profit in Britain* (Aberdeen University Press, Aberdeen, 1991), p. 104.
42 Ray Fitzwalter and David Taylor, *Web of Corruption* (Granada, London, 1981), pp. 138–9.
43 Reginald Maudling, *Memoirs* (Sidgwick & Jackson, London, 1978), p. 143.
44 Alan Doig, *Westminster Babylon*, p. 166.
45 Ray Fitzwalter and David Taylor, *Web of Corruption*, p. 247.
46 Ibid., p. 149.
47 Alan Doig, *Corruption and Misconduct*, p. 135.
48 Select Committee on Members' Interests, HC 490.
49 Ray Fitzwalter and David Taylor, *Web of Corruption*, p. 247.
50 Ibid., p. 251.
51 House of Commons, *Hansard*, 1 November 1974.
52 Adam Raphael, *My Learned Friends* (W. H. Allen, London, 1989), p. 112.
53 Alan Doig, *Corruption and Misconduct*, p. 151.
54 House of Commons, *Hansard*, 17 April 1964.
55 Adam Raphael, *Observer*, 17 October 1976.
56 Adam Raphael, *My Learned Friends*, pp. 114–15.
57 Select Committee on Conduct of Members, 1976–7, p. 10.
58 Ray Fitzwalter and David Taylor, *Web of Corruption*, p. 251.
59 Royal Commission on Standards of Conduct in Public Life 1974–6, Command Paper 6524, para. 307.
60 House of Commons, *Hansard*, 20 October 1976.
61 Ibid., 1 November 1976.
62 Select Committee on Members' Interests, HC 490.
63 Adam Raphael, *My Learned Friends*, p. 123.
64 Select Committee on Members' Interests, HC 490.
65 House of Commons, *Hansard*, 26 July 1977.

66 Ibid.
67 Ibid., 15 June 1979.
68 Andrew Roth, 'The Business Background on MPs', *Parliamentary Profiles* (London, 1981), p. ii.
69 *Tatler*, October 1988.
70 *World In Action*, Granada TV, 15 January 1990.
71 *Observer*, 7 June 1987.
72 *House Magazine*, 18 July 1987.
73 *World In Action*, Granada TV, 15 January 1990.
74 Ibid.
75 *Financial Times*, 7 March 1990.
76 *Guardian*, 7 March 1990.
77 As of 1991. Parliamentary salaries are linked to a Civil Service rate and now increase automatically each year.
78 *Observer*, 26 October 1986.
79 *World In Action*, Granada TV, 15 January 1990.
80 Ibid.
81 *Lymington Times and New Milton Advertiser*, 1 July 1989.

2: Abroad on Business

1 Richard Crossman, *The Diaries of a Cabinet Minister, 1968–70*, Vol. 3 (Jonathan Cape, London, 1977), p. 406.
2 Letter from John Browne's then solicitors, Gordon Dadds and Co., to Theodore Goddard, Elizabeth Browne's solicitors, 31 October 1983.
3 Select Committee on Members' Interests, HC 135, answer to question 528.
4 Ibid., p. x.
5 Memorandum from John Browne to Julian Wathen, deputy chairman of Barclays Bank PLC, 24 June 1980.
6 See House of Commons, *Hansard*, 23 January 1981, col. 552, 11 March 1981, col. 942.
7 Ibid., 12 May 1981, cols. 683–5.
8 Select Committee on Members' Interests, HC 135, answer to question 843.
9 Letter to Ian Andrew, Abu Dhabi Investment Authority, Abu Dhabi, United Arab Emirates, 7 July 1978.
10 Letter to Mohammad Kaki, president of Ahmad and Mohammad

Salek Kaki group of companies, Riyadh, Saudi Arabia, 3 November 1981.

11 Select Committee on Members' Interests, HC 135, p. 130.

12 'Agreement for the Services of J. E. D. de la Valette Browne', contract signed by Browne on behalf of his company, Falcon Rose Ltd, with Selco East Consultants Ltd.

13 Letter to Mrs Thatcher, 15 April 1981.

14 Letter from Peter Dance, Davy McKee Corporation, to John Browne, 16 April 1981.

15 Letter from John Biffen, Secretary of State for Trade, to John Browne, 17 June 1981.

16 Memorandum of meeting headed: 'Selco East Consultants Ltd Meeting with Tarmac'.

17 Letter from John Browne to Ambassador Stephen Egerton, 5 June 1981.

18 Letter from John Browne to Philip Chidiac, Selco East Consultants, 23 February 1982.

19 Interview with *Southern Evening Echo*, 9 May 1989.

20 *Observer*, 31 May 1989.

21 Select Committee on Members' Interests, HC 135, statement by Charles Chidiac, p. xxviii.

22 Ibid., p. 113.

23 Letter from Charles Chidiac to John Browne, 26 June 1985.

24 Letter from John Browne to Philip Chidiac, 23 February 1982.

25 Letter from John Browne to Charles Chidiac, 12 February 1982.

26 Attendance note of High Court hearing, 30 November 1983.

27 House of Commons, *Hansard*, 30 July 1982, col. 1475.

28 Ibid., col. 1468.

29 Ibid., 25 November 1982, col. 1011.

30 Select Committee on Members' Interests, HC 135, p. xx.

31 Ibid., answer to questions 654 and 687.

32 Interview with *Southern Evening Echo*, 7 May 1989.

33 Interview with author.

34 Attendance note of High court hearing, 30 November 1983.

35 Ibid.

36 Letter from Withers and Co., John Browne's solicitors, to Theodore Goddard, Elizabeth Browne's solicitors, 31 January 1984.

37 Letter from John Browne to Jacques Rossier, Swiss Bank Corporation, 18 February 1981.

38 'House of Commons Stationery', Serjeant-at-Arms rules, 1986, p. 3.
39 Letter from John Browne to Herr William Wirth, Crédit Suisse, 16 April 1981.
40 Letter from John Browne to Desire Kettaneh, 16 April 1981.
41 Telex from Withers and Co., John Browne's solicitors, to Theodore Goddard, Elizabeth Browne's solicitors, 23 May 1984.
42 Letter from Emmet Stephenson to John Browne, 16 July 1984.
43 Letter from John Browne to Iqbal Mamdami, Trans Arabian Bank, 22 October 1981.
44 Company accounts of Falcon Finance Management Ltd, 1983, 1984, 1985.
45 *Today*, 8 October 1990.
46 Ibid., 10 August 1989.
47 *Observer*, 21 January 1990.
48 *Daily Mirror*, 1 March 1990.
49 *Observer*, 21 January 1990.
50 House of Commons, *Hansard*, 23 April 1985 (written answer, 394–7w), 25 April 1985 (written answer, 521–2w), 15 January 1986 (written answer, 585w).
51 Register of Members' Interests, 13 January 1986.
52 House of Commons, *Hansard*, 12 November 1986, col. 86.
53 *Daily Telegraph*, 31 December 1981.
54 *Sunday Times*, 6 July 1980.
55 Annual accounts of Shenley Trust Services Ltd.
56 Letter to Sir Peter Emery from Mr T. M. Molatlwa, Minister of Foreign Affairs, 14 August 1981.
57 Agreement between Shenley Trust Services and Bophuthatswana government, signed on 7 May 1982.
58 Under the strict application of the rules, Sir Peter was not obliged to declare the Bophuthatswana consultancy as a foreign payment. Although Rule 7 clearly states that 'any payments ... from or on behalf of foreign governments, organisations or persons' should be declared, they would need to be disclosed only if the MP has engaged in parliamentary activity on behalf of his client.
59 Agreement between Shenley Trust Services and Bophuthatswana government, signed on 7 May 1982.
60 Letter from Sir Peter Emery to Labour Research Department, 12 June 1984.

61 Letter from Gillian Craig of Shenley Trust Services Ltd to Bernard Johnson, 11 May 1984.
62 *The Times*, 18 October 1983.
63 Letter from S. K. Gopane, Secretary for Foreign Affairs, to Jamie Guise, Shenley Trust Services, 13 July 1984.
64 *Exmouth Herald*, 13 June 1986.
65 Quoted in letter from President Mangope to Owen Kelly, Commissioner of Police, City of London, 29 October 1987.
66 Letter from Norton, Rose, Botterell and Roche, Bophuthatswana solicitors, to President Mangope, 13 August 1987.
67 Letter from R. C. F. Gillanders, Fraud A Division, Crown Prosecution Service, to Norton, Rose, Botterell and Roche, 3 September 1987.
68 Letter from President Mangope to Owen Kelly, Commissioner of Police, City of London, 29 October 1987.
69 Select Committee on Members' Interests, HC 44-viii, p. 211.
70 Ibid.
71 *Mafeking Mail*, October 1989.
72 Letter from T. J. Andrews, Southern African Department, Foreign Office, to Ruth Rees, 27 November 1989.
73 *Independent*, 25 February 1990.

3: In the City

1 *Daily Telegraph*, 5 July 1965.
2 Letter to Herbert Bowden, chairman of the Committee of Privileges, Third Report, 1964–5: 12 July 1965.
3 Anthony Sampson, *The Changing Anatomy of Britain* (Hodder & Stoughton, London, 1983), p. 312.
4 *Independent on Sunday*, 24 June 1990.
5 Ibid.
6 Andrew Roth, *Parliamentary Profiles, A–D*, p. 10.
7 *Guardian*, 7 March 1990.
8 Register of Members' Interests, 8 January 1990.
9 Andrew Roth, *Parliamentary Profiles, A–D*, p. 70.
10 See *Labour Research*, May 1990. After several years of non-disclosure, Rupert Allason, David Ashby and John Wilkinson did declare these shareholdings in 1991.
11 See House of Commons, *Hansard*, written question on 18 July 1979, 748w.

12 *The Times*, 2 April 1987.
13 Ibid., 4 April 1987.
14 Letter to *The Times*, 10 November 1987.
15 Alan Doig, *Westminster Babylon*, p. 296.
16 *Observer*, 5 April 1987.
17 *The Times*, 1 October 1987.
18 Ibid., 6 October 1987.
19 BBC TV Breakfast Time, 7 October 1987.
20 House of Commons, *Hansard*, 24 March 1981, col. 875.
21 Ibid., col. 878.
22 Ibid., 22 February 1982, cols. 678–85. Sir Nicholas declared these interests in the debate.
23 Ibid., col. 686.
24 Ibid., 14 January 1986, col. 1013.
25 Ibid.
26 Ibid.
27 Letter from Bryan Gould to Mrs Thatcher, 14 February 1986.
28 Letter from Mrs Thatcher to Bryan Gould, 16 February 1986.
29 See Dominic Hobson, *The Pride of Lucifer* (Hamish Hamilton, London, 1990), p. 201.
30 *Guardian*, 28 January 1987.
31 Ibid.
32 See Dominic Hobson, *The Pride of Lucifer*, p. 312.
33 *The Economist*, 22 December 1990.
34 *Spectator*, 20 April 1991.
35 Annual Review, Price Waterhouse, 1990.
36 *Computer News*, 7 April 1988.
37 Paul Foot, *Daily Mirror*, 8 June 1990.
38 House of Commons, *Hansard*, 30 March 1988, col. 1109.
39 Paul Foot, *Daily Mirror*, 8 June 1990.
40 Jock Bruce-Gardyne, *Ministers and Mandarins* (Sidgwick & Jackson, London, 1986), p. 66.
41 Unpublished evidence to Select Committee on Members' Interests by Ian Greer, 3 April 1990.
42 See Select Committee on Members' Interests, HC 561. Also interview by the author with Ian Greer.
43 Case study document prepared by Ian Greer Associates on British Airways account.
44 See Jock Bruce-Gardyne, *Ministers and Mandarins*; see also *Independent*, 20 November 1987.

45 *Independent*, 20 November 1987.

46 House of Commons, *Hansard*, 16 July 1987, cols. 1281–2.

47 Evidence to Select Committee on Members' Interests by David Burnside, Director of Public Affairs at British Airways, HC 518.

48 *Sunday Times*, 26 May 1985.

49 Ibid.

50 Ibid.

51 Register of Members' Interests, 13 January 1986.

52 *Independent on Sunday*, 27 May 1990.

53 *Observer Magazine*, 14 October 1990.

54 *Mail on Sunday*, 25 February 1990.

55 *Daily Telegraph*, 26 February 1990.

56 Evidence to Select Committee on Members' Interests, HC 518, p. 25.

57 Ibid.

58 *Western Daily News*, 28 July 1984.

59 House of Commons, *Hansard*, 25 July 1984, col. 1138.

60 Ibid., col. 1146.

61 Anthony Steen declared his British Midland Airways interest in debates on 21 November 1984, 28 March 1985, 27 January 1986, 9 April 1986, and 17 November 1987. But he did not declare his interest during long interventions on 14 February 1985 and 24 July 1987. Nor did he declare his consultancies during questions to the Transport Secretary on 20 July 1987 and 30 November 1987. Under the current rules he was not obliged to do so.

62 *The Supply of Beer* (Monopolies and Mergers Commission, HMSO 1989).

63 Marketing Strategies for Industry (UK) Ltd, Mitcham, Surrey.

64 Monopolies and Mergers Commission report and statement by Francis Maude, Minister for Consumer and Corporate Affairs, Department of Trade and Industry, House of Commons, *Hansard*, 21 March 1989, cols. 492–3.

65 Press conference, 21 March 1989.

66 House of Lords, *Hansard*, 14 June 1989, col. 1443.

67 Dr Rob Baggott, *Alcohol, Politics and Social Policy* (Gower Press, London, 1990), p. 67 (figures compiled by 'Action on Alcohol Abuse').

68 An indication of the amount of time MPs give to their commercial

interests was given by Roger Gale when he disclosed that between February 1986 and February 1987 he spent twenty-five days with Scottish and Newcastle Breweries PLC. He became a parliamentary consultant to the company in 1986.

69 *Independent*, 18 July 1989.
70 Jeremy Paxman, *Friends in High Places—Who Runs Britain* (Michael Joseph, London, 1990), p. 258.
71 Labour Research Department report, July 1989.
72 *World In Action*, Granada TV, 15 January 1990.
73 Ibid.
74 House of Lords, *Hansard*, 10 July 1989, col. 13.
75 'Drink: Trouble Brewing', Brook Productions for Channel 4, January 1990.

4: The Privatisation of Power

1 House of Commons, *Hansard*, 14 April 1981, col. 195.
2 Argument by Professor Peter Hennessy, author of *Whitehall* and *Cabinet Government*. Quoted in *New Statesman*, 22 December 1989.
3 Evidence to Select Committee on Members' Interests, HC 44.
4 Letter to chairman of Association of Health Authorities, 20 August 1981.
5 House of Commons, *Hansard*, 15 December 1982, col. 459.
6 *Bradford Telegraph and Argus*, 5 November 1983.
7 *Private Eye*, 4 November 1983.
8 *Bradford Telegraph and Argus*, 13 October 1983.
9 *Daily Mirror*, 27 October 1983.
10 *Private Eye*, 4 November 1983.
11 Ibid.
12 Michael Brown, *Sunday Correspondent*, 11 March 1990.
13 *Scotsman*, 19 March 1988.
14 *Review of the Year—May 1983 to April 1984*, report by Michael Forsyth Associates.
15 Ibid.
16 The seven MPs were Michael Ancram (1,491 shares), Peter Hordern (902), Charles Irving (3,254), Anthony Marlow (285), Hugh Rossi (2,862), Fred Silvester (250) and Sir William van Straubenzee (2,000).
17 House of Commons, *Hansard*, 5 March 1984, 450w.

18 Ibid., 26 March 1984, 58w.
19 Evidence to Select Committee on Members' Interests, HC 44.
20 *Health and Social Services Journal*, 4 April 1985.
21 Paul Foot, *Daily Mirror*, 26 February 1987.
22 House of Commons, Early Day Motion, No 145, 30 April 1984.
23 House of Commons, *Hansard*, 8 June 1982, col. 20, 13 December 1983, col. 827.
24 Early Day Motion 895, 'Local Government Competitive Tendering', 18 July 1985. The motion was also signed by Sir Marcus Fox and Sir Geoffrey Finsberg.
25 House of Commons, *Hansard*, 18 July 1985, col. 478.
26 Letter to the author.
27 House of Commons, *Hansard*, 6 July 1987, col. 129.
28 Ibid., col. 109.
29 'Reversing Clause 4—A Policy for Denationalisation', written by Tim Eggar, Kenneth Carlisle and Michael Grylls (Conservative Political Centre, January 1984).
30 House of Commons, *Hansard*, 11 March 1985, col. 7.
31 Minutes of meeting on 'Privatisation', 27 June 1985.
32 Ibid., 2 July 1985.
33 By 1988 Peter Rost had picked up six consultancies and two directorships (Register of Members' Interests, 1989).
34 House of Commons, *Hansard*, 8 March 1983, col. 786. Rost declared his interest when proposing the amendment.
35 Ibid., cols. 794–5.
36 Minutes of meeting on 7 July 1988, compiled by S. Perning.
37 Note by S. Perning, Danish Board of District Heating (DBDH), 14 November 1988.
38 Translation of article in Danish trade paper *Berlingske Erhverv*, December 1988.
39 Letter to S. Perning from A. Bainbridge, 12 October 1988.
40 Letter from A. Bainbridge to Mogens Larson of DBDH, 11 November 1988. Quoted in legal submission document.
41 Minutes of meeting of Major Energy Users Council (MEUC), 15 December 1988.
42 Ibid.
43 House of Commons, *Hansard*, 20 December 1988, col. 299.
44 Ibid., 6 April 1989, col. 442.
45 *Guardian*, 16 December 1988.
46 Memorandum and minutes of meetings of Hill Samuel 'Privatis-

ation Advisory Role' committee, 27 June 1985, 2 July 1985.

47 Ibid.

48 Ibid.

49 Ibid.

50 Standing Committee, Water Bill, 17 January 1989, col. 654.

51 *Western Mail*, 8 June 1990. Raffan declared this interest in the 1991 Register of Members' Interests.

52 Ibid.

53 Letter from Barry Chattington to John Browne, quoted in Select Committee on Members' Interests, HC 135.

54 Letter from John Browne to David Scholey, S. G. Warburg, 30 June 1981.

55 Letter from Harry Clark to John Browne, 30 October 1981.

56 Letter from John Browne to Sir Richard Cave, 18 March 1982.

57 House of Commons, *Hansard*, 25 March 1982, col. 1084.

58 Ibid., col. 1085.

59 Letter from John Browne to Sir Richard Cave, 20 April 1982.

60 House of Commons, *Hansard*, 20 April 1982, cols. 215–16.

61 Ibid.

62 'Aims and Methods of 3 C's Ltd', company document written November 1982.

63 Minutes of board meeting of 3 C's Ltd, 16 June 1982.

64 Memorandum and record of conversation between Kenneth Baker and John Browne, 15 December 1982.

65 Letter from Kenneth Baker to John Browne, 10 January 1983.

66 'Replies to the Questions from the Inquiry into Cable Expansion and Broadcast Policy', May 1982. The first line of the document states: '3 C's was formed eighteen months ago by J. Browne MP . . .'

67 Select Committee on Members' Interests, HC 135, p. 99.

68 House of Commons, *Hansard*, 2 December 1982, col. 457.

69 Ibid., col. 473.

70 Standing Committee D on Cable and Broadcasting Bill, 22–4 May 1984.

71 House of Commons, *Hansard*, 8 May 1990, col. 131.

72 Ibid.

73 Ibid., col. 128.

74 Ibid.

75 *PR Week*, 22 February 1990.

76 Ibid.

77 *Independent on Sunday*, 6 January 1991.

5: Selecting Your Interests

1 Evidence to Select Committee on Procedure, Session 1989–90: HC 19, vol. 2, p. 21.
2 Ibid. (answer to question 161).
3 House of Commons, *Hansard*, 14 December 1943, col. 1402.
4 Erskine May, p. 684.
5 Letter to Select Committee on Members' Interests, HC 108, p. 13.
6 Ibid., pp. 7–8.
7 House of Commons, *Hansard*, 30 November 1989, col. 870. Technically Wiggin was not obliged to declare his interest as he was making an intervention.
8 *Sunday Correspondent*, 8 April 1990.
9 Letter to Select Committee on Members' Interests, HC 108, p. 10.
10 Select Committee on Environment, Session 1989–90, HC 680, p. 10.
11 Evidence to Select Committee on Members' Interests, HC 108, p. 4.
12 *Independent on Sunday*, 13 May 1990.
13 Select Committee on Trade and Industry report on Information Technology, 1 February 1988.
14 Select Committee on Trade and Industry, Session 1988–9, 19 July 1989, HC 532.
15 *Independent on Sunday*, 13 May 1990.
16 Letter to Select Committee on Members' Interests, HC 108, p. 14.
17 House of Commons, *Hansard*, 8 February 1989, col. 1047.
18 Ibid., 18 December 1989, col. 95.
19 Ibid., 19 October 1988, col. 975.
20 Evidence to Select Committee on Members' Interests, HC 506, p. 18, by Michael Mates, chairman of Defence Select Committee.
21 'Scrutiny', BBC TV, 10 March 1991.
22 House of Commons, *Hansard*, 16 December 1985, col. 42.
23 Select Committee on Defence, Session 1985–6: 5 February 1986, HC 169, p. 171.
24 House of Commons, *Hansard*, 16 January 1986, cols. 1206–7.

25 See Magnus Linklater and David Leigh, *Not With Honour* (Sphere, London, 1986), pp. 161–2.
26 Andrew Roth, *Parliamentary Profiles.*
27 Evidence to Select Committee on Members' Interests, HC 506, p. 39.
28 House of Commons, *Hansard,* 5 April 1990, 833w.
29 *Daily Mirror,* 19 March 1990.
30 Select Committee on Members' Interests, HC 506, p. 35.
31 *Daily Mirror,* 19 March 1990.
32 Select Committee on Defence Report on Low Flying, Session 1989–90: 14 May 1990, HC 120, p. 176.
33 Select Committee on Members' Interests, HC 506, p. xviii.
34 Ibid., p. 14.
35 Ibid.
36 Michael Mates effectively admitted this during the Select Committee inquiry when he said: 'They could only have been aware by consulting the Register. Whether they did or not I do not know.'
37 Evidence to the Select Committee on Defence Inquiry on Low Flying, Session 1989–90: HC 120, p. 26.
38 Evidence to Select Committee on Members' Interests, HC 506, p. xviii.
39 SGL Brochure issued on 26 February 1990.
40 Evidence to Select Committee on Members' Interests, HC 506, p. 20.
41 Resolution of the House of Commons, 22 May 1974.
42 Evidence to Select Committee on Members' Interests, HC 506, p. 20.
43 *Independent on Sunday,* 11 March 1990.
44 House of Commons, *Hansard,* 15 May 1990, col. 746.
45 Several press reports, notably *Independent,* 30 March 1990.
46 *The Times,* 25 May 1990.
47 See Select Committee on Members' Interests, HC 506.
48 *Guardian,* 11 August 1990.
49 Public Accounts Committee, 1979–80, 25th Report, 'The Royal Hospital for Sick Children', p. 36.
50 Grant Jordan, ed. *The Commercial Lobbyists,* pp. 101–2.
51 Evidence by Sir Marcus Fox to Select Committee on Members' Interests, HC 44-vii, p. 198.
52 Ibid.

53 Evidence to Select Committee on Members' Interests, HC 518-vi, p. 91.
54 House of Commons, *Hansard*, 23 March 1989, col. 1291.
55 McCarthy and Stone document, 'A Balanced View—Response to Allegations Made by Nigel Griffiths, MP'.
56 Interview with the author.
57 The letter, dated 5 April 1989, was sent by John McCarthy to the following MPs: Denzil Davies, Alistair Darling, Lawrence Cunliffe, Jeff Rooker (Labour), Michael Jack and Teddy Taylor (Conservative).
58 Evidence to Select Committee on Members' Interests, HC 44-vii.
59 Standing Committee C, Licensing (Amendment) Bill, 8 April 1987, cols. 15–16.
60 House of Commons, *Hansard*, 9 November 1987, col. 77.
61 Standing Committee C, 8 April 1987, col. 15.
62 Ibid., 22 April 1987, col. 56.
63 Ibid., 8 April 1987, col. 16.
64 House of Commons, *Hansard*, 27 February 1987, col. 515.
65 Ibid., 22 April 1987, col. 678.
66 *Independent*, 23 April 1987.
67 Standing Committee H, 30 January 1990, cols. 126–7. Henry Bellingham declared his interest in the Commons and in Standing Committee.
68 House of Commons, *Hansard*, 30 April 1990, col. 802.
69 Select Committee on Members' Interests, HC 108, pp. 21–2.
70 Ibid., p. 12.
71 Ibid., p. 13.

6: The Agents of Influence

1 Evidence to Select Committee on Members' Interests, HC 518-vi, p. 85.
2 *Financial Times*, 23 December 1985.
3 *The Times*, 12 July 1988.
4 Speaker Clifton-Brown, House of Commons, *Hansard*, 13 December 1949, cols. 2519–20.
5 House of Commons, *Hansard*, 12 December 1949, col. 2353, 5 December 1949, col. 1535.
6 *Campaign*, 14 March 1969.
7 Francis Noel-Baker, 'The Grey Zone: The Problems of Business

Affiliations of Members of Parliament', *Parliamentary Affairs*, vol. 15, 1961–2.
8 Andrew Roth, publisher and editor of 'Parliamentary Profiles'.
9 *Sunday Times*, 6 October 1968; see also Alan Doig, *Corruption and Misconduct*, p. 215.
10 *Yorkshire Post*, 2 July 1976.
11 Ibid.
12 Schlozman and Tierney, 1986, p. 261. Quoted in Grant Jordan, *The Commercial Lobbyists*, p. 1.
13 *Reader's Digest*, January 1989.
14 Select Committee on Members' Interests, HC 44-x, p. 257.
15 Lloyd-Hughes Associates company profile, 1981.
16 Ibid.
17 Ibid.
18 Schlozman and Tierney, 1986, p. 294. Quoted in Grant Jordan, *The Commercial Lobbyists*, p. 24.
19 Alan Doig, *Westminster Babylon*, p. 307.
20 *The Economist*, 5 March 1988.
21 *Observer*, 15 November 1987.
22 *Sunday Telegraph*, 17 March 1985.
23 *Observer*, 1 July 1984.
24 Register of Members' Interests, 14 January 1991.
25 Rob Baggott, *Alcohol, Politics and Social Policy*, pp. 67–8.
26 Letter to *Labour Research*, July 1984.
27 Ibid.
28 Ibid.
29 *World In Action*, Granada TV, 15 January 1990.
30 Evidence to Select Committee on Members' Interests, HC 44-vii.
31 TV Eye, Thames TV, 26 April 1984.
32 Evidence to Select Committee on Members' Interests, HC 44-vii, p. 202.
33 Ibid., p. 198.
34 Ibid., p. 197.
35 Ibid., p. 203.
36 Ibid., pp. 198, 200.
37 Evidence to Select Committee on Members' Interests, HC 44-viii, p. 217.
38 TV Eye, Thames TV, 26 April 1984.
39 Select Committee on Members' Interests, HC 44-viii, p. 225.
40 *Independent*, 13 April 1987.

41 Select Committee on Members' Interests, HC 44-viii, p. 218.

42 Ibid., p. 216.

43 House of Commons, *Hansard*, 9 April 1987, col. 450.

44 Select Committee on Members' Interests, HC 44-viii, p. 220.

45 Ibid., p. 219.

46 Ibid., p. 218.

47 *Sunday Times*, 2 October 1983.

48 *Newsnight*, BBC TV, 9 December 1985.

49 Ibid.

50 *Guardian*, 13 September 1985.

51 *Newsnight*, BBC TV, 9 December 1985.

52 Ibid.

53 Ibid.

54 Ibid.

55 Ibid.

56 *Observer*, 15 December 1985.

57 *PR Week*, 1 February 1990.

58 *Independent on Sunday*, 11 March 1990.

59 *PR Week*, 1 February 1990.

60 Newsnight, BBC TV, 9 December 1985.

61 Grant Jordan, ed., *The Commercial Lobbyists*, p. 56.

62 TV Eye, Thames TV, 26 April 1984.

63 Evidence to Select Committee on Members' Interests, HC 389-i.

64 TV Eye, Thames TV, 26 April 1984.

65 *Observer*, 9 April 1989.

66 Evidence to Select Committee on Members' Interests, HC 518-vi, p. 10.

67 Evidence to Select Committee on Members' Interests, HC 561, p. viii.

68 Letter to Select Committee on Members' Interests, HC 389-i.

69 Evidence by Ian Greer to Select Committee on Members' Interests, HC 389-i, p. 3.

70 Ibid., p. 4.

71 Ibid., p. 1.

72 *Independent on Sunday*, 27 May 1990.

73 *PR Week*, 22 October 1988.

7: Ministers and the Money Men

1 Letter to Tony Benn, 15 January 1986.

2 Letter to Mrs Thatcher, 21 January 1986.
3 House of Commons, *Hansard*, 15 January 1988, col. 410.
4 Ibid., 3 June 1937, col. 1229.
5 *The Economist*, 30 July 1898.
6 House of Commons, *Hansard*, 14 February 1899, col. 971. Quoted in D.C.M. Platt, *The Commercial and Industrial Interests of Ministers of the Crown*, Political Studies, vol. ix, 1961.
7 House of Commons, *Hansard*, 16 August 1895, cols. 171–2.
8 Ibid., 7 August 1896, col. 148.
9 Ibid., 14 April 1896, col. 879.
10 Ibid., 15 February 1899, col. 202.
11 D.C.M. Platt, *Commercial and Industrial Interests*.
12 House of Commons, *Hansard*, vol. 66, cols. 987–8.
13 G. R. Searle, *Corruption in British Politics*, pp. 48–9.
14 Ibid., p. 59.
15 Ibid., pp. 56–7.
16 Ibid.
17 Ibid., p. 103.
18 House of Commons, *Hansard*, 20 March 1906.
19 Alan Doig, *Corruption and Misconduct*, p. 101.
20 House of Commons, *Hansard*, 11 October 1912.
21 Alan Doig, *Corruption and Misconduct*, p. 102.
22 House of Commons, *Hansard*, 19 June 1913, cols. 556–7.
23 Simon Haxey, *Tory MP*, p. 36.
24 G. R. Searle, *Corruption in British Politics*, p. 413.
25 Simon Haxey, *Tory MP*, p. 32.
26 *Questions of Procedure for Ministers*, Cabinet Office Document, p. 15, paras. 67–9.
27 Ibid., p. 16, para. 74.
28 Alan Doig, *Corruption and Misconduct*, p. 224.
29 Ibid.
30 House of Commons, *Hansard*, 25 June 1973, col. 855.
31 Ibid., 22 October 1979, col. 63.
32 'At the Mercy of the Unscrupulous', Fulcrum Productions for Channel 4, 23 November 1989.
33 Ibid. No action or charges have been brought against any individual.
34 Fulcrum Productions for Channel 4, 23 November 1989.
35 *Daily Telegraph*, 24 March 1986.
36 *Mail on Sunday*, 23 March 1986.

37 House of Commons, *Hansard*, 25 March 1986, col. 781.
38 *Observer*, 13 April 1986.
39 Ibid.
40 Interview, Paul Lashmar, *Observer*, 13 April 1986.
41 House of Commons, *Hansard*, 27 April 1987, col. 6.
42 *The Times*, 31 March 1987.
43 *Labour Research*, April 1987.
44 Ibid., June 1987.
45 *Questions of Procedure for Ministers*, p. 16.
46 *Daily Mirror*, 17 May 1990.
47 *Guardian*, 27 August 1990.
48 *Labour Research*, October 1990.
49 *Guardian*, 21 December 1985.
50 Report to the US Securities and Exchange Commission by Blue Arrow PLC, May 1989.
51 *The Times*, 1 August 1990.
52 London *Evening Standard*, 13 June 1990.
53 *Financial Times*, 14 June 1990.
54 *Guardian*, 14 June 1990.
55 *Financial Times*, 14 June 1990.
56 *Observer*, 17 June 1990.
57 *Independent*, 7 March 1990.
58 *The Times*, 22 March 1990.
59 *Guardian*, 2 February 1990.
60 *Daily Telegraph*, 3 February 1990.
61 *Independent*, 6 February 1990.
62 *The Times*, 7 February 1990.
63 *Financial Times, Daily Telegraph* and *The Times*, 27 April 1990.
64 *The Times*, 7 February 1990.
65 *Daily Telegraph*, 11 September 1990.
66 *The Times*, 13 February 1990.
67 *The Times*, 15 May 1990.
68 Press release by N. M. Rothschild and Sons, 29 May 1990.
69 Paul Foot, *Daily Mirror*, 18 January 1991.
70 *The Times*, 2 June 1990.
71 *Guardian*, 4 June 1990.
72 London *Evening Standard*, 15 June 1990.
73 House of Commons, *Hansard*, 14 June 1990, col. 470.
74 Ibid., 20 November 1962, col. 999.

75 Evidence to the Royal Commission on Standards of Conduct in Public Life, 1974–6, Command Paper 6524.
76 Letter to John Prescott, Shadow Cabinet Minister, 13 June 1990.
77 *Independent*, 14 June 1990.
78 London *Evening Standard*, 13 June 1990.
79 *Guardian*, 14 June 1990.
80 Correspondence quoted in *The Times*, 30 July 1990.
81 House of Commons, *Hansard*, 20 June 1968, col. 171.

8: Conclusion: Whom Does Your MP Serve?

1 Select Committee on Members' Interests, HC 44-viii, p. 218.
2 Quoted in *Lymington Times and New Milton Advertiser*, 1 July 1989.
3 *Guardian*, 27 August 1990.
4 Ibid.
5 *The Times*, 22 March 1990.
6 *Independent*, 12 September 1989.
7 Ibid.
8 *The Economist*, 18 April 1896.
9 Letter to *Sunday Telegraph*, 24 March 1985.
10 *World In Action*, Granada TV, 15 January 1990.
11 Andrew Roth, *Parliamentary Profiles S–Z*, p. 708.
12 Letter from Tim Sainsbury to W. M. Moffatt, 13 July 1989.
13 *Brighton and Hove Leader*, 1 March 1990.
14 Ibid.
15 *The Times*, 20 January 1990.
16 *World In Action*, Granada TV, 15 January 1990.
17 Letter from James Hastings to Lord Douglas-Hamilton, 19 January 1988. Quoted in report of Standing Committee of Housing (Scotland) Bill, 21 January 1988, col. 8.
18 Select Committee on Members' Interests, HC 408, p. 5.
19 House of Commons, *Hansard*, 17 December 1985, col. 240.
20 *World In Action*, Granada TV, 15 January 1990.
21 Adam Raphael, *Observer*, 1 December 1985.
22 *Financial Times*, 19 November 1987.
23 Select Committee on Members' Interests, HC 44-x, p. 247.
24 House of Commons, *Hansard*, 17 December 1985, col. 217.
25 Select Committee on Members' Interests, HC 110, p. 4.

26 Official Complaints Procedure of Select Committee on Members' Interests.
27 *World In Action*, Granada TV, 24 April 1989.
28 Letter from Peter Viggers to Councillor Silvester, 31 January 1991.
29 Royal Commission on Standards of Conduct in Public Life 1974–6, July 1976, Command Paper 6524, para. 307.
30 House of Commons, *Hansard*, 20 October 1976, col. 1446.
31 Ibid., 1 December 1987, col. 570w.
32 Ibid., 2 April 1990, col. 393w.
33 Graham Zellick, 'Bribery of Members of Parliament and the Criminal Law', *Public Law* (1979), pp. 31–58.
34 *Halsbury's Laws of England* (3rd ed., 1959), vol. 30, para. 1317. Quoted in Graham Zellick, *Public Law*.
35 *Digest of the Criminal Law*, 1878, p. 118.
36 Graham Zellick, *Public Law*, pp. 35–8.
37 Ibid., p. 42.
38 Ibid., p. 43.
39 House of Lords, *Hansard*, 8 December 1976, col. 650.
40 Royal Commission on Standards of Conduct in Public Life, 1974–6, Command Paper 6524, para. 311.
41 Criminal Code, RSC 1970. Quoted in Graham Zellick, *Public Law*.
42 Paper by Nora Lever, Principal Clerk on Private Members' Business in Canadian Parliament, October 1987.
43 Graham Zellick, *Public Law*, p. 56.
44 Nora Lever paper, p. 17.
45 See Appendix 2 for full list.
46 Labour Party policy statement on the environment, 'Putting People First', 27 August 1986. Quoted in Geoffrey Cannon, *The Politics of Food* (Century Hutchinson, London, 1987), p. 301.
47 Alan Doig, *Westminster Babylon*, p. 20.
48 *House Magazine*, 6 March 1989.

Select Bibliography

Alan Doig: *Corruption and Misconduct in Contemporary British Politics* (Penguin, London, 1984)
——*Westminster Babylon* (Allison & Busby, London, 1990)
Ray Fitzwalter and David Taylor: *Web of Corruption* (Granada, London, 1981)
Simon Haxey: *Tory MP* (Victor Gollancz, London, 1939)
Grant Jordan, ed.: *The Commercial Lobbyists—Politics for Profit in Britain* (Aberdeen University Press, 1991)
D. C. M. Platt: 'The Commercial and Industrial Interests of Ministers of the Crown', *Political Studies*, volume 9, 1961
Adam Raphael: *My Learned Friends* (W. H. Allen, London, 1989)
G. R. Searle: *Corruption in British Politics, 1895–1930* (Clarendon Press, Oxford, 1987)
Graham Zellick: 'Bribery of Members of Parliament and the Criminal Law', *Public Law* (1979), pp. 31–58

INDEX

A Note on the Author

Mark Hollingsworth has been a journalist on Granada Television's *World In Action* since 1988. Before that he worked for TVS on the current affairs programme *Facing South*. He has also written for numerous publications, notably the *New Statesman*, and the *Observer*.

His previous books are *The Press and Political Dissent*, published by Pluto Press in 1986, *Blacklist–The Inside Story of Political Vetting* (with Richard Norton-Taylor), published by Hogarth Press in 1988, and *The Economic League–The Silent McCarthyism* (with Charles Tremayne), published by Liberty in 1989.

Born in 1959, he was educated in South Africa and lives in south London.